Master Builders of Byzantium

Master Builders of Byzantium

Robert Ousterhout

Princeton University Press

Princeton, New Jersey

Published by Princeton University Press
41 William Street
Princeton, New Jersey 08540

In the United Kingdom:
Princeton University Press
Chichester, West Sussex

http://pup.princeton.edu

Publication of this book has been aided by a grant
from the Millard Meiss Publication Fund of the
College Art Association of America

Designed and composed in Garamond No. 3
by Wilsted & Taylor Publishing Services
Printed by CS Graphics

Printed and bound in Singapore

10 9 8 7 6 5 4 3 2 1

Library of Congress Cataloging-in-Publication Data
Ousterhout, Robert G.
Master builders of Byzantium / Robert Ousterhout.
p. cm.
Includes bibliographical references and index.
ISBN 0-691-00535-4 (cloth : alk. paper)
1. Building—Byzantine Empire. 2. Architecture, Byzantine.
I. Title.
TH16.093 1999
723′.2—dc21 99-29652
CIP

CONTENTS

PREFACE

The present study addresses the working methods of Byzantine masons. It was inspired by years of teaching architectural history and the constant challenge of making the past accessible to the pragmatically oriented students in a professional school. One useful approach is to present historical architecture so that it reflects all of the concerns of its builders. As I discovered, although many popular books address the subject of the "architect in history," none of them devotes more than a few sentences to the Byzantine period.

As the premise of this study was being formulated, I found it necessary to write a variety of position papers before the subject at hand could be properly addressed, as well as detailed analyses of various monuments before they could be included in a more general study. My investigation began with an examination of Late Byzantine construction techniques. Under the title *Constantinople as an Architectural Center 1261–1453*, I was aided by a Fulbright Fellowship in 1986–87. I subsequently shifted the focus, and with the title *Innovation in Byzantine Architecture*, I received additional support from the Graham Foundation during a sabbatical in 1990. Under the title of *Byzantine Masons at Work*, most of the text was written while I was an Associate in the Center for Advanced Study at the University of Illinois at Urbana-Champaign in 1994; it was completed during a sabbatical in 1997.

During these years, I have been assisted in many ways by the School of Architecture, the Research Board, the Beckman Institute, and the Office for International Programs and Studies at the University of Illinois. I have also benefited from years of friendly cooperation with the Ephoreia of Byzantine Antiquities at Kavala, Greece, and its director, Charalambos Bakirtzis, and by the collegiality and hospitality of numerous colleagues in Greece and Turkey. I have also learned a great deal from discussions with my teachers Slobodan Ćurčić and George Stričević; with my colleagues W. Eugene Kleinbauer, Carol Krinsky, Marylee Coulson, Nancy Patterson Ševčenko, John Philip Thomas, Eunice

Dauterman Maguire, Henry Maguire, and Anthony Cutler; and with many of my students. I am indebted to Denis Sullivan, Alexander Kazhdan, Lee Sherry, and particularly Alice-Mary Talbot for sending so many useful textual references my way. In addition, two important publications appeared during the course of my study, and these facilitated the research: *The Oxford Dictionary of Byzantium* (Oxford, 1991), edited by A. Kazhdan; and W. E. Kleinbauer's *Early Christian and Byzantine Architecture: An Annotated Bibliography and Historiography* (Boston, 1992). I have also benefited from the excellent libraries at the University of Illinois and Dumbarton Oaks. In Istanbul, the libraries of the American Research Institute in Turkey and the German Archaeological Institute have been particularly useful. I am grateful to the staffs of all of these institutions. Finally, I thank Vassilis Marinis for preparing the index.

As this study was first beginning to take shape during a year in Greece and Turkey in 1986–87, I made the acquaintance of several individuals whose research has influenced my own in very many ways—as my bibliography will testify—and who have subsequently become valued colleagues and dear friends. I dedicate this study to them: Charalambos Bakirtzis, Paul Mylonas, Yıldız Ötüken, Thanasis Papazotos, and Giorgos Velenis. Thanasis Papazotos's premature death prevented him from seeing the finished study, but he has remained a constant source of inspiration throughout its preparation.

Master Builders of Byzantium

The Problem of Byzantine Architecture

Byzantine architecture may be approached from several different points of view: as a historical reflection of a set of economic and social conditions, as a setting for the rituals by which a certain society defined itself, or as "a succession of complex artifacts and aesthetic experiences." Each approach has its own validity, but this study examines Byzantine architecture from the point of view of its builders. The study identifies several problems that Byzantine masons must commonly have encountered in the process of design and construction and addresses these problems based on a careful analysis of the surviving buildings and of the limited written evidence.

"Byzantine" is here defined as the medieval civilization of the eastern Mediterranean with its capital in Constantinople. This study focuses on the period of the ninth through the fifteenth century, which is bounded in very general terms by the end of the Iconoclast Controversy in 843 and by the fall of Byzantium to the Ottomans in 1453. Although the Byzantine Empire continued in an unbroken line from Late Antiquity, the social disruptions of the Transitional period, which extends from the late sixth through the early ninth century, effectively marked a transformation of Byzantine society and its institutions. I prefer to call this period of social change the Transitional period, a name that is more positive than "Dark Ages" and less restrictive than "Iconoclast period." As shall be proposed in the following chapters, both the architecture and the process that led to its creation were considerably different after the Transitional period from those periods that had existed before it. The period under discussion is broken by the Latin Occupation of 1204–61, when the forces of the Fourth Crusade seized power, but in terms of cultural production this does not mark a dramatic shift. The architecture of the Middle Byzantine period (843–1204) and of the Late Byzantine (or Palaiologan) period (1261–1453) are similar in form and concept, and they are best discussed together.

No existing study examines the full range of concerns of a Byzantine builder. G. Downey's "Byzantine Architects: Their Training and Methods," in the 1946 *Byzantion*, is concerned primarily with a definition of terms. A. Choisy's outdated *L'art de bâtir chez les Byzantins* (Paris, 1883) concentrated on structure. Neither study takes into consideration the radical transformation of Byzantine society and its architecture in the Transitional period. Among more recent publications, W. E. Kleinbauer's important study, "Pre-Carolingian Concepts of Architectural Planning," in *The Medieval Mediterranean: Cross-Cultural Contacts*, ed. M. J. Chiat and K. L. Reyerson (St. Cloud, Minn., 1988), is full of valuable information concerning the architectural profession in Late Antiquity. Although it deals with the later periods, A. Petronotis's *O Architekton sto Byzantio* (The architect in Byzantium) (Thessaloniki, 1984) is brief and limited in scope. G. Velenis's dissertation, *Ermeneia tou Exoterikou Diakosmou ste Byzantine Architektonike* (Observations on exterior decoration in Byzantine architecture) (Thessaloniki, 1984), comes close to my goals, but it is limited to a discussion of construction techniques and their relationship to the outward appearance of a building. P. A. Rappoport's *Building the Churches of Kievan Russia* (Aldershot, 1995) has also been very useful, providing a wealth of archaeological information—the sort of detailed information we lack for most Byzantine sites. Because the early builders of Kievan Rus' learned masonry construction directly from Byzantine masons, many of Rappoport's technical observations are valid for Byzantine architecture as well. Similarly, J.-P. Adam's *Roman Building: Materials and Techniques* (Bloomington, 1994) provides much useful scientific information that is also applicable to the Byzantine period.

One of the premises of this study is that the nature of the architectural profession changed during the Transitional period, and a clear understanding of the transformation is essential for the appreciation of the architecture after that time. Unlike the architect (*mechanikos*) of classical antiquity, who had a liberal arts education and a theoretical approach to design, a Byzantine mason (*oikodomos*) was limited in his education to practical training gained within the context of a workshop. Throughout the text, the terms *architect* and *mason* are used according to these specific meanings. A workshop (*ergasterion*) is defined as a team or company, an association of craftsmen; the Greek word *ergasterion* had the same double meaning in Byzantine times as the word *workshop* does in English today: it could refer either to the building where labor occurred or to the group of workers.

The education of a Byzantine mason was based on practice rather than on theory. He was thus rooted in established architectural conventions. What methods were employed in the process of designing and laying out a new building? What were the respective roles of patron, mason, and artist in the design process? And where within this relatively conservative environment was creativity allowed or encouraged?

I propose to address these issues in the following study. In defining the parameters of my inquiry, I incur a debt to J. J. Coulton's *Ancient Greek Architects at Work* (Ithaca, N.Y., 1977), although it deals with a very different period of history. If my opening sentences sound familiar, it is because I cribbed some of them from Coulton. Discussion focuses on the architecture of Constantinople and areas under its influence because the Byzantine capital was always the center of building activity, and it concentrates on church architecture because the vast majority of surviving Byzantine buildings are churches. Through an examination of the best monuments, it is possible to understand the full range of experience of a Byzantine builder. Because of the limited textual material, the scope of the study is expanded a bit wider, both geographically and thematically, to bring together relevant written sources related to architecture. There is considerably more information from the Balkans that might have been included here, but it merits a separate study.

The treatment of the subject is far from exhaustive. In all aspects, there are certainly many more monuments that would be appropriate to include in the discussion, just as there are texts that have escaped attention. Nevertheless, it represents a beginning, and the primary intention is to define the parameters of inquiry. It is hoped that the study will stimulate further investigation into how the Byzantines conceived and built their distinctive architecture—what W. B. Yeats called their "monuments of unageing intellect."

CHAPTER ONE

Defining the Byzantine Church

A new kind of Byzantine church appeared in the ninth century or perhaps slightly earlier. Unlike the great basilicas of earlier times, it was small and intimate, with a centrally positioned dome and a lavishly decorated interior (figs. 1–4). Hundreds of such buildings survive in modern Greece, Turkey, southern Italy, and throughout the Balkans, and they are perhaps our best reminders of the cultural achievements of the Middle Byzantine (843–1204) and Late Byzantine (1261–1453) periods.

The Transformation of a Society and Its Architecture

The development of a new type of church architecture was but one of the many results of the radical transformation of society in the eastern Mediterranean during the period of the seventh through the ninth centuries. The Byzantine Empire suffered territorial losses and economic hardship, and the decline of cities effectively disrupted the traditions of public, urban life that had characterized the Late Antique and Early Christian social order.[1] This period is best known, however, for the controversies concerning religious images. During the period of Iconoclasm, which lasted (with a short interruption) from 726 to 843, the debates were primarily theological, concerning the nature and veneration of religious images. Were icons "graven images" to be abjured and outlawed, as the Iconoclasts believed, or should they be officially permitted parts of Orthodox devotion, as the Iconophiles believed?[2] The disputes that raged throughout the period divided and ultimately redefined Byzantine society. One of the results of the Iconophile victory in 843, called the "Triumph of Orthodoxy," was the development of a theology of images that both established their place in Byzantine worship and fostered the development of the decorative program of the Byzantine church.

The transformation of society had numerous other manifestations. The sixth through the ninth centuries witnessed the decline of cities, trade, and commerce, as well as a gen-

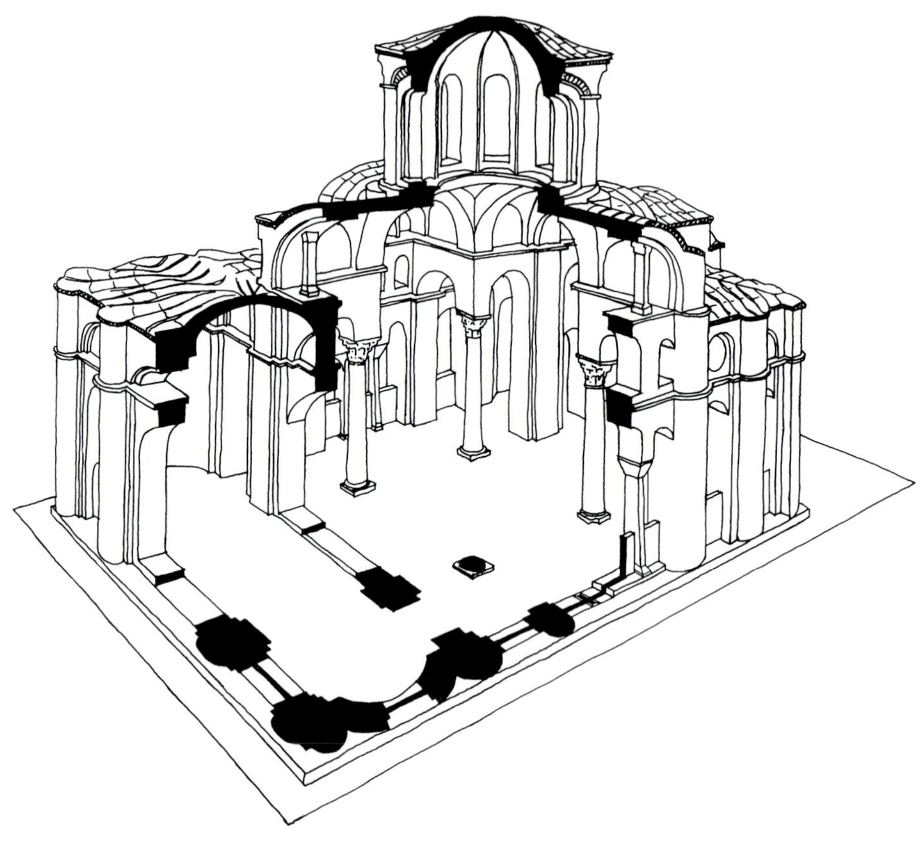

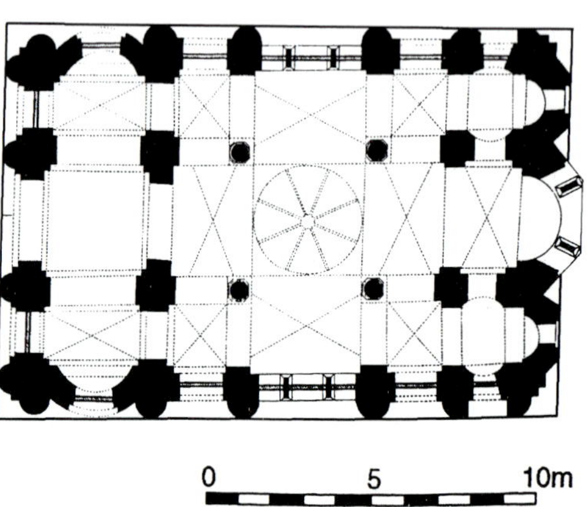

FIG. 1. Cutaway perspective view of the Myrelaion (Bodrum Camii), Istanbul

FIG. 2. Plan of the Myrelaion

FIG. 3. Exterior view of the Myrelaion, from the north

eral population decline. At the same time, monasticism became an important force within Byzantine society. Related to the demographic transformation, the pattern of patronage shifted away from the large basilicas, which had been under the jurisdiction of the episcopal authorities, to smaller, private and monastic foundations, accompanied by a fundamental change in the nature of worship. The processional liturgy of pre-Iconoclastic times gave way to a ceremony that became more closed and centralized in the later periods.[3] The structure and symbolism of the Byzantine liturgy encouraged the development of the compact, centralized, domed church.

Because the church building was the primary setting for the display and veneration of religious images, it is not surprising that both devotional practices and church architecture were transformed to serve the religious concerns of a changing, more closed society. In the Early Christian period, worship had been focused in immense basilicas that could house thousands, such as Saint John in the Stoudion and Hagia Sophia.[4] The service was an active one characterized by entrances and lavish processions, with both the celebrants and the congregation moving between the atrium and the interior of the basilica. By the Middle Byzantine period, however, devotion had become increasingly private, based on

FIG. 4. View into the vaulting of the Myrelaion

the interaction, in the form of prayer, between an individual worshiper and a religious image that represented the holy figure to whom the prayer was directed. The privatization of Byzantine worship resulted in the small, personal scale of most churches as well as in the addition of numerous ancillary spaces and private chapels.

The ninth century witnessed a gradual revival of culture and the emergence of significant patronage stimulated by a growing economy, fiscal reforms, and a systematization of the bureaucracy. The legislation of the preceding period had insisted on uniformity in an attempt to maintain order through the turbulent times, and this policy clearly extended into religious matters. The insistence on uniformity also affected the nature of most Byzantine institutions in the period that followed, including artistic production. For example, it is difficult to talk about a standard decorative program for the Early Christian church, whereas, rightly or wrongly, this has been the usual approach to Middle Byzantine monumental art.[5] Whether or not we call it a Feast Cycle, there is a uniformity to both subject matter and organization that suggests a sort of codification: as Orthodox belief was rethought and redefined, so too was its visual expression (see fig. 5).

FIG. 5. Interior view of the katholikon of Daphni monastery (near Athens), looking east

Similarly, there is a uniformity and conservatism in the architecture of the period, which was built to address similar spiritual concerns.

Although certain features identify a church as Byzantine, and most architectural scholarship has emphasized the standardization of forms in the Middle Byzantine period, it is incorrect to say that there was a standard Byzantine church. Certainly a Byzantine church is easily recognized and distinguished from an Early Christian basilica, from a contemporaneous Romanesque or Gothic church, or even from an Islamic mosque. Byzantine masons did not, however, simply create a formula and repeat it without alteration. Each church was built with specific desires and requirements in mind, and these were taken into consideration in the design of the building. Was it for public, private, or monastic use? Were burials to be included? Was it to be decorated with frescoes or mosaics? Was the site regular or irregular? Were there older foundations or walls that could be reused? What building materials were available? Byzantine religious architecture was, above all, a *responsive* architecture, easily adapted to the special necessities of location, function, and decoration, and this responsiveness often led to new formulations.

tophoria, serving as functional extensions of the bema. Architecturally the three spaces were similar; they were interconnected, and normally all three opened into the main worship space. A screen limited the view into the tripartite sanctuary. This barrier, the templon or iconostasis, in later times at least—perhaps by the fourteenth century—contained the major icons of the church.

The organization of the Middle Byzantine sanctuary differed considerably from its Early Christian predecessor, reflecting changes in the liturgy. The creation of the tripartite sanctuary, introduced already in the late sixth century, corresponded to the closed, centralized nature of the developed liturgy.[11] It had receded from the nave and had been given its own architectural definition. The furnishings also reflected changes: the stepped, theater-like synthronon of the Early Christian period was either reduced to a single row of seats or eliminated altogether, apparently because the number of concelebrating clergy had decreased. In addition, the central feature of the Early Christian synthronon, the bishop's throne, also vanished, reflecting the decline of spontaneous preaching in favor of standardized readings.

At the west side of the church, the Early Christian atrium also disappeared. It had served as a gathering place for the processions and had provided a transition from the street. Its role in Middle Byzantine times was assumed by the narthex, or entry vestibule, which similarly provided a transition from the exterior, albeit in a closed rather than in an open form. Normally the narthex was long, low, and narrow. The narthex was also the designated area for some special functions, such as baptisms, burials, and services in honor of the dead. With additional functions assigned to the narthex, particularly in monastic churches, its size could be expanded and an additional outer narthex, or exonarthex, could be added to the west.[12] Often open in form, the exonarthex resembled a porch.

Between the narthex and the sanctuary stood the main worship space of the church, called the naos, from the ancient Greek word for temple. The Middle Byzantine naos usually had a centralized design, and the term is often used in modern scholarship to distinguish it from the nave of an Early Christian church, which was longitudinal in its organization. In the naos the congregation gathered, standing through the lengthy services. Normally square in plan, the naos could take on a variety of forms, often subdivided by piers or columns. The dominant feature of the naos was a central dome that focused attention on the space immediately beneath it. The dome created a directional ambivalence in the interior. While the plan reveals a processional axis, beginning at the western entrance and terminating at the apse, the dome created a central focus and a vertical axis. Most Byzantine churches juxtaposed longitudinal and centralized planning schemes.

This architectural juxtaposition conformed to the necessities of the mature Byzantine worship service. There were really two performance areas. More sacred activities were restricted to the bema, centered at the altar. The other performance area was the central space of the naos, accentuated by the dome. As the processional nature of the early service was transformed, the processional axis of the Early Christian church was de-emphasized; this helps to explain the centralized design of most Byzantine churches. The solea, a fence that marked the final line of the processional axis as it entered the sanctuary, disappeared. Similarly, the ambo, a free-standing pulpit in the nave, was usually eliminated. The liturgy was reduced to a series of appearances, and for most of the service, the templon effectively separated the clergy from the congregation.[13] The centrally positioned dome highlighted the appearances of the celebrants at the door of the templon. At the same time, the active participation of the congregation was curtailed. The liturgical service began with antiphons rather than with processions, and the service ended with the distribution of sanctified bread rather than with communion, which was celebrated only rarely.[14]

These elements, related to the regular liturgical functioning of the church, may be regarded as standard, and they are clearly represented in the design of the Myrelaion church in Constantinople (built ca. 920), which can be taken as the "textbook" example (see figs. 1–4).[15] Nevertheless, not every church was so equipped. In some regions, the narthex was not standard. Occasionally the pastophoria were combined into a single space or reduced to a niche in the bema. Some churches lacked domes, and basilicas with wooden roofs continued to be constructed.

To be sure, many churches were much more complicated. Subsidiary chapels, or parekklesia, provided additional spaces for worship, commemoration, or burial.[16] Lateral aisles allowed easy access to all parts of the building. Sometimes lateral porches of light construction were included.[17] Some large congregational churches were equipped with galleries on an upper level; even small churches occasionally had galleries to provide a private space for the devotions of the founder.[18] In the Late Byzantine centuries, belfries became common.[19]

In spite of the uniformity of design, the Byzantine architect had any number of variables to work with, such as types of vaults, choice of materials, fresco or mosaic decoration, surface articulation, proportions, additional chapels, and so forth. The greatest variations occur in the naos, perhaps because the naos gave the church its individual expression. From the ninth century onward, the most common type of church was the cross-in-square church. The terms *four-column church* and *quincunx* have also been applied to this type; in German it is known as a *Kreuzkuppelkirche* (cross-domed church), and in French as an *église à croix inscrite* (inscribed cross church).[20] None of these terms adequately describes the three-dimensional form of the building type, nor do they address its range of design possibilities. The terminology is understandably confusing for the uninitiated. The word *quincunx* is derived from the pattern of five dots on a die and might better suggest a five-domed church; and in English-language scholarship, the term *cross-domed church* denotes something else entirely: a domed church with a cruciform plan. Most important, unlike the Early Christian basilica, whose far simpler spatial organization may be adequately understood from a floor plan, a Byzantine church must be comprehended as a three-dimensional entity, an object that both exists in space and molds and defines the spaces it contains. It is thus incorrect to refer to a cross-in-square plan, because a plan is two-dimensional, and the basic components of a cross-in-square church are only fully recognizable when expressed in three dimensions.

The cross-in-square church may be typified by the Myrelaion church (figs. 1–4). In this system, forms are massed in a pyramidal manner, the vaults cascading downward from the high, centrally positioned dome. Normally the dome rises above a drum. A ring of windows around its base helps to concentrate the natural light at the center of the church. Below this, vaults extend outward in four directions; this is the cross, set within the square of the plan below it. The eastern arm connects with the vault of the bema. Below, the dome is supported on four piers or, more commonly, columns that subdivide the interior space into nine units, or bays. The four corner bays of the naos are the smallest and have the lowest vaults. Normally these correspond with the vaulting heights of the narthex to the west and of the pastophoria to the east.

Many sources have been proposed for the origins of the cross-in-square church, ranging from Sasanian fire temples to Roman audience halls, in spite of their great chronological and geographical distance from the heartland of the Byzantine Empire.[21] The assumed relationship is based on the fallacy that if two objects look alike, they must be related. Most scholars have abandoned these notions, concluding instead that the cross-in-square church evolved from an existing ecclesiastical architecture during the Transitional period. In addition, it does not require a linear evolutionary framework to track the transformation of Byzantine architecture from the sixth to the ninth century. Most buildings from this period are not firmly dated, and this has added to the confusion. But in general, churches became smaller. Although Hagia Sophia set the standards for future developments, it was too large, too cumbersome, too costly, too experimental, and too complicated to be copied in full. Nevertheless, the introduction of a dome above the main worship space marked an important transformation in church design, altering significantly the impression both on the interior and on the exterior of the church. The Myrelaion's dome is only about 3.3 meters in diameter, or just about ten Byzantine feet—one-tenth that of Hagia Sophia. Nevertheless, both buildings juxtapose a longitudinal axis with a vertical axis, giving emphasis to the two most important performance spaces of the interior.

Cyril Mango suggests that the cross-in-square church was developed in a monastic context in Bithynia—that is, in the hinterland of Constantinople—during the period of Iconoclasm.[22] The small scale and unified interior would have suited a small, unisex monastic congregation of fewer than one hundred individuals. The columns do not really create aisles, so the congregation would have been united within the naos. A few examples of early cross-in-square churches still survive along the south shore of the Sea of Marmara, most notably the church now known as Fatih Camii (Mosque of the Conqueror) in Trilye. Sometimes called Hagios Stephanos, its date in the early ninth century can now be confirmed (figs. 7–9). The ruined church of Saint John at Pelekete may be a bit earlier.[23]

The Fatih Camii offers a useful contrast to the Myrelaion. Although it similarly utilizes the cross-in-square format, the details are not fully coordinated, and the vaulting forms are simpler. The tripartite east end (the south chapel is now destroyed) is slightly wider than the naos. More important, because the heavy pilasters of the interior isolate the corner bays, the unified impression that characterized the Myrelaion's interior is lacking.[24] The scale is similarly small, with the dome slightly more than 4.5 meters in diameter.

Several other churches from Asia Minor exhibit experimental solutions. A church from Side, on the south coast of Asia Minor, for example, had a cross-in-square format, but was apparently adapted to utilize existing foundations. Called "Church H" by its excavators, it was dated to the seventh or eighth century primarily on the basis of its plan (fig. 10).[25] According to the excavators, the city of Side was abandoned by the ninth century, so the church must have been built before then. Constructed on the site of an older church, of which only the foundations of the apse were uncovered, Church H was part of a larger building complex of uncertain purpose, never completely excavated. Whether or not the proposed dating is correct, the plan exhibits the same awkwardness as does the church in Trilye: the east end is not well coordinated with the naos, and, in this example, the pastophoria, or side chambers, are square and without apses. Thick walls isolate the western corner spaces, and the transitions from one part of the building to another are clumsy. The church comprises a disparate mix of components. In this example, the reuse of older foundations and a restricted setting may be partially to blame. Unfortunately, none of this can be clarified from the brief excavation report, and the published plan implies that the church was built in one period. Finally, the small scale is noteworthy: the dome of Church H would have been very close in size to that of the Myrelaion.

The underlying order to the system of the cross-in-square church is much more readily seen in the mature form of the Myrelaion. The roof profile establishes a hierarchy of forms and, as was common, the internal spatial and structural divisions are expressed on the

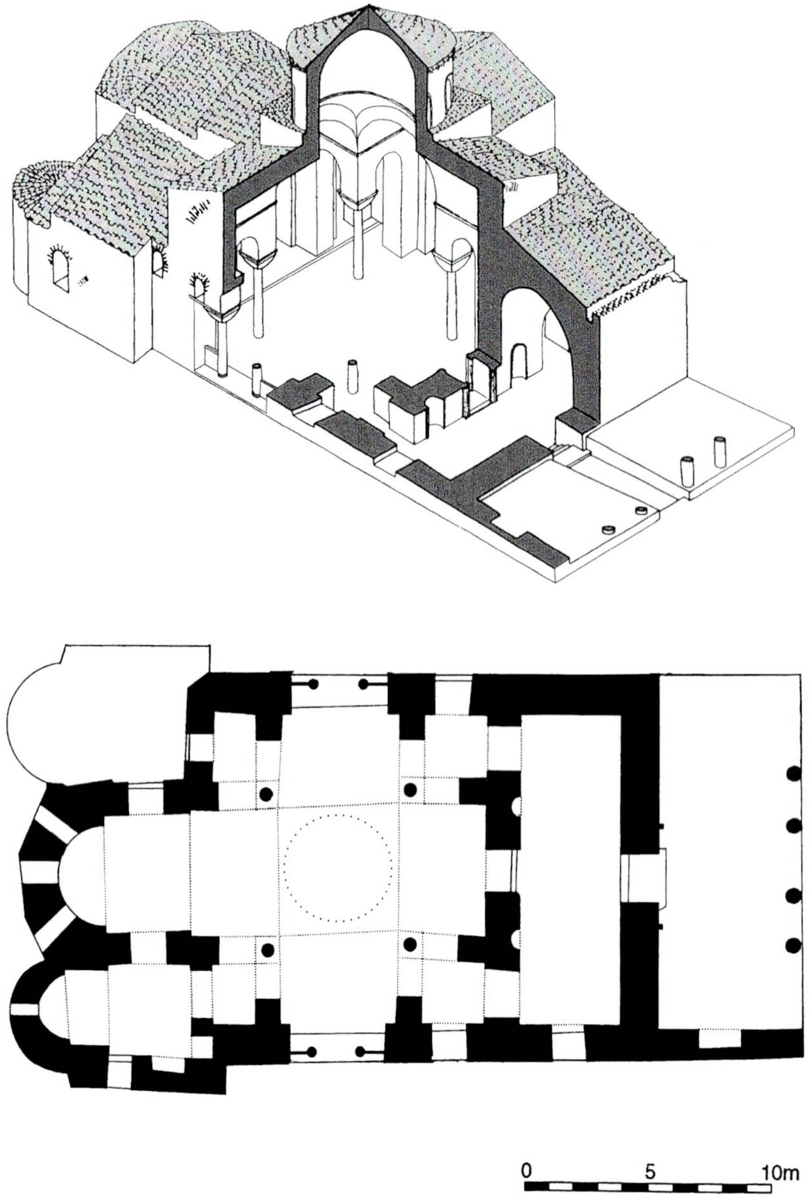

FIG. 7. Cutaway view of the Fatih Camii, Trilye

FIG. 8. Plan of the Fatih Camii

FIG. 9. Detail of the north facade of the Fatih Camii, after restoration

external facades. Pilasters correspond to the internal walls and supports; blind arcades reflect the heights of the vaults inside. This clear and rational system allows one to discern the internal disposition from the external articulation.

The system was also flexible. Piers could replace columns for greater stability. The plan could be shortened so that the eastern corners of the square merged with the tripartite sanctuary, or it could be reduced even further, to a two-column plan. Examples of all these variations existed, even within one region, such as Cappadocia, Bithynia, or Bulgaria (figs. 11A–F).[26] Variations may be so extreme as to call into question the adequacy of our terminology. However, in the Constantinopolitan examples of the cross-in-square church, the nine-bay naos almost invariably formed an indissoluble unit, squarish or slightly oblong in plan, to which the tripartite sanctuary and the narthex were joined.

The Myrelaion church has been taken as a typical example of the mature cross-in-square church, and an understanding of it prepares us for the numerous possibilities within the building type. But it shortchanges the Myrelaion to simply dismiss it as typical because in many ways it is unique, and the question of its origin has never been properly addressed. The church was constructed about 920 as a palace chapel attached to the private residence of the emperor Romanos I Lecapenos (fig. 12). The palace was constructed on a platform created by a giant rotunda—apparently the remains of a Late Roman palace—and the juxtaposition of the Late Roman and the Middle Byzantine phases

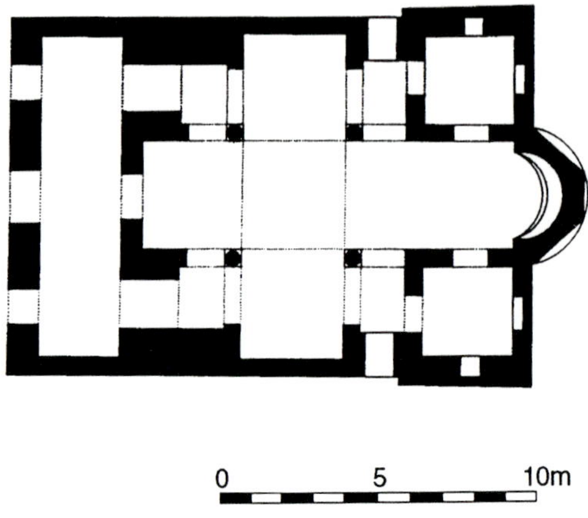

FIG. 10. Plan of Church H at Side

dramatically illustrates the changes in scale that architecture had undergone. To adjust the church to the height of the palace, a tall substructure was constructed for it, creating a lower level similar in plan to the upper level. This has provided the present Turkish name to the building: Bodrum Camii, or "Basement Mosque." Excavations indicate that the lower level served simply as a substructure throughout the Middle Byzantine period, but in the Late Byzantine period, the lower level was adapted to serve as a funerary chapel.[27] A corbeled walkway extended around the church on the main level, and the design of the building was remarkably open.

Most unusually, Romanos constructed the Myrelaion as a mortuary chapel to house the remains of his family members and of himself. Historians report that he had ancient sarcophagi brought into the building for this purpose, but unfortunately there is no evidence as to where within the building they were placed. In any event, Romanos thus broke with the tradition of his predecessors for burial at the church of the Holy Apostles. Later he converted the palace and its chapel into a nunnery. In function and setting, then, the building was far from typical.

Similarly, some of the architectural forms are unusual within the context of a cross-in-square church. For example, in the interior the vaults are elaborated: the dome and drum have a fluted surface, forming what is known as a "pumpkin dome," and the cross arms of the naos are topped by groin vaults rather than by simpler barrel vaults (see fig. 4). On the exterior, the proportions are tall, and the impression is dominated by the heavy half-columns engaged to each set of stepped pilasters. Although half-columns appear in other Byzantine examples, none are as massive as these, and it is unclear whether their primary

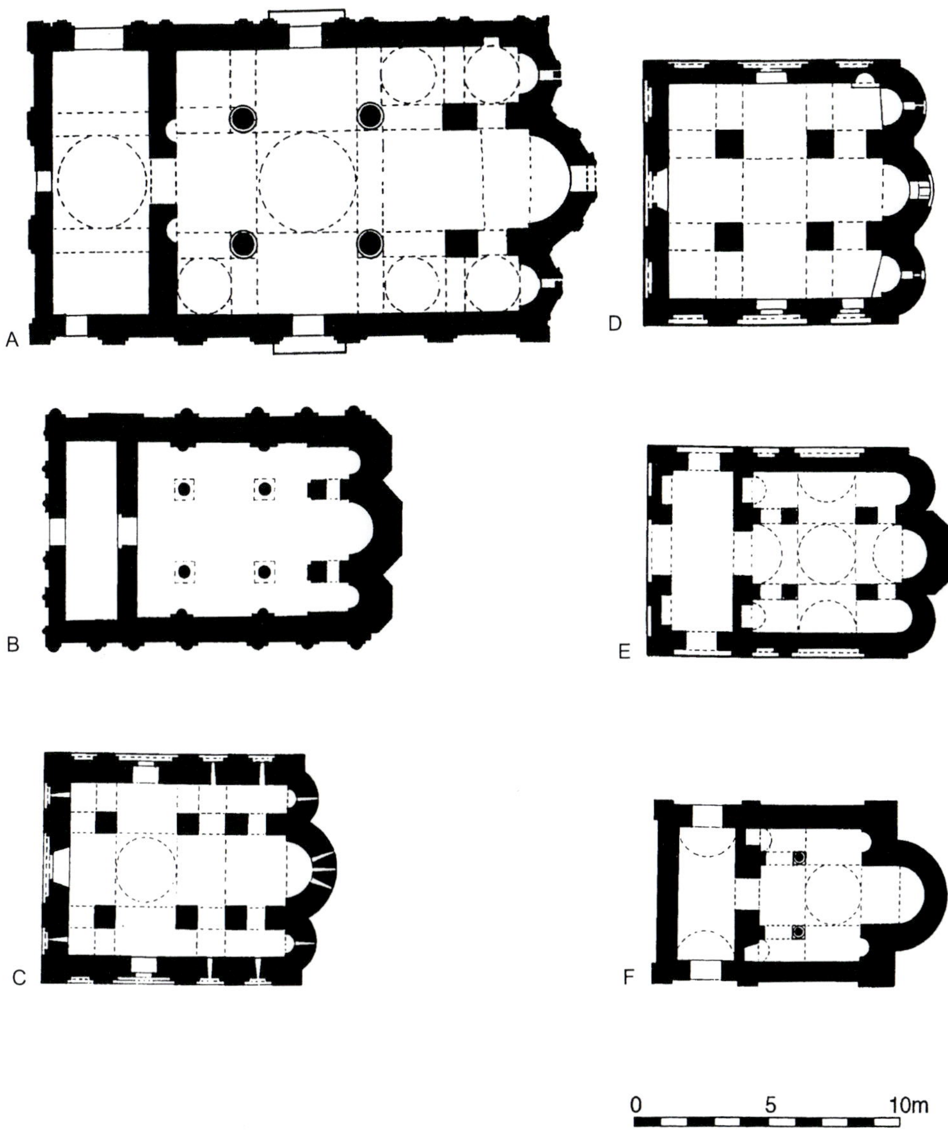

FIG. 11. Comparative plans of cross-in-square churches from Bulgaria:

A. Saint John Aliturgitos at Nesebar

B. Church at Bjal Brjag no. 1. at Preslav

C. Church of Saint George at Koluša

D. Church of Saint John the Theologian in the Zemen monastery

E. Church no. 4 in Selište, at Preslav

F. Church no. 3 in Selište, at Preslav

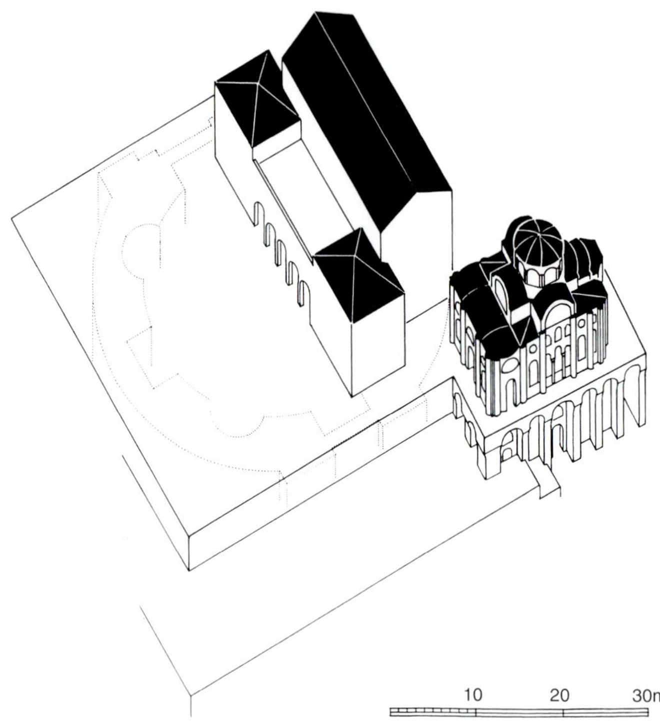

FIG. 12. Hypothetical reconstruction of the Myrelaion palace

function is formal (to articulate the facade) or functional (to strengthen the structure at critical points). The small, round windows are also unusual.[28] The designer was not simply perfecting a common building type. He was also addressing special site requirements and special functions, developing an architectural vocabulary appropriate to its setting and to the elevated status of the patron.

Of course the bricks and mortar formed only a portion of the final product, which was often lavishly embellished. A Byzantine church was normally decorated with frescoes or mosaics. Many have lost their decoration: for example, in Istanbul and elsewhere in Turkey churches were converted to mosques, and the Christian decorations were suppressed. These buildings were also given prayer niches to reorient them to Mecca and minarets for the call to prayer. The Myrelaion was converted to a mosque after the fall of Constantinople to the Ottomans, and it has subsequently been devastated by both fires and heavy-handed restorations. The original columns have been replaced with stone piers. The marbles and mosaics have vanished, although some tesserae, marble pieces, fragments of *opus sectile*, and glazed ceramic tiles were found in the excavations.[29] It is difficult to realize the elegance of the original when all that is left is the skeleton. But originally the Byzantine church and its decoration functioned together, the one enhancing the other, forming an artistic unity, a *Gesamtkunstwerk*, and it gives a false impression if we discuss the architectural forms without considering the decorative surfaces.

The pyramidal system of spaces in the cross-in-square church lent itself to an expression of the hierarchical system of Orthodox belief. The common church type and a standard system of decoration seem to have been developed simultaneously. More than fifty years ago, Otto Demus proposed that there was an underlying organizational system that controlled the decoration of a Middle Byzantine church, and although his thesis requires some modification, it is worth reviewing.[30] The church can be viewed as having three zones, with the holiest at the top. The dome, with its connotations of heaven, was given to the holiest figure, Christ, usually represented as a bust in a roundel. The Patriarch Photios described the dome decoration of the ninth-century church of the Virgin at Pharos this way: "On the very ceiling is painted in colored mosaic cubes a man-like figure bearing the traits of Christ. You might say that he is overseeing the earth and devising its orderly arrangement and government, so accurately has the painter been inspired to represent the Creator's care for us."[31] This image of Christ is usually called the Pantokrator, or "ruler-of-all" (see fig. 5).[32] In the drum of the dome, he is surrounded by his acolytes, usually angels or prophets. The second most important space, the apse, is usually devoted to the Virgin Mary, normally shown holding the Christ child and often flanked by angels.

The second zone is devoted to narrative scenes of the life of Christ. Demus called this the Feast Cycle because many of the scenes were selected from the calendar of the twelve major celebrations of the church, although it may be better to call them scenes from the lives of Christ and the Virgin. These scenes commonly appear in the vaults and wall areas of the crossarms. Some narrative scenes were also represented in the narthex. These pictures helped to transform the church mystically into an image of the Holy Land, where the events depicted had occurred.

The lowest zone comprised the Choir of Saints, as a Byzantine writer described it, the "choir of apostles and martyrs and prophets and patriarchs who fill the naos with their holy icons."[33] This "choir" was frequently grouped by type: sainted priests, church fathers, and patriarchs appeared in or near the apse; the martyrs appeared in the naos; and holy monks appeared in the western part of the church. These figures were represented as busts, half-length portraits, or life-size standing figures. Often unframed, they seem to occupy the same space as the viewer. In effect they became a part of the congregation that peopled the church.

Like the architectural forms, the subject matter of the decoration could also vary, depending on its context and medium. Certain elements were standard, but the selection and placement of scenes and of individual saints were subject to great variation, and

FIG. 13. Interior view of the Barbara church at Göreme, looking east

there was often a good deal of overlapping between zones. In the later period, the decorative program was expanded, and the number of scenes multiplied. Occasionally the lives of saints were illustrated as well. In both the art and the architecture, the final product resulted from the interplay of fixed and variable elements within a conservative framework.

Although the forms were flexible, a certain sanctity was associated with them that exceeded their structural or functional roles. This may explain the consistency, if not the conservatism, in Byzantine planning. It also explains why, even in Cappadocia in central Turkey, where the churches were carved into the soft rock formations, this standard church type was often maintained.[34] Being carved rather than built, a Cappadocian church could have taken on any form. Structural elements such as columns and domes were unnecessary for the stability of the church. But this was how a church was meant to be. In some churches, like the naively decorated Barbara church in Göreme, the artist painted the vaults to look as if they were constructed of blocks of stone (fig. 13). In other words, the conservatism in architecture may be in part the result of the meanings associated with certain architectural forms. The church as an established and recognizable image was sanctified in the same way as the image of a saint on an icon. It is not simply coincidence that the controversies of the Iconoclast period resulted both in a theology of icons and a standard church type.

How did the Byzantine viewer regard the church? Lavishly decorated and carefully arranged, the church could become the image of heaven, of the cosmos, or of the Holy Land. It was a symbolically flexible framework whose meanings shifted with the ceremonies it housed, a vessel to enhance and to comment on the ritual. The Mystagogical

History, attributed to Patriarch Germanos of Constantinople (715–30), gives a lengthy interpretation of the church building and its components as well as the furnishings and the liturgical vestments. Although written in an earlier age, it is still appropriate in this context:

> The church is a heaven on earth wherein the heavenly God "dwells and walks." It typifies the Crucifixion, the Burial, and the Resurrection. It is glorified above Moses' tabernacle of testimony. . . . It was prefigured by the patriarchs, foretold by the prophets, founded by the apostles, and adorned by the angels.

The text then explains the symbolism of its various parts:

> The apse is after the manner of the cave of Bethlehem where Christ was born, and that of the cave where he was buried. . . . The altar is the place where Christ was buried, and on which is set forth the true bread from heaven, the mystic and bloodless sacrifice, that is, Christ. . . . It is also the throne upon which God, who is borne up by cherubim, has rested. At this table too he sat down at his Last Supper.[35]

This flexible symbolism helped to transport the worshiper and to create a sense of the real presence of the events commemorated or reenacted in the worship service. Because the focus of the celebration was variable, the symbolism of the building and its parts was able to shift as well.

A well-known eleventh-century text, the Protheoria of Nicholas of Andida, insists upon a direct, symbolic relationship between the life of Christ and the liturgy, with the events represented in chronological order.[36] As a proof of this symbolic relationship, the author cites the authority of the icons, which were a part of the church decoration, "handed down to the holy churches of God in a good and pious way together with the sacred liturgy. . . . In them are related for the pious to see all the mysteries of the Incarnation of Christ from the coming of the archangel Gabriel to the Virgin, to the Lord's Ascension into heaven and his Second Coming."[37] According to Nicholas of Andida, the church, with its decorative program and its liturgical celebrations, was to be understood as a unit. The liturgy, like the pictorial program of the naos, represented the full life of Christ. Viewed in this way, the liturgy could be understood as a series of "icons" of the major events of Christ's earthly life. The system of Orthodox belief was reflected both in the decorative cycle and in the liturgy, and both were structured by and interacted with the architectural framework.

Byzantine Architecture Viewed from a Twentieth-Century Perspective

The standard approach to Byzantine architecture has been typological—that is, buildings are classified according to ground plan, definition of space, and other formal criteria.

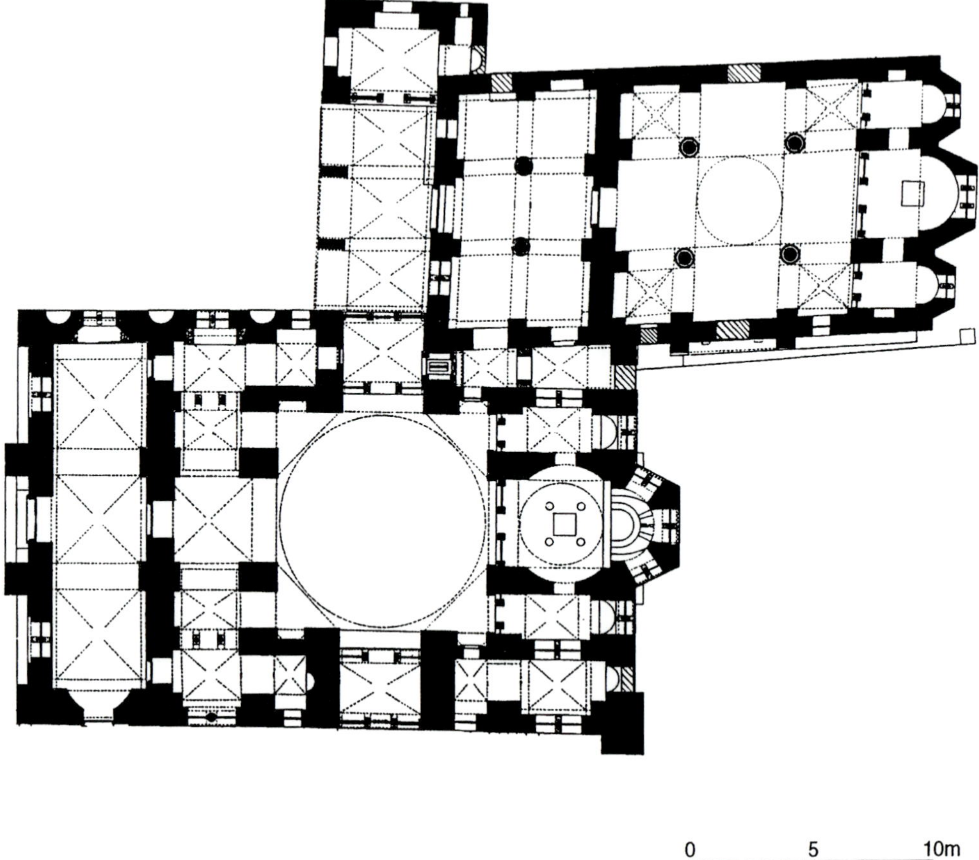

FIG. 14. Plan of the Theotokos church and the katholikon at Hosios Loukas monastery, Phokis

Typology provides an easy system of categorization that is useful for supplying a simple description of a building, but it should not be taken as an end in itself. As Cyril Mango states, "Buildings are labeled and pigeon-holed like biological specimens according to formal criteria: where a resemblance is found a connection is assumed even across a wide gulf in time and space."[38] A simplistic system of classification may thus set up artificial categories and can easily misdirect scholarly inquiry.

When used properly, typology can be a useful indicator of relationships. The tenth-century church of the Theotokos at the monastery of Hosios Loukas, for example, stands as the earliest securely dated cross-in-square church in Greece, displaying all of the features that one sees in contemporaneous churches in Constantinople and vicinity (figs. 14–15). At the same time, its construction technique and decorative details are of local derivation. Here it is possible to suggest an association with the Byzantine capital for

FIG. 15. View of the Theotokos church from the southeast

the origin of the design and the presence of a mason from the capital—or one familiar with its architecture—directing a team of local masons. Typology, however, has limited application. The church of Saint John at Hymettos (ca. 1120) near Athens employs a similar plan. But by the time of its construction, the cross-in-square church type was widely diffused, and its selection may tell us no more than the fact that the mason had four columns of the same size at his disposal.[39]

Occasionally, typological differences may be a good indicator of distance between centers of production. For example, the Çanlı Kilise in Cappadocia displays any number of features that would appear to be derived from the architecture of Constantinople (figs. 16–17). However, its abbreviated cross-in-square design eliminates the extra spaces given to the tripartite sanctuaries that are standard in the capital, and the original building did not have a narthex. Both features distinguish this building from those of the capital, in spite of its Constantinopolitan flavor.

In most instances, however, a typological approach tells us very little about the original context of the building, nor can it serve unaided as an indicator of date. If we exclude the annexed chapels, the church of Christ Pantepoptes in Constantinople (figs. 18–19), built shortly before 1080, is virtually indistinguishable from the Theotokos of Lips (figs. 20A–B, 21), built about 907. This degree of formal conservatism is unheard of in con-

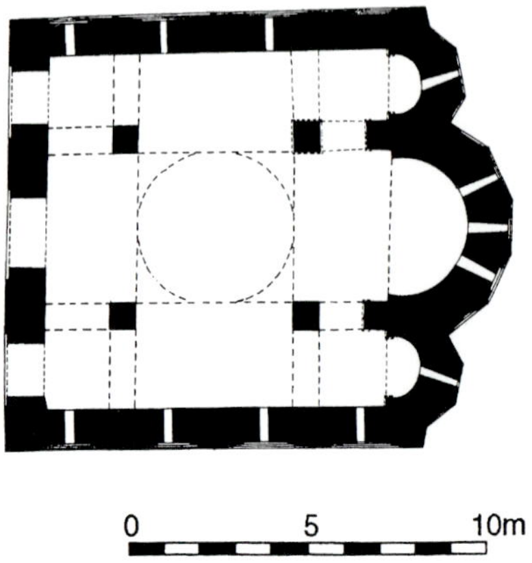

FIG. 16. Reconstructed Phase I plan of Çanlı Kilise near Akhisar

FIG. 17. South facade of Çanlı Kilise

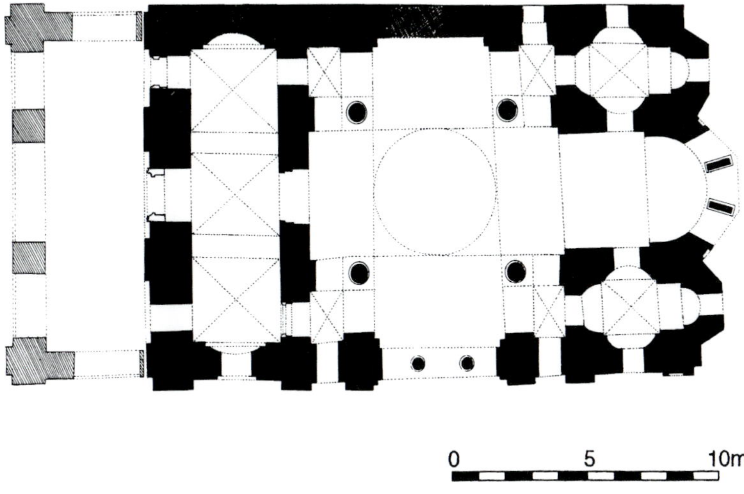

FIG. 18. Plan of the church of Christ Pantepoptes (Eski Imaret Camii), Istanbul

temporaneous Western European architecture—or, for that matter, in almost any other culture.

The typological approach does not take into consideration workshop practices. At Hosios Loukas and at Çanlı Kilise, for example, the construction technique and the building design tell very different stories. A single workshop may have been capable of constructing buildings of different plans, types, and vaulting solutions, but techniques of wall construction remain relatively constant within a region and within a workshop. Although it is perhaps the easiest way for a scholar to begin the study of Byzantine architecture today, a typological approach may not reflect its actual developments.

Some attempt has been made to associate different types of buildings with different functions, and certainly a functional approach to Byzantine architecture makes some sense. For example, the so-called Athonite triconch seems almost invariably to have been used for monastic worship (see figs. 58–60). The development of the lateral apses, or choroi, has been viewed in direct relationship to the necessities of monastic worship, housing the monastic choirs who sang the liturgy. However, the development of the Athonite triconch may best be understood as a regional phenomenon limited to Mount Athos, where about twenty examples are preserved, and to related areas in northern Greece and in the Balkans. No similar triconches are preserved in other monastic settlements, such as Mount Papikion or Bithynia, or in areas around Constantinople. Although the Athonite triconch plan may be identifiable as monastic, most monastic churches have different plans.[40]

FIG. 19. South facade of Christ Pantepoptes

The cross-in-square church type may have had its origins in the monastic realm, which was one of the most vital parts of society during the Transitional period. Still, this does not explain the wide diffusion of the building type and its use for a variety of different purposes—as palace churches or as burial chapels, for example. Robert Bergman has suggested that the cross-in-square church type was used primarily by the aristocracy.[41] But this hypothesis confuses function with scale. Like the Myrelaion, most buildings of this type are small, with a dome about three to five meters in diameter. The type is ideally suited to a small scale, and thus to housing a small congregation, and the cross-in-square type was selected for a variety of private or semi-private foundations ranging from imperial to monastic in their patronage.

The important point is that scale is normally omitted from such discussions of function and typology. Because of the physical limitations of the printed page, most books reproduce floor plans to the same size rather than at the same scale. Scale is the hardest aspect of architecture to convey without an actual site visit, but it was probably the critical factor in the selection of a plan or a building type. From a purely practical point of view, buildings of different sizes demanded different structural systems, and thus the development of various church "types" may have come about from a consideration of scale.

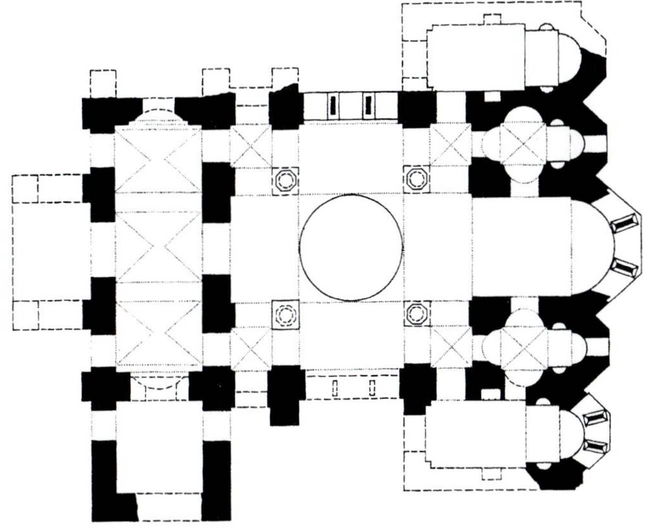

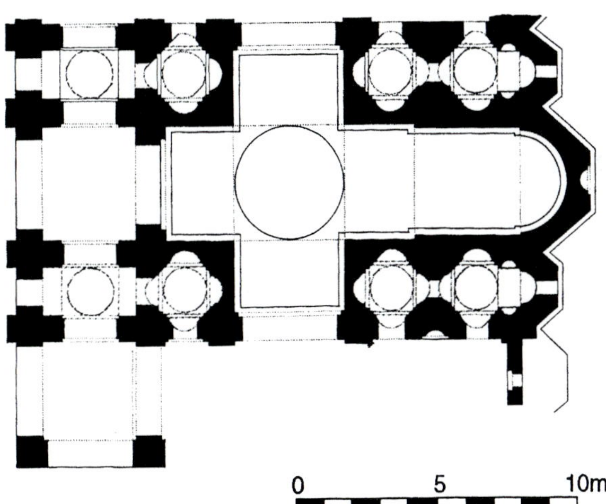

FIG. 20. Plans at (A) ground and (B) gallery levels of the church of the Theotokos of Lips (Fenari İsa Camii, north church), Istanbul

FIG. 21. Reconstruction of the Theotokos of Lips, seen from the northwest

Scholars of an earlier generation attempted to develop an evolutionary model of the cross-in-square church, seeking its ancestry in the cross-domed church and ultimately in the domed basilicas of the Justinianic period. Obviously, all of these building types share certain features. In each church, there is a centrally positioned dome above a building that is inherently rectilinear, with a dominant axis expressed in the plan, terminating in the apse. In general terms, this pattern of development makes some sense: of the three, the domed basilica make the earliest appearance in the main line of architectural developments in such buildings as Justinian's Hagia Eirene and the late ninth-century church at Dereağzı in southwest Turkey. Both had spacious basilican plans with structural systems that were modified for the support of a large dome over the nave.

The cross-domed churches, with barrel vaults positioned on all four sides, presented a more developed structural system for bracing the central dome, as well as a somewhat more compact and centralized plan. This type appeared in a number of buildings from the Transitional period, as in the reconstruction of Hagia Eirene after the earthquake of 740 (fig. 22). It may also be seen in the Koimesis church in Nicaea of the seventh or eighth century and in Hagia Sophia in Thessaloniki of the seventh century (fig. 23). Dendrochronology has recently provided secure dates for several of these buildings.[42] In

FIG. 22. Interior of Hagia Eirene, Istanbul, looking east

the same period one finds a number of smaller and more compact examples of cross-domed churches with enclosed spaces at the corners, such as the church now known as Atik Mustafa Paşa Camii in Istanbul (fig. 24), possibly ninth-century in date. Looking at the plans alone, it is tempting to hypothesize that the treatment of the corner support is an indicator of change, progressing from closed pier (Nicaea) to open cluster pier (Thessaloniki) to corner chapel (Atik Mustafa Paşa Camii) and ultimately to the earliest examples of the cross-in-square church (Fatih Camii at Trilye and Church H at Sardis) (fig. 25).[43] However, the chronology does not support this linear pattern of evolution, and it is perhaps wisest to view the period of the sixth through the ninth centuries as one of experimentation and transformation. In architectural terms, the time under consideration in our study may be regarded as one of standardized production following a period of transition.

Architecture Viewed from a Byzantine Perspective

The following two descriptions of churches are preserved in Byzantine texts, written at different times and for different purposes. Neither building survives, but the texts are

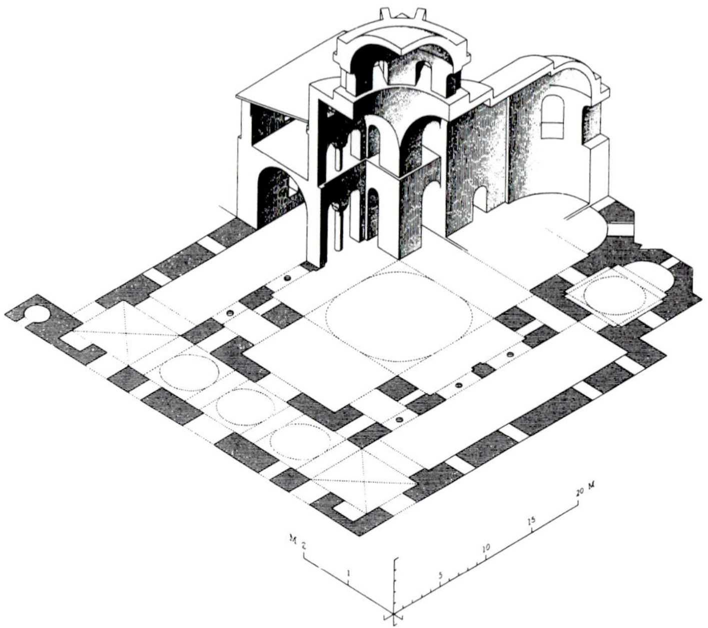

FIG. 23. Cutaway view of Hagia Sophia, Thessaloniki

well known to Byzantinists and have been the subjects of much discussion. The first text is an *ekphrasis*, a piece of evocative writing that often describes a work of art or architecture and may be found in many types of literature.[44] This *ekphrasis* was written by the tenth-century emperor Constantine VII Porphyrogennetos, and the subject is the Nea Ekklesia (New Church) built about 880 on the grounds of the Great Palace in Constantinople. The church was dedicated to Christ along with the archangels Michael and Gabriel, the prophet Elijah, the Theotokos, and Saint Nicholas.

> This church, like a bride adorned with pearls and gold, with gleaming silver, with the variety of many-hued marble, with compositions of mosaic tesserae, and clothing of silken stuffs, he [Basil] offered to Christ, the immortal Bridegroom. Its roof, consisting of five domes, gleams with gold and is resplendent with beautiful images as with stars, while on the outside it is adorned with brass that resembles gold. The walls on either side are beautified with costly marbles of many hues, while the sanctuary is enriched with gold and silver, precious stones, and pearls. The barrier that separates the sanctuary from the nave, including the columns that pertain to it and the lintel that is above them; the seats that are within [the sanctuary] and the steps that are in front of them, and the holy tables themselves—all of these are compacted of silver suffused with gold, of precious stones and costly pearls. As for the pavement, it appears to be covered with silken stuffs of Sidonian workmanship: to such an extent has it

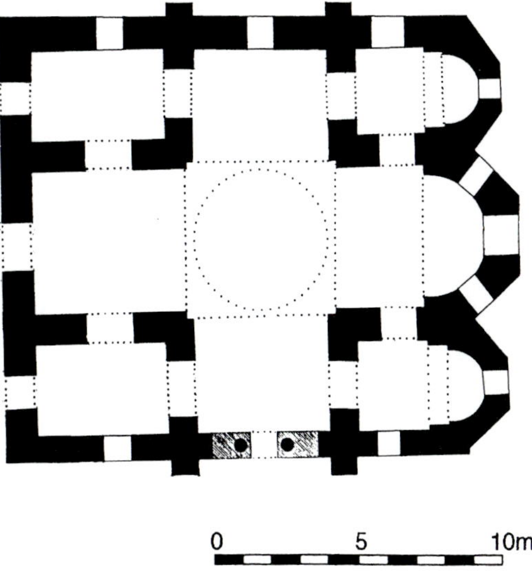

FIG. 24. Plan of Atik Mustafa Paşa Camii, Istanbul

> been adorned all over with marble slabs of different colors enclosed by tessellated bands of varied aspect, all accurately joined together and abounding in elegance. . . . Such is the church with regard to its interior.[45]

The second text is part of a legal document, the *Inventory of the So-called Palace of Botaniates*. It is also remarkably precise in its descriptions, but in this instance because of its legal function. It records the contents of a dilapidated estate in Constantinople that once belonged to the Botaniates family, which was handed over to the Genoese in 1192. The palace was close to the place called Kalubia, apparently near the modern quarter of Sirkeci. The text contains a detailed description of the palace's church, and, although it is long, it is worth citing in its entirety:

> The holy church is domed with a single apse and four columns—one of Bithynian marble. The frieze and the curve of the apse are revetted with marble, along with the vaults. The L-shaped spaces to the west are incrusted with Nikomedian tiles, along with the cornice. Above there are images in gold and colored mosaic, as with the dome and the four vaults—three with windows. The partition of the sanctuary consists of four posts of green marble with bronze collars, two perforated railings, a marble entablature, and a gilded wooden templon. Over the altar with its four straight sides there is a ciborium resting on four slender columns and screened off by two rails, two railings with lattice doors and windows. Above the west

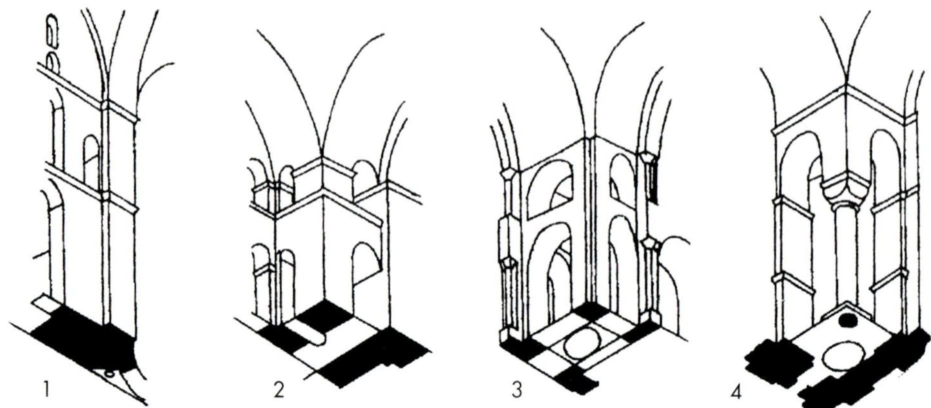

FIG. 25. Diagram suggesting a false evolutionary development of corner pier supports

> door is a carved marble icon. The floor consists of an interlace of green slabs and *opus sectile* and a border of Phlegmonousian marble. To the south is an extension in the shape of an arch [or: having an arch], decorated with images, with a conch decorated with mosaic. Its partition consists of three slender columns, [paneling known as] a *harmosphenion*, and a marble entablature. The two entrances have marble rails, and the other is closed. The floor is of white marble with *opus sectile* and roundels. The outer semi-circular terrace, which is decayed, has two reed-like columns and a marble floor. To the north there is an extension in the shape of an arch, decorated with images, a conch that is not shut off, and a floor of plain marble. The partition towards the west consists of columns and two railings with latticed doors and two reed-like columns, a rail, two lattices, and the window panes missing in the clerestory.[46]

What do these texts tell us? Older generations of scholars attempted to use these and similar texts to reconstruct lost works of architecture. At least four very different plans have been recommended for the Nea Ekklesia, with disagreements concerning the disposition of domes and interior spaces.[47] For the Botaniates church, scholars differ as to whether it had lateral apses or side chapels. But neither text clearly delineates the plan of the church, nor do they mention the construction materials. Both concentrate on the details, the decorative features, and the surface coverings.

As a part of a work of literature, an *ekphrasis* had a literary function that took precedence over the exactness of the recording. For example, the architectural descriptions in the eleventh-century *Chronographia* of Michael Psellos were introduced to illustrate the character of the imperial patrons, who, according to Psellos, were usually wasteful and extravagant.[48] In romances like *Digenes Akrites*, descriptions of architecture assist in the creation of an exotic setting.[49] In the *Vita Basilii*, the architectural descriptions help to establish the piety of the emperor and to illustrate his renewal of the empire.

This is not to say that a Byzantine description of a work of architecture does not reflect the truth, and most are remarkably accurate, as Wulff once demonstrated by comparing *ekphraseis* with surviving buildings.[50] But an *ekphrasis* emphasized perceptual understanding and is better understood as an expression of spiritual realities than as an archaeological record.[51] The description of the Nea Ekklesia, read in context, provides a reflection of its patron, Basil I. Taken out of context, it may appear incomplete. Nevertheless, it includes the salient features that would make the building distinctive in the eyes of the Byzantine reader, whose world was filled with many such edifices. But for us, something is missing: we can envision the atmosphere, the rich materials, and some of the details, but the overall form remains vague.

Not all Byzantine architectural descriptions were literary exercises; our second text comes from a legal document. The information provided in monastic foundation documents (*typika*) is similarly precise, as would have been necessary for laying out the regulations for life in the monastery. For example, the *typikon* of the Kosmosoteira monastery in Greek Thrace, written by the Sebastokrator (Crown Prince) Isaak Komnenos in 1152, provides numerous details about the construction materials, the disposition of components, the decoration of the church, and the care and maintenance of its fittings.[52]

In the palace inventory, the meaning of some of the terms is obscure, and parts of the description are a bit confusing. But like the *ekphrasis*, the description is dominated by the itemization of costly materials and furnishings; the plan and the construction materials go unmentioned. In both texts, the overall form recedes into the background and vanishes from sight behind the wealth of detail.

Perhaps the emphasis in such descriptions of buildings indicates a general medieval attitude toward architecture. That is to say, the parts can stand for the whole, or even assume greater importance than the whole. Indeed, this is exactly what Richard Krautheimer concluded in his study of early medieval copies of works of architecture.[53] In architectural copies, some (but not all) elements of the prototype are singled out for repetition, but the scale and the plan are almost invariably altered in the transfer. The details are the features that make each building distinctive; the individual details represent the whole. Although a general conservatism prevailed in terms of design and construction in Byzantine architecture, it was the finish materials, the decoration, and the furnishings that gave a building its particular character. Appreciating the emphasis on specific detail in Byzantine descriptions is one key to understanding Byzantine attitudes toward architecture.

The same attitudes appear in Byzantine representations of architecture. Often, as in the Vatican Homilies of James the Monk, or the Sinai Homilies of Gregory Nazianzenos, or in a liturgical roll from Patmos, figures are set within a framework that resembles a church, topped by domes and vaults.[54] Materials and patterns are carefully defined. The settings are sometimes referred to—incorrectly—as the cross-section of a church, and attempts have been made to identify some of them as specific buildings. But although the details are carefully rendered, the overall form of the buildings remains vague. It would be impossible to draw a ground plan from any of these illustrations. On the other hand, representations of specific buildings are limited to the identifying details, as in the scene of the Arrival of the Relics of John Chrysostom at the Holy Apostles in Constantinople in the Menologion of Basil II.[55] In the background, the church of the Holy Apostles is represented only by the distinctive profile of its domes.

Anthony Cutler has recently emphasized that originality is a culturally constructed notion.[56] Indeed, it is difficult to discuss the artistic production of another culture without resorting to the language of our own. Words such as *abstract*, *responsive*, *originality*, and *creativity* have particular meanings in contemporary usage—and perhaps had no real counterpart in the Byzantine vocabulary—and they are here employed guardedly. Nevertheless, the great *variety* one finds in Byzantine architecture requires an explanation. Accordingly, an examination of the creative process in Byzantine architectural production might be guided by the same principles that are evident in the descriptions and illustrations of the buildings just discussed. The details of a building were accorded greater significance and were thus given greater attention than the whole. Creativity on a small scale, involving only certain parts of a building, might have led to new formulations on a larger scale, and they might even have altered the way a building was envisioned. For example, a focus on the small scale, or on the details, may have led to an emphasis on the mosaic or fresco program and its manipulation, to a decorative treatment of the masonry construction, or to small changes in the basic schema of the building. The introduction of new features on a small scale, involving only a part of the building, would also make sense within the conservative framework of workshop practices. The creativity of the Byzantine mason must be understood in different terms than the creativity of the Late Antique architect—or than that of our contemporary builders. Thus it is important to emphasize detail as a guide to Byzantine architecture after the Transitional period. As Cyril Mango stated, "The chief contribution of Middle Byzantine architecture consisted in the elaboration of a type of church that was, in its own way, perfect."[57] The type thus remained relatively conservative, but the numerous elaborations indicate the creative input of individual masons and workshops. In sum, not only architectural forms but also the process by which they were created experienced fundamental changes at this time.

CHAPTER TWO

The Mysterious Disappearing Architect and His Patron

The builders of the great monuments of Byzantine architecture are most often anonymous figures who fail to appear in the historical record. Considerably more is known about their patrons because the texts tell us more about them. Historians are sometimes even able to reconstruct patrons' personalities, although the implications of this for the study of architecture are far from clear. Nevertheless, a text-oriented history of Byzantine architecture tends to emphasize patronage because the texts document patronage. It is easy to overlook the fact that a text may tell us next to nothing about the building itself, or about the builder, his working method, and the process of building. As with so many other aspects of Byzantine art, connecting text and artifact is a problematic exercise. In an attempt to rediscover the mysterious Byzantine architect, it is important to examine the evidence from the texts.

Architects and Their Patrons

The Early Christian period has left some information about architects—enough to determine that the practices of Roman times were continued perhaps as late as the seventh century. For example, in the sixth century, Cassiodorus provides the following formula for a palace architect: "When we are thinking of rebuilding a city, or of founding a fort or a general's quarters, we shall rely on you to express our ideas on paper. The builder of walls, the carver of marbles, the caster of bronzes, the vaulter of arches, the plasterer, the worker in mosaic, all come to you for orders, and you are expected to have a wise answer for each."[1] The architect is advised to "study Euclid—get his diagrams well into your mind, study Archimedes and Metrobius." All of this suggests that a proper Early Christian architect was both well trained and highly regarded, and that he followed much the same course of education that Vitruvius prescribed in the first century B.C.[2] Throughout the literature of the fourth through the seventh centuries, architects are praised, names are recorded, and the architect seems to have achieved a certain social standing. For example, Anthemius and Isidorus, the architects of Hagia Sophia in Constantinople, were men of status, the equivalent of university professors, with direct access to the emperor.

The picture is considerably different in the Middle and Late Byzantine periods, when builders are of considerably lower stature. In Alexios Makrembolites's "Dialogue between the Rich and the Poor," written between 1342 and 1344, masons are included among the poor.[3] Masons are rarely mentioned by name in either texts or inscriptions, and when named, it is usually as an incidental detail in a text with another purpose. Some histories and hagiography provide information about architecture in the form of *ekphraseis*, but architectural practices are difficult to piece together from the written evidence. In the *ekphraseis* of the Middle and Late Byzantine periods, the structure of the building seems to vanish amid the luxurious ornamentation and details. Similarly, those responsible for the construction seem to have vanished as well. They go unmentioned and unnamed in most of the documents of the period, whereas the *ktetores*, or founders, are given all the credit. But this may happen in almost any period: it is still commonplace to say that Justinian built Hagia Sophia, or that Louis XIV built Versailles, in spite of the fact that historians know quite a bit about the actual architects, who were lauded in their own day. Like Louis, Justinian clearly understood the symbolic implications of a building program, and both rulers were interested in—and presumably personally involved in—the process of building. But neither was an architect.

The relative status of patron and mason is nicely illustrated in a Latin manuscript of the *Chronicon Santa Sophiae*, which shows Justinian directing a mason in the completion of the dome of Hagia Sophia (fig. 26).[4] The contrast of scale says it all: Justinian is huge, even larger than Hagia Sophia. The tiny mason stands on the ladder holding a trowel and a roofing tile; he turns nervously to receive the emperor's instructions. Although this is a Western European manuscript, it follows in the Byzantine tradition, as the subject matter of the manuscript might suggest. Similar signative discrepancies in scale between patron and builder are evident in numerous other manuscripts, such as the Manasses World Chronicle and the Hamilton Psalter.[5]

It was common in a Byzantine *ekphrasis* for the building to be seen as a reflection of the character of the patron. For example, Procopius glorified Justinian's architectural production as a part of his panegyric to the emperor: he dominates the text, just as he dominates the illustration in figure 26. Procopius attributes major decisions to the emperor, while minimizing the contribution of the architects. According to Procopius, when structural problems occurred during construction, the builders despaired of finding a solution themselves and turned to the divinely inspired emperor for guidance.[6] In contrast, it has been suggested that the ninth-century author of the *Diegesis*, a semi-legendary account, attempted to do exactly the opposite—that is, to emphasize the

FIG. 26. Detail of an illuminated manuscript depicting Justinian directing the construction of Hagia Sophia. Vatican Library, Rome (MS lat. 4939, fol. 28v)

structural problems in order to diminish the reputation of Justinian, and possibly to criticize indirectly a contemporary imperial builder.[7]

As in Procopius's sixth-century panegyric to Justinian, the tenth-century *Vita Basilii*, which celebrates the deeds of Emperor Basil I (reigned 867–86) and was apparently written by his learned grandson Constantine Porphyrogennetos (reigned 913–59), includes a lengthy account of the emperor's architectural patronage. In general, the text emphasizes Basil's just government, while the discussion of architecture emphasizes his piety and his renewal of the empire:[8] "Between his warlike endeavors which he often, for the sake of his subjects, directed to a good end like a president of athletic contests, the Christ-loving emperor Basil by means of continuous care and the abundant supply of all necessary things, raised from ruin many holy churches that had been rent asunder by prior earthquakes or had fallen down or were threatening immediate collapse on account of the fractures [they had sustained], and to the solidity he added [a new] beauty."[9] There follows a catalogue of Basil's numerous restorations and building projects, without mention of an architect.

The eleventh-century writer Michael Psellos described examples of lavish architectural patronage to emphasize the weak or wasteful characters of the imperial patrons, following a formula that had been established in Roman times. His account of Constantine IX Monomachos's construction at the Mangana, "In the catalogue of the emperor's foolish excesses . . . the worst of all [was] the building of the church of Saint George the Martyr,"[10] seems to echo Suetonius's account of Nero's golden house: "His wastefulness showed most of all in the architectural projects."[11] Both buildings are said to have been encrusted with gold and surrounded by lavish gardens. In contrast, John Kinnamos's very brief characterization of the early twelfth-century Empress Eirene notes her patronage as evidence of her devotion: "[Empress Eirene] passed her whole life benefiting persons who were begging something or other from her. She established a monastery in the name of the Pantokrator, which is among the most outstanding in beauty and size. Such was this empress."[12]

Byzantine hagiography follows a similar pattern, and the churches constructed by Byzantine saints are seen as physical manifestations of their holiness. Usually in such descriptions it is the saint who calls the shots, as a combination of patron, contractor, and master mason. The saint follows divine authority, assuring that the building is constructed in accord with God's plan. The sixth-century *vita* of Saint Nicholas of Sion, for example, made his authority explicit. Wanting to depart for the Holy Land in the middle of a construction project, Nicholas proposed to halt the work in his absence and to dismiss the craftsmen and stonemasons. His brother Artemas objected: "How so? Can't I direct the craftsmen?" Nicholas was firm: "No! God granted me this grace, the stone obeys me, and I do as I wish."[13] The workers agreed and departed. When Artemas attempted to continue the quarrying with new workers, they were unable to move a single block until the saint returned.

For the several churches built by Saint Nikon of Sparta in the tenth century, no architect is mentioned, and the divinely inspired saint directed the work himself. At the beginning of the construction of the church of Saint Photeine at Sparta, the saint's gathering of workers, materials, and donations is said to have been "sufficient to win the favor of the saint and for the work to be in accord with God's plan."[14] At about the same time, at the Lavra monastery on Mount Athos, Athanasios also organized and directed the workmen.[15] Although the laborers are called *oikodomoi*, the common word for trained builders, their contribution is never made specific: they fade into the background because the text—and thus the building—is all about Athanasios, who visited the construction site regularly to oversee the work.

With very few exceptions, however, patrons must have lacked expertise and specialized skills related to building, and it is possible that most often their contribution to the final product amounted to little more than determining the scale and the budget. Beyond this is only speculation. For example, Emperor Constantine IX Monomachos was a knowledgeable and involved patron. He is said to have regularly visited the construction site

FIG. 27. Mosaic depicting Theodore Metochites presenting the church to Christ, Chora monastery (Kariye Camii), Istanbul

at the Mangana, altering the plan and expanding the project several times (although Psellos credits his interest to the fact that his mistress lived nearby).[16] Psellos praises the final product, but the exact nature of Constantine's contribution remains unclear.[17] Similarly, in the early fourteenth century, Theodore Metochites was apparently personally involved in the reconstruction and redecoration of the Chora monastery (fig. 27), and his position in the coordination of such a large, multimedia endeavor begs speculation.[18] But the input of the patron must by necessity remain an indeterminate element in our analysis of Byzantine architecture. Whatever his or her contribution, in the end the masons held the responsibility of translating the patron's wishes into buildable architectural terms. Patrons such as Theodore Metochites, or Justinian in an earlier age, could have provided "hothouse conditions," an unlimited budget, and perhaps a few suggestions—but the masons did the rest.

Byzantine Builders

Until the sixth century, or perhaps slightly later, the term for an architect was *mechanikos* or *mechanopoios*, often translated as "engineer." The title indicates a broadly based, academic education similar to that specified by Vitruvius in Roman times. The education in *mechanike theoria* is also clarified by Pappus of Alexandria in his *Synagoge*, written about

FIG. 30. Mosaic illustrating the construction of the Tower of Babel. Cappella Palatina, Palermo

Here we may begin to reconstruct a chain of command for an imperial project, in which a government official—who was certainly *not* an architect—is placed in charge of the project, presumably with a master mason (or master masons) under his command.

In another instance, during the restoration of Constantinople by Michael VIII following the reconquest of the city from the Latins in 1261, the emperor appointed a monk named Rouchas to restore the church of Hagia Sophia: "And placing in charge the monk Rouchas, a man efficacious in this type of affair [*andra drasterion epi tois toioutois*] he rearranged the sanctuary, the ambo, and the solea, and reconstructed other parts with imperial funds."[39] Although it is possible that Rouchas was a mason, the context suggests that he was instead the imperial overseer.

A chain of command between the imperial patron and the workers is clearly recorded in a sixth-century provincial building project. The church of the Theotokos (the "Nea Ekklesia") in Jerusalem was constructed by Justinian and Theodora in the 530s. Cyril of Scythopolis writes that a *mechanikos* named Theodore was responsible for the actual construction of the church, while the tax clerks (*trakteutai*) at the praetorian prefect's office were to take care of the finances for the project. At the same time, Peter, the archbishop of Jerusalem, was given final authority, but a certain Barachos, bishop of Bakatha, was charged with supervising the construction.[40] Thus, between the patron and the project architect were a variety of named intermediaries; none of them were architects.

Building contracts (*homologiai*) and other documents are also occasionally mentioned in relationship to building projects. These are frequently noted in the *Book of the Eparch*, a tenth-century code governing the guilds of Constantinople.[41] Both written and verbal contracts between the patron and the contractor or overseer of a project are noted; both are regarded as binding. Similarly, in the tenth-century *vita* of Hagios Germanos, the author recorded a contract that established the wage Germanos was to pay the workers.[42] The late eleventh-century *typikon* of Gregory Pakourianos also mentions receipts issued to document successfully completed work.[43]

It is possible to surmise that, in addition to a master mason, a workshop of masons had a supervisor or some sort of official to attend to the finances and the non-architectural decision making. This was the role taken by Barachos and Eustathios, and probably by Rouchas, Nikephoros, Stephen, Petronas, and Patrikios in the earlier examples. Clearly, when names are mentioned, they identify individuals from the upper part of the hierarchical structure of a building project. But the same language ("X built Y," or "X was responsible for the construction of Y") might identify the patron, the government representative, or the manager—as well as the mason. Possibly two roles, architect and manager, were played by the same individual in a small project, but in most projects, there was likely some division of leadership.

Workshops and Guilds

Apart from a few rules governing the organization of guilds, very little is known about the activities or the constitution of a workshop of builders in the Middle or Late Byzantine periods. Our best source is the *Book of the Eparch*, from the tenth century, which gives some of the regulations governing craftsmen at that time.[44] Artisans were organized into guilds (*systemata*, or *somateia*), which, in the tenth century, were privileged corporations with voluntary membership, and which were protected from the competition of non-guild members. In many ways, they were similar to the later medieval guilds of Paris. Byzantine guilds were subject to governmental control, but direct services to the state appear to have been minimal.[45] Urban guilds played a role in imperial triumphs and other ceremonies.[46] The guild system continued into the following centuries but became less strict.[47] During the Middle Byzantine centuries at least, the guilds were an active political force within Constantinople.[48] There are indications that some sort of professional corporation continued in the thirteenth and fourteenth centuries.[49] For example, Georgios Marmaras of Thessaloniki is identified consistently with his title, *protomaistor ton oikodomon* or *protomaistor ton domitoron* (master of the builders), in several documents from Mount Athos (1322–27) that do not concern architecture.[50] This seems to have been a professional title, suggesting the existence of a permanent workers' organization within the city.[51] On the other hand, workshops (*ergasteria*) were also temporary associations of workers from various professions who were brought together for a specific project. Unfortunately, the relationship between the guild system and the individual workshops is not clear.

According to the *Book of the Eparch*, competition was restricted by the precise definition and limitations placed on the guild's activities.[52] For example, the artisan was held responsible for his work, and he was not allowed to embark on another project before completing the one at hand. At the same time, workers were also protected from the improper behavior of the client. Special skills were demanded of builders: "Those who build walls and domes or vaults of brick must possess great exactitude and experience lest the foundation prove unsound and the building crooked or uneven." For brick buildings, builders were held accountable for ten years after construction, and with mudbrick construction, they were accountable for six years, barring natural disasters.[53]

Workshop Size and Make-up

Workshops are usually assumed to have been temporary organizations, formed to complete a specific task. For certain, the relationship between workers with complimentary skills, or between workers and apprentices, continued over a period of years. The presence of apprentices is important in this respect, because in a "professionally illiterate" society, workshops were the method of transferring acquired knowledge from one generation to the next. The fact that workshops spanned several generations helps to account for the continuity in Byzantine architecture.

The head of a workshop or of a guild was called the *maistor* or *protomaistor*, which is usually translated as "master mason" or "master builder." The *Diegesis*, a semi-legendary account of the ninth century, credits the building of Justinian's church of Hagia Sophia to one hundred master builders (*maistores*), each directing one hundred workers, with fifty master builders and their teams working simultaneously on each half of the building.[54] But this account is clearly fabulous: the *Diegesis* also claims that the design of the church was revealed to the emperor by an angel. It is plausible that the magnitude of the workshops fantasized in the *Diegesis* was meant to contrast with the workshops of its author's time, just as the scale of Middle Byzantine architecture contrasted with that of the Justinian period.

In another example, given by Theophanes, Constantine V wanted to restore the aqueduct system for Constantinople in 766–67; therefore, he called artisans from the various regions of the empire.[55] The numbers may appear equally fabulous, but this was an extensive undertaking: one thousand masons (*oikodomoi*) and two hundred plasterers (*christai*) from Asia and Pontus; five hundred clay-workers (*ostrakarioi*) from Greece and the islands; five thousand laborers (*operai*) and two hundred brickmakers (*keramopoioi*) from Thrace. Moreover, "He set taskmasters over them including one of the patricians."[56] By contrast, although numbers are not given in the discussion of an Isaurian workshop of stonemasons in Antioch during the early sixth century, which is mentioned in the *vita* of Saint Symeon the Younger, one has the impression of a small, itinerant workforce in which the workers took care of each other.[57] In the sixth-century *vita* of Saint Nicholas of Sion, the hagiographer writes that eighty-three craftsmen (*technitai*) were working on the church.[58] On the other hand, at Peristerai, near Thessaloniki, Saint Euthymios built the church of Saint Andrew in the ninth century with the assistance of only three or four laborers.[59]

One of the post-Byzantine *hypomnemata* (commentaries) associated with the monastery of Hosios Loukas is accepted by several scholars as presenting some important evidence for the early history of the monastery, although almost all of the attention has been focused on the evidence for dating the existing churches.[60] For a church completed in the year 966, the emperor sent experienced masons (*oikodomoi*) from Constantinople under the supervision of an overseer (*epistates*) who held the ranks of *patrikios* and *Domestikos ton Scholon*, and two hundred men. They were instructed to build a church "as beautiful as Hagia Sophia, but not so large." In the team were eighty of the most experienced master builders (*oi pleon empeiroi kai megaloi technitai* 80, *oi protomaistores*) with eighty apprentices (*mathetas*).[61] The text poses several problems: the numbers are certainly exaggerated, no specialized skills are identified, and no names are given. Still, it suggests something of the hierarchy that existed within a construction project.

The evidence from Western Europe in the Gothic period is much more detailed, but considering the vastly different scale of projects of the East and West, it would be misleading to reconstruct a Byzantine workshop on a Western model.[62] Some basic features of Western medieval practice are worth considering, however. For example, it was common in the West for the supervision of a project to be divided between a clerk of works, who was responsible for the administrative and financial aspects, and the master mason, who directed the actual construction. In comparison to a master mason, a clerk had some formal education, came from a higher social class, was paid considerably better, and could hope for advancement. A master mason, on the other hand, was regarded as a craftsman in spite of his talent. He normally lacked education other than his experience in the workshop, where he would have learned through the oral transmission of the tra-

The *typikon* of the Monastery of the Resurrection at Constantinople (ca. 1295–1324), written by Constantine Akropolites, records several significant details concerning the monastery's restoration by Constantine's father, George Akropolites. Salaries were paid to the workers, and, until expenses grew excessive, careful records were kept. "Specially assigned secretaries recorded in detail on paper the gold pieces delivered to the supervisors of the project, as is customary for those who undertake large projects."[78] The text also suggests the problems of financing a large architectural endeavor. After sixteen thousand gold pieces were spent in the course of a year, George ordered the ledgers to be abandoned, and in the end, George had to take money from the inheritance of his son to complete the project.[79] Thus Constantine declares that he paid the wages of the workers, even though he was still a small child when the work was completed.

In a legal case in fifteenth-century Thessaloniki, payments, quantity of materials, and the number of workers are all recorded.[80] Payments are also included in the mathematical textbooks: in examples, the construction of a house requires between six and twenty days. In one problem the builder is paid twenty *aspra* for each day that he works, but owes thirty *aspra* for each day that he does not work; in another equation the builder earns one thousand *aspra* for the entire project.[81] It is not clear how hypothetical these problems are.

In the tenth century, Athanasios of Athos cured a group of masons from a mysterious paralysis, tonsured them, and put them to work—thus apparently eliminating the necessity of payment.[82] According to his *vita*, Athanasios regularly ascended the scaffolding to oversee the work. Of the workers, who are called both *technitai* and *oikodomoi*, only one is mentioned by name: a man named Daniel is singled out not because of his contribution to the construction but because he had a vision after the saint's death.[83] At Mount Galesios in the following century, the stylite saint Lazaros similarly served as both master mason and contractor. He directed the planning and construction of a new trapeza, or dining hall, apparently while standing on the top of a column, from which he could literally oversee the work.[84] At least part of his workforce consisted of monks from the monastery.

In the fourteenth century, Dionysios of Athos directed the construction of the monastery named after him, Dionysiou, in several phases.[85] Dionysios acted as a general contractor, organizing the workers and the building materials. In the earlier phases of construction at the monastery, all of the work was carried out by the monks alone: they built cells and a chapel, and added winter cells on the west side of the mountain, another church, a storehouse at seaside, and a tower to guard against pirates.[86] In a later and apparently more prosperous period, Dionysios hired workmen (*ergatai*), who assembled the necessary building materials and then summoned the builders (*oikodomoi*). Through their efforts, Dionysios was able to erect a new church dedicated to Saint John Prodromos, a fortification wall, new cells, a refectory, and an aqueduct.[87] A clear distinction is made between the laborers (presumably unskilled) and the team of builders (presumably skilled).

A document from the monastery of Iviron on Mount Athos (dated 1421) records the work done on a garden in Thessaloniki whose ownership was contested. Three *oikodomoi*, Andreas Kampamares, Argiros Xifilinos, and Georgios Monomachos, made various improvements and constructed a fountain and a water channel (*hydrochetos*) with the help of others. Andreas testified that, after the flooding from the fountain, he employed ten unskilled workers (*ergatai*) to clean up, and then for the repair, he hired four skilled workers (*technitai*) along with twenty unskilled workers (*ergatai*) at a cost of fifty aspra (which also included the price of two squared timbers to brace the fountain). The other *oikodomoi* declared that when they enlarged another fountain and seven water channels (repairing five and adding two new ones) in 1416–17, they employed fourteen trowels (*mystria*), twenty workers (*ergatai*), seven buckets of plaster (*asbestes*), three buckets of either potsherds or seashells (*ostraka*), and one bottle of linseed oil (*linelaion*) worth two *aspra*, at a total cost of twenty *aspra*.[88] The document is rare because of the information it provides about the size of the workforce, the materials necessary, and the costs. It also distinguishes among the roles assigned to *oikodomoi*, *technitai*, and *ergatai* respectively.

Although most references to masons and builders say nothing about them and fail to provide names, they are found in a wide variety of locations. Byzantine masons were at work in Kievan Rus' in the tenth and eleventh centuries and were clearly responsible for the introduction of both masonry construction and a Byzantine architectural vocabulary, but the references to their presence are extremely vague; they are usually referred to as "masters," following the Greek *maistores* or *mastores*. The Laurent'ev Chronicle of 989 and the Ipat'ev Chronicle of 991 record simply that Vladimir brought Greek masters to construct the Tithe church in Kiev.[89] At the katholikon of the Dormition in the Monastery of the Caves in Kiev, the *Paterikon* reports that a local team of workmen was headed by four masters from Constantinople.[90] The names of only four masons have been recorded for pre-Mongol Rus'; none of them was a Byzantine, although Greek masters were at work in Kiev, Chernigov, and Pereslavl in the eleventh century, and at work in Kiev, Vitebsk, and Pskov in the twelfth century.[91] Rappoport assumes that the Byzantine team working in Kiev in the 1030s was large and included numerous specialists, but this is without textual basis.[92]

In Ottonian Germany, the chapel of Saint Bartholomew at Paderborn was said to have been constructed by Byzantine workmen: *per graecos operarios construxit*. This phrase has elicited a great deal of speculation. Although the chapel is suggestive of Byzantine forms and is unique in Ottonian architecture, the exact contribution and point of origin of the Byzantine masons remains unclear.[93] Similarly, in the ninth century, Emperor Leo V is said to have sent "workmen and excellent masters in architecture" to construct the church of San Zaccaria in Venice.[94] Workers from Constantinople might also have participated in the construction of Madinat al-Zahra in Spain in the tenth century.[95]

There are also some mentions of masons traveling within the Byzantine Empire. In the tenth century, an Armenian architect named Trdat was at work in Constantinople, repairing the dome of Hagia Sophia.[96] In the eleventh century, Constantinopolitan masons were sent to Chios to build the katholikon of Nea Moni[97] and to Jerusalem to rebuild the Holy Sepulcher.[98] There are also the references (noted earlier in this study) of masons being brought to Athos. Similarly, in the twelfth century at Patmos, Christodoulos imported builders for the construction of the monastery.[99] Furthermore, in 1361, John V ordered two *technitai* to be sent from Athos to Lemnos to repair the fortifications.[100]

The many recorded instances of the movement of masons merit comment, as they seem to contradict the regulations specified by the *Book of the Eparch*. In some instances, these may be dismissed as topoi, meant to emphasize the significance of the building project. For example, it is possible to dismiss as hyperbole Procopius's assertion that for the reconstruction of Hagia Sophia, "Justinian began to gather artisans (*technitai*) from the whole world."[101] In other instances, however, workers must have been "summoned from afar" out of genuine need, such as for the reconstruction of the Aqueduct of Valens by Constantine V. This assertion is in agreement with the recorded depopulation of Constantinople and Thrace in the eighth century, which required new inhabitants to be brought in.[102] In other instances, such as in Kievan Rus' or Jerusalem, the presence of Byzantine workers may have been a part of a program of Byzantine cultural or ideological expansion. Although the *Book of the Eparch* suggests that under normal circumstances workshops did not travel, Byzantine history is full of unusual circumstances. In addition, imperial patronage often included the provision of both materials and craftsmen. Finally, there probably were not active workshops of builders in every part of the empire; thus at Athos, Patmos, and elsewhere, it was necessary to bring in trained personnel. This may have become standard practice by the Late Byzantine period, as it seems to have been the norm in the Late Byzantine Balkans.[103]

Many masons are mentioned by name in the Late Byzantine period, but this may be the result of several factors: records and inscriptions have survived better from this period; at the same time, the scarcity of trained builders may have increased their individual importance; or perhaps the recording of masons' names echoes contemporaneous developments in the West, where the emergence of distinctive architectural and artistic personalities is evident. For example, several names may be associated with surviving monuments in Macedonia: at the church of Bogorodica Ljeviška in Prizren, an inscription (ca. 1310) names two *protomaistores*, Nicholas and Astrapas, who are usually identified as the builder and the artist. At Dečani, a *protomaistor*, George, and his brothers, Dobroslav and Nicholas, constructed the entrance tower and the refectory. An inscription at Chilandar monastery on Mount Athos mentions builders named Michael and Barnabas; the former may be the same as the painter Michael, whose inscription is known from the frescoes of the church of the Peribleptos in Ohrid.[104]

In addition to those already mentioned, there are also references to builders from the *Acts* of the monasteries of Mount Athos, in which the builders are mentioned by name, but no further details are given. For example, the *oikodomoi* Demetras, Eustathios, and Nikon are noted at Lavra.[105] The *oikodomoi* Manouilos Vivlodoitis and Theodoros Malakis are mentioned at Chilandar in 1296.[106] *Protomaistoros ton oikodomon* or *protomaistoros ton domitoron* (master of the builders) Georgios Marmaras of Thessaloniki is mentioned in documents at Chilandar, Iviron, and Zographou in 1322, 1326, and 1327 respectively.[107] Another *protomaistor*, Demetrios Theophilos, is mentioned at Docheiariou in 1389.[108] In the early fifteenth-century inscriptions from the Gattilusi family holdings in the north Aegean, a certain Constantine *maistor* (or *mastoras*) is named four times, twice in inscriptions at Samothrace and twice in inscriptions at Enez.[109] In Constantinople, Nikephoros Gregoras notes the presence of *tektones* in 1348, and two *leptourgoi* (carpenters or sculptors of wood), named Giorgios and Stylianos, are mentioned in documents of the 1360s.[110] Masons and carpenters are also mentioned at Kerinia on Cyprus and at Trebizond in the fourteenth century.[111] There are certainly many other references.

In her study of inscriptions and donor portraits in thirteenth-century Greece, Sophia Kalopissi-Berti has observed that artists are mentioned when they are of the same social standing as the patron, or when the artist and patron are one and the same.[112] The same may hold true for builders or project supervisors: Patrikes and Nikephoros, for example, whatever their roles, clearly had an elevated status and are mentioned in connection with their imperial patrons. Saints Nikon and Lazaros assumed the dual roles of both patron and builder. On the other hand, the masons mentioned in the documents from Mount Athos would have had a social standing similar to that of the monks who hired them.

It is easier today to recognize the individualizing traits of a workshop than it is to determine its size or to identify its members. The remarkable uniformity in Byzantine architecture can be attributed to the consistency in workshop practices within a given region, as has long been recognized.[113] Indeed, more than a century ago, Auguste Choisy credited the influence of the workshop system for the traditional and regional character that is often still evident in Byzantine art.[114] Although much that Choisy wrote has been superseded, this observation still rings true.

CHAPTER THREE

Drawing the Line and Knowing the Ropes

In designing their buildings, Byzantine masons probably did *not* utilize architectural drawings—neither for the design nor for the codification of ideas. This suggestion has important implications for our understanding of Byzantine architecture. Today, our analysis of a historical building usually begins with drawings—the plan, the elevations, the sections. Although this may be the best way to develop a conceptual understanding of a building in its final form, this method of analysis may not properly represent the way a building was initially conceived by its builder.

This chapter attempts to reconstruct Byzantine design methodology. It examines the evidence for the use of architectural drawings and related on-site calculations, as well as for the application of geometry, modular units, proportional systems, and standards of measurement to determine the overall form of the building and to position its most significant features. Lacking texts that address these issues directly, it is impossible to say with any precision what was involved in the design process during the Middle and Late Byzantine periods. Nevertheless, several aspects may be confirmed through an examination of limited written sources and archaeological evidence. Still, we must be cautious not to assume that builders historically worked in the same manner as architects do today.

Rather than relying on plans, a Byzantine mason drew upon practical experience. Within the workshop, masons learned both construction methods and standard architectural forms that could be easily adapted to the specific requirements of location, function, and decoration. Modular measurements, geometry, and, in some occasions, a simple form of quadrature (proportional relationships developed through a system of geometric figures) may have been employed to establish the plan and the elevation. Standard measurements also seem to have been employed in numerous surviving buildings, and proportional relationships may have been an important concern in establishing the overall dimensions of a building. Thus, to reconstruct the design process, it is important also to examine the Byzantine knowledge of arithmetic, geometry, surveying, and systems of measurements.

Drawings, Preplanning, and "Knowing the Ropes"

Historians are not entirely lacking in useful texts, although there is none that addresses the practice of architecture directly. Byzantine hagiography, however, is an almost untapped resource for architectural information, and some insight into the design process may be gleaned from a careful reading of texts. For example, in the tenth century, Saint Nikon directed the construction of a church dedicated to Saint Photeine at Sparta, as noted in the previous chapter. Because the actions of the saint are described in some detail, his legend provides a useful starting point for our discussion.

> When the great man was in labor with a great and passionate desire to raise a divine church from the very foundations to the Savior and Master of all, he considered it of great importance to erect a most sacred and most beautiful house as far as he could. A divine vision from heaven revealed to him its building, and he seized the occasion and was now about to proceed to the task.

Having placed his trust in God, he went to the central church and instructed the congregation and clergy to accompany him in procession to the marketplace.

> During the journey, the saint put three stones on his shoulders and carried them, and no one could conjecture what the burden of the stones meant to him. But when he had come to the marketplace, having put the stones on the ground he said: "Here, my children, it has been decided by God, as has been revealed to me in my lowliness, that a church be built in the name of our Lord Jesus Christ and his praiseworthy mother and the eminent martyr Kyriake, for the aid and salvation of all your city."

The people followed his instructions and cleared the site of rubbish and gathered building materials. Some provided money, while others

> agreed to contribute what was most suitable and to share in the great expense with labor and the task was considered by them desirable and quite worthy. . . . And so in a short time a great deal of material was collected and one or another had lavished upon the holy man the necessities for the building. And these were of the most beautiful material, so that this was sufficient to win the favor of the saint and for the work to be in accord with God's plan. He began the building, having earlier delineated (*hypograpsas*) it with a rope; he constructed the colonnades (*stoes*) below and above, bringing to bear a technical skill even more ambitious than his physical skill. Then, having enclosed the building on all sides, he affixed the roof.[1]

FIG. 31. Detail of an illuminated manuscript showing land being measured with ropes, illustrating Joshua 18–19. Vatican Library, Rome (MS gr. 746, fol. 372r)

Additional details of the construction process are described in the subsequent chapter of the *vita*. At this point, some comments are in order concerning the instigation of the project. First, the plan was marked with stones and then laid out (*hypograpsas*) with a rope. The latter seems to have been standard practice throughout the Middle Ages: land measurements were done with ropes (see fig. 31),[2] and military camps were laid out using similar procedures.[3] In the Armenian foundation rite, twelve unpolished stones were first placed at the four corners of the church, then the officiating bishop took the architect's measuring line and marked out the space of the foundation.[4] The same practice is known from Western Europe: in the famous Dream of Gunzo, Saints Peter, Paul, and Stephen use ropes to show a comatose abbot the plan and measurements of the new church at Cluny monastery (figs. 32–33).[5] To lay out a building, one simply had to "know the ropes." Significantly, no mention is made of architectural drawings, and the planning was apparently done on the site, "in accord with God's plan."

The use of ropes suggests a similarity between the process of surveying and the process of laying out a building on-site. Treatises concerning land measurement mention two instruments, which were also standard units of measurement: the *orgyia* and the *schoinion*.[6] Both would have been prepared and carried by the surveyor. The *orgyia* was a reed or stick, normally about 2.1 meters long, which could be divided into nine *spithamai* or 108 *daktyloi*.[7] Texts recommend that the *schoinion* be made out of a thick hemp to keep it from stretching.[8] Divisions into *orgyiai* were marked on it with string. Before the time of Michael IV (mid-eleventh century) the *schoinion* was normally divided into ten *orgyiai*, with a total length of 21.1 meters; however, after Michael IV's reign, a length of 21.7 meters became more common.[9] Texts recommend that each extremity of the rope be affixed with an iron ring that could be attached to a stake when the rope was stretched.

FIG. 32. Detail of an illuminated manuscript illustrating Gunzo's dream at Cluny monastery. Bibliothèque Nationale de France, Paris (MS lat. 17716, fol. 43)

FIG. 33. Detail of an illuminated manuscript showing Gunzo relating his dream to Abbot Hugh. Bibliothèque Nationale de France, Paris (MS lat. 17716, fol. 43)

Interestingly, the texts also recommend that the process of recording the land measurements be accompanied by a verbal description, noting significant natural features and directions.[10] Although the standard of measure may have been different for buildings—usually the *pous*, or foot, was used, divided into sixteen *daktyloi*—a similar process of marking and measuring can be envisioned.

The text of Saint Nikon prompts the question: Did Byzantine masons utilize architectural drawings? None is mentioned in the *vita* of Nikon, and the phrase "in accord with God's plan" (*kata gnomen Theou*) sounds more to our purposes in the English translation; it actually refers to God's knowing—his judgment—rather than to his blueprint. It is known from Vitruvius that Roman architects utilized "plans, elevations, and perspectives,"[11] and that this practice continued at least through the seventh century, when architects were still trained in the classical tradition.[12] In the sixth century, Paul the Silentiary praised the architect Anthemios, who was "skilled to draw a circle and set out a plan."[13] In the same period, Cassiodorus's formula for the palace architect also notes the significance of setting out ideas on paper.[14] In the texts, such a plan is called a *skariphos*, in contrast to the *thesis*, which was marked on the site; Mark the Deacon records that at the early fifth-century cathedral of Gaza, "The holy bishop had engaged the architect Rufinus from Antioch, a dependable and expert man, and it was he who completed the entire construction. He took some chalk and marked the outline (*thesis*) of the holy church according to the plan (*skariphos*) that had been sent by the most pious Eudoxia."[15] The use of such drawings may explain the remarkable similarities in plans and proportions of churches at widely separated locations in the Early Christian centuries.[16] Although no proper drawings have been preserved from this period, an enigmatic sketch of the plan of an Early Christian basilica was found on a brick that had been reused at the medieval church of Saint Sofia in Ohrid (fig. 34).[17] If Koco's identification is correct, this may be the only surviving plan from the Early Christian period.

The architectural profession was transformed in the Transitional period, with the theoretical orientation of the university-trained architect giving way to the practical orientation of the workshop-trained master builder. Did design practices continue unchanged? There are no clear references to Byzantine architectural drawings in the period after the Transitional period, and it would appear that, for most examples, drawings were *not* used.

After the Transitional period, there are a few vague references to drawings in Byzantine texts, but our interpretation of them is complicated by the lack of a technical specificity in the language, and the references must be understood in context. For example, in the *vita* of the eccentric eleventh-century stylite Lazaros Galesiotes, the saint directed the construction of a new refectory in his monastery, which was located near Ephesus. "When the builders were about to raise our refectory, our father, standing on top of his

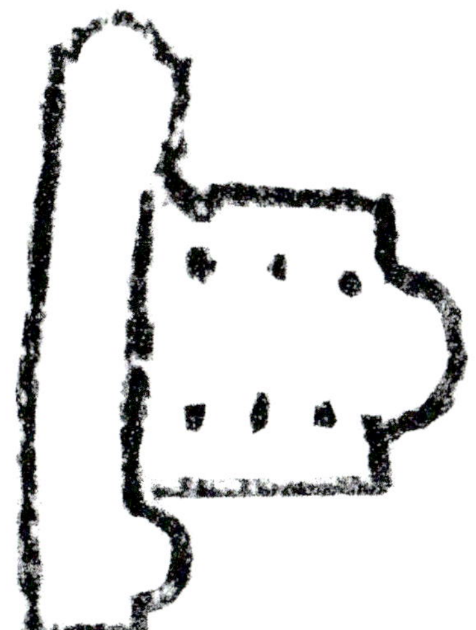

FIG. 34. Architectural drawing on an Early Christian brick, found in the narthex of Saint Sophia, Ohrid

column, indicating with the fingers of his right hand, delineated the length and breadth for the builders."[18] One of the brothers complained that the "form of the work" (*schematismos tou ergou*) was absurdly large for their small community, to which the saint responded, in effect, "If you build it, they will come."

Several points are noteworthy here. First, it is difficult to either prepare or use a drawing while standing on the top of a column. Second, only with the plan delineated on the ground could the monk's observation on scale be made. Finally, the word *daktylodeikton*, meaning "indicated with the fingers," sounds similar to the gestures of Gunzo as he explains the plan of the church to Abbot Hugh in the manuscript from Cluny (see fig. 33). One gets the impression that Lazaros is pointing out the coordinates from on high, and the brethren are scurrying around to mark them on the site. Taken out of context, the phrase *schematismos tou ergou* sounds as if it were referring to a working plan, but in context, it does not.

A similar event is recorded in the *vitae* of the Bithynian Saint Ioannikios (ca. 752–846). In the Metaphrastes version of the *vita*, the saint determined the plan (*tes oikodomes schema*) of a church of the Prodromos for the builders.[19] Again, the phrase *tes oikodomes schema* sounds as if it were referring to something like a blueprint, but the context is similar to that just mentioned, and the evidence is at best equivocal. In another version of the *vita*, written by Peter of Atroa, Ioannikios "had drawn (*schematisas*) the place and outlined (*diagrapsas*) the edifice" for the church of the martyr Eustathios. Afterwards he instructed the workers and departed for the desert.[20] Again, it seems that the action of delineating the building is taking place at the site, with the saint drawing on the ground, although the sentence could be interpreted either way. In either case, it suggests that some degree of planning took place before the construction began but that it occurred at the building site and not necessarily with a drawing on paper.

Although there is no evidence of floor plans, the on-site work should also be considered the "drawing"—that is, a necessary part of the process used to coordinate the various features of the design before the construction began. Like a blueprint, the marking of the plan on the building site indicates that many features of the building must have been determined before construction began. Marking the plan of the building full-scale on the site was probably a common practice. The plan sent to Gaza was chalked onto the ground, although based on a drawing. The *vita* of Saint Symeon the Younger, from the sixth century, records that the plan of a trefoil martyrium was traced on the ground.[21] A similar situation is recorded in the apocryphal *Acts of the Apostle Thomas* of perhaps the third century. Thomas, a carpenter, was taken to India, where he began to build a palace for the king: "And the apostle took a reed and drew, measuring the place, and the doors he set toward the sunrising . . . and the windows toward the west.[22] John Harvey, who adamantly believes that no building could be designed without a proper architectural drawing, presents this as evidence for a drawing sketched with a reed pen on paper, but the context suggests otherwise.[23] Perhaps it is more important to think of design and construction not as two separate exercises but as interrelated and simultaneous activities; as Coulton insists for ancient Greek architecture, planning continued through the construction process.[24]

This view is reinforced by surviving markings in several Late Antique buildings. The numerous inscribed lines on the podium of the Temple of Apollo at Didyma have been subjected to intensive scrutiny. They appear to be a part of the process of designing the profiles for the column bases and even for determining the entasis of the columns.[25] The lines indicate that the final design details were determined long after the construction was underway. If the temple had been completed, presumably these lines would have been smoothed over. Similarly, a series of curved lines was discovered on the floor of the sixth-century church of the Holy Cross at Resafa (fig. 35).[26] Analysis of these lines has determined that they correspond to the arcades of the nave. Thus, the details of the elevation were only calculated after the floor of the nave was laid. In many ways, these details resemble a Gothic tracing floor. What survives is not a complete rendering of the elevation but what would have been necessary for the masons to determine the shape of the voussoirs for constructing the arcades.

There is also a third, unpublished example to add to this list, and doubtless there are others. At Çanlı Kilise in western Cappadocia, from the eleventh century, similar curved lines, inscribed with a compass, were found on the inner wall of the narthex, accompanied by radiating lines (fig. 36). The curves corresponded with the arches of the facade,

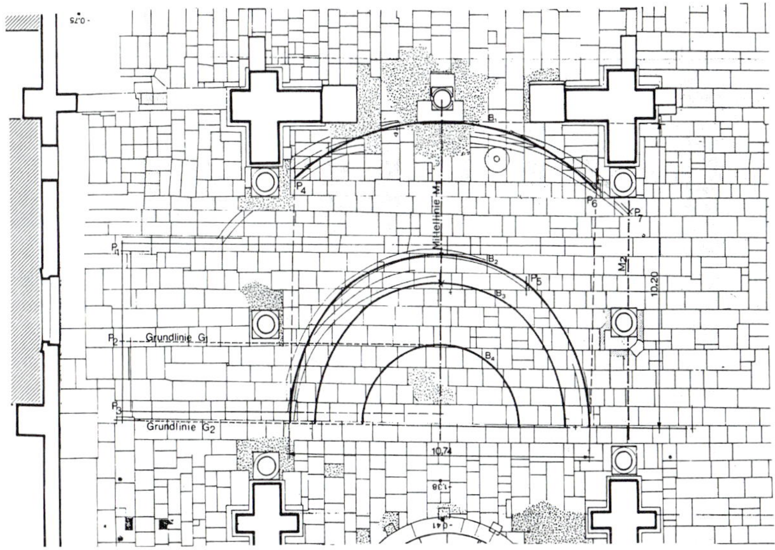

FIG. 35. Incisions from the floor of the church of the Holy Cross, Resafa

and they must be remnants of a similar process of calculating the stereotomy of the voussoirs, with the radiating lines marking the division between voussoirs. These remnants of the design process would have disappeared when the narthex was plastered and painted.

A treatise on military machinery, the *Poliorcetica* of the tenth-century writer known as Heron of Byzantium, also provides some insight into the role of drawings in the transmission of ideas, and it is worth examining in some detail. Heron indicates that his text derives from the writings of the Roman architect Apollodorus and other classical sources.[27] But he explains that he must differ from them in the manner of presentation, because the technical vocabulary of the ancients was unfamiliar to his audience and—more importantly for us—because a classical illustration, which he calls a *schema*, would not provide the necessary information for actual construction. Heron says that he will clarify his text with illustrations, with what he calls a *schematismos*. Denis Sullivan has compared the illustrations accompanying the text of Heron (fig. 37), from the eleventh or possibly tenth century, with those representing the same siege engines in a text of Apollodorus (fig. 38), which is closer to the original.[28] Heron has transformed abstract, two-dimensional diagrams into realistic, three-dimensional, narrative illustrations—and his careful phrasing clearly indicates that he is making a distinction between the two. It is also noteworthy that the drawings of machines *not* based on antique prototypes are nonsensical (fig. 39). The point is that the Byzantine audience understood pictures

FIG. 36. Incisions on the west wall of the narthex at Çanlı Kilise, Akhisar

as *representational*, but they did not understand either the meaning of a conceptual diagram or the purpose of a working drawing.[29] And this is precisely what a blueprint or architectural drawing is—a conceptual diagram. Consequently, one may suspect that if the Byzantines did not understand them, they did not use them.

Elsewhere in the *Poliorcetica*, Sullivan suggests that Heron may not have understood the terms for plan and elevation (*to keimenon kai to orthomenon*). He copies the terms from Apollodorus in the description of an observatory, but without the accompanying ancient technical drawings, which have not been preserved elsewhere.[30] In figure 39, the illustrations instead show the observatory twice, once fully raised, and once partially raised.[31] Accordingly, Sullivan translates these terms as "the flat and the upright view," which may be more appropriate for the tenth-century understanding of the terms.

In spite of misunderstandings, the illustrations in military treatises are the closest in function to architectural drawings. A late tenth-century treatise describes the process of laying out a military camp. Measurements are done by surveyors (*minsouratores*) with a measuring cord stretched from the centerpoint of the camp, and instructions are provided for establishing the boundaries and then subdividing the camp.[32] The accompanying drawings (fig. 40) are sketchy and oversimplified, however, and they do not always correspond to the far more detailed description in the text. As George Dennis notes, they simply repeat a formula that appeared in the *Strategikon* of Maurice from several centuries earlier.[33] In fact, one could easily lay out the camp from the description alone, but not from the illustration.

An unusual entry in the *Acts* of the Patriarchate of Constantinople records a court case

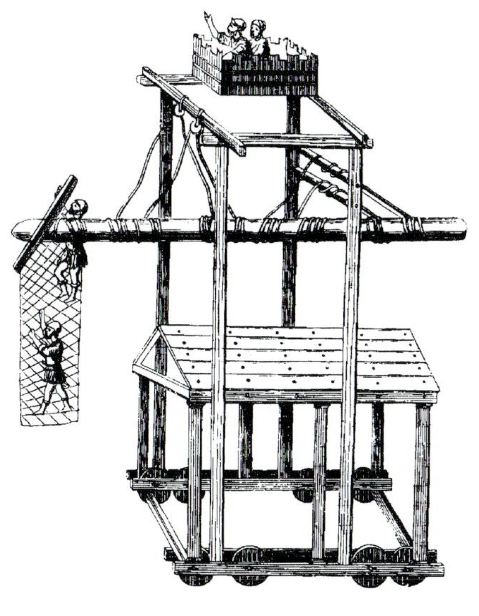

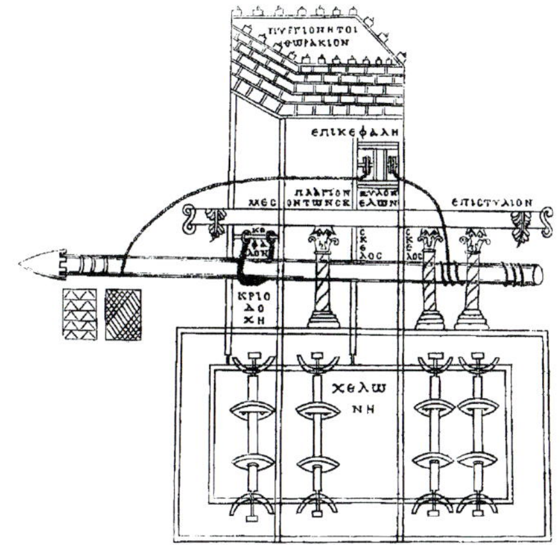

FIG. 37. Drawing based on a detail from a treatise on siege engines showing the Ram of Hegetor. Vatican Library, Rome (MS gr. 1605)

FIG. 38. Drawing based on a detail from a treatise on siege engines showing the Ram of Hegetor. Bibliothèque Nationale de France, Paris (MS suppl. gr. 607)

FIG. 39. Drawing based on a detail from a treatise on siege engines showing a lookout tower. Vatican Library, Rome (MS gr. 1605, fol. 22v)

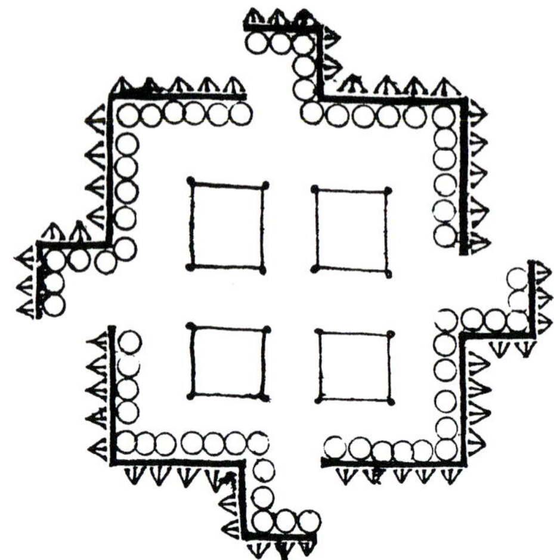

FIG. 40. Drawing based on a detail from a military treatise showing the plan of a camp. Vatican Library, Rome (MS gr. 1164, fol. 236v)

in which a drawing was presented as evidence in a dispute over property rights. The position of mills and a canal were shown by means of a *katagraphe*—a drawing or diagram of some sort.[34] One suspects that this was similar to the drawings of military camps—that is, useful to make a very simple point, but no more. In fact, the same term, *katagraphe*, is used to refer to a diagram of infantry positions in another tenth-century treatise, and it is also found in the *Poliorcetica* in reference to the accompanying illustrations.[35]

There is some evidence for the use of architectural drawings in the Muslim world at this time, as well as for the development of the plans on the site. When the Abbasid calif al-Mansur founded the city of Baghdad in 762, the historian al'Ya'qubi noted the tracing of the plan directly on the ground. According to the historian al-Tabari (839–923), the plan of the city was delineated with a combination of ashes, cotton seeds, and naphtha, which were subsequently ignited so that the calif could better visualize the buildings.[36] When the same calif wanted to transfer the site of the markets of Baghdad in 774, "he then had a large garment brought, traced on it the plan of the market," replicating the details and ownership of the original.[37] Similarly, the architect of the Ibn Tulun mosque in Cairo, dated 876, was provided with parchment onto which he could draw the plan so that the ruler could understand the design.[38]

The history of Baghdad by al-Khatib al-Baghdadi (1002–1071) describes a detailed drawing sent to the Byzantine ruler, which represented "Baghdad's land, markets, thoroughfares, palaces, and canals on both the east and the west sides. . . . When the king was drinking he would call for the illustration and drink a toast, looking at the drawing. . . . He used to say: I have never seen an illustration of a better built place."[39] Here, however, it is not clear if the drawing was an actual plan or—more likely—a cityscape, similar to those in the sixth-century Madaba mosaic map or the Ottoman city views of Matrakci.[40]

A unique manuscript recently discovered in the Great Mosque at San'a includes two architectural drawings of sorts, one of which is shown here in reconstruction (fig. 41).[41] Dating perhaps to the tenth century, the drawings represent mosques seen simultaneously in plan and elevation as a series of superimposed arcades. Oleg Grabar discusses these at length and concludes that they should be understood as drawings of architecture rather than as architectural drawings. While possessing a certain conceptual sophistication, they are evocative of architecture rather than representations of existing buildings or details for a building to be constructed.[42]

In the Islamic texts that tie the use of drawings to the construction of buildings, there are several references to historical rulers drawing the plans. The Ghaznavid ruler Ma'sud (reigned 1031–41) is said to have drawn architectural plans on paper: "He built with his own knowledge of geometry and drew the lines with his own exalted hand."[43] The Kubadabad Palace near Konya is said to have been designed by the Seljuq ruler 'Ala'al-Din Kayqubad in 1236, who drew the design of each palace structure.[44] There are numerous references to drawings (*tarh*) in the fourteenth century among the Ilkhanids, and there is one drawing from the late thirteenth century, perhaps the earliest surviving architectural drawing from the Islamic world. Quite different in concept from the San'a illustrations, the drawing is incised on a plaster slab and shows the projection for a *muqarnas* vault (fig. 42).[45] The evidence is compelling for the use of architectural drawings among the Ilkhanids in the late thirteenth and fourteenth centuries. But were the incidents from before that time singled out for mention because of their unusual nature? Were they references to standard practices and should they be understood as evidence of a continuous tradition? The former is most likely. When the earliest surviving Ottoman architectural drawings appear in the late fifteenth century, they seem to have been created under the influence of the design procedures of Renaissance Italy, rather than having developed out of an indigenous tradition.[46]

According to the evidence assembled by Wachtang Djobadze, architectural practices in medieval Georgia were somewhat different from the ones that are reconstructed in Byzantium.[47] According to his reading of the hagiographical literature, church construction was based on plans that had been traced. Ep'rem Mcire (eleventh century) writes that Nino the Illuminator of Georgia (fourth century) drew the plan of a church that was later built by architects and masons. Basil Zarzmeli likewise says that Serapion traced the plan of a church and gave it to the architect and mason. After training the laborers, they built the church as it had been outlined in the plan.[48] Djobadze also points out the unique tenth-century capital in the church at K'orogo showing the donor hold-

FIG. 41. Reconstruction drawing of a manuscript illumination depicting the plan and elevation of a mosque. Manuscript House, San'a, inv. no. 20–33.1

ing the plan of the church (fig. 43). The plan itself is enigmatic: it seems to fit with the exterior sculptural program that shows the process of constructing the church (see fig. 102). On the other hand, the exceptional simplicity of the church at K'orogo should not have required a plan. It may thus simply be a *presentation* image, similar to the more common models of churches with which donors are sometimes depicted. In general, however, the differences in the use of materials—the finely cut ashlars of Caucasian churches versus the rougher brick and stone of Byzantine churches—may have necessitated a difference in construction practices.[49]

Geometry

Discounting—or at least downplaying—the use of architectural drawings, how then were buildings designed, and how were ideas transmitted? A useful approach toward architectural design in the Middle Ages may be the combination of geometry and mem-

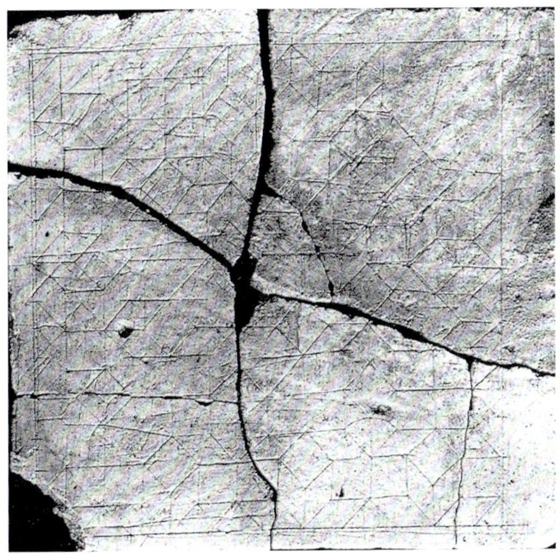

FIG. 42. Plan of a *muqarnas* quarter vault inscribed on a plaster slab found at Takht-i-Sulayman, Iran

FIG. 43. Sculpted capital depicting the donors with the plan of the church, from the church of the Virgin at K'orogo

ory.[50] In his studies of Islamic architecture, Yasser Tabbaa notes that geometry could have contributed to the "codification and dissemination of architectural ideas," whereas he interprets memory in a more poetic way to refer to the "collective consciousness of a culture."[51] More pragmatically, memory is also professional retention, the experience of a mason—his mental record of building types, components, and construction techniques, both as he observed them and as they had been passed down to him in a workshop tradition.

The geometric underpinnings of Islamic architecture have been frequently discussed, and Tabbaa's approach works well within an Islamic context.[52] However, a geometric basis for Byzantine architecture has never been as convincingly argued, and most of the writings on the subject have only clouded the issue. Even our geometrical terminology gives a false impression: a cross-in-square church is rarely square, but more likely rectangular or trapezoidal. But the Byzantines were aware of geometry, and as Hans Buchwald has observed, it could have been applied in three different ways: to determine the shape of secondary forms and decorative details; to create an underlying scheme that controls the positions of the most significant architectural features; and/or to define the primary architectural form of the building.[53]

In Byzantine architectural decoration, geometry was very often a controlling element. Almost all architectural sculpture can be divided into geometric components, which can be either sketched on the surface by the sculptor prior to carving or delineated with a template.[54] Complex patterns must have been designed with the use of a ruler and compass. But it is much more difficult to reconstruct the design process on a larger scale—that is, of the building itself. For this, it is important to first look in more detail at Byzantine geometry.

In the sixth century, the theory-based architects clearly had a firm grasp of geometry, and this is evident in their buildings. Anthemios of Tralles, the architect of Hagia Sophia, had a sophisticated understanding of descriptive geometry and had written a treatise on conic sections.[55] Theory and practice must have separated in the later centuries. The elite continued to copy and write learned treatises for their libraries, but these were probably never read by the "professionally illiterate" artisan. As Krumbacher gloomily noted, "the Byzantines were unproductive for nearly half a millennium in the fields of arithmetic, geometry, land surveying, and astronomy.[56]

Certainly geometry continued to be studied after the Transitional period, but its impact on architecture was more likely of a practical nature rather than of a theoretical one. An eleventh- or twelfth-century manuscript on geometry, copied from earlier authors, includes a number of architectural problems.[57] The manuscript is illustrated with a variety of geometric diagrams, but there is nothing resembling a working drawing or a concept sketch for the design of a building. The problems of an architectural nature are di-

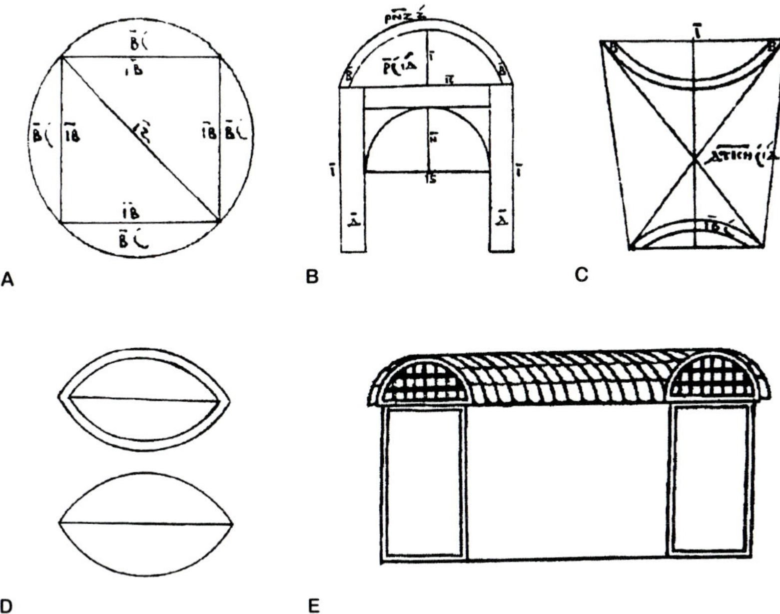

FIG. 44. Drawings based on architectural diagrams from a Byzantine treatise on geometry. Topkapı Library, Istanbul (MS 1, fols. 46r, 48v, 49v, 50r, 51r):

A. Pendentive dome
B. Masonry wall pierced by arch
C. Barrel vault with pitched roof
D. Conch of apse
E. Roof covered with tiles

rected toward calculating the quantity of materials necessary, rather than toward designing the plan or elevation of a building.

Various formulas are given in mathematical terms for determining the surface and volume of domes, barrel vaults (*kamarai*), cross-vaults (*tetraseirai*), spandrels (called "nails" —*onycha* or *dionycha*), and conches.[58] One particularly problematic formula determines the volume of a pendentive dome, identified as the measurement of a dome or vault (*metresis tetrastoou etoi tetrakamarou*) on a square base (fig. 44A).[59] Many of the formulas seem quite practical in their orientation: for example, how to approximate the mass of brickwork required in the construction of a wall pierced by an arch (fig. 44B); how to calculate the amount of brick to form a barrel vault, as well as the rubble necessary to form a pitched roof above it (fig. 44C); how to calculate the amount of brick to form the conch of an apse, as well as the area of the inner surface to be covered with mosaic (fig. 44D); and how to determine the number of roofing tiles necessary for covering a house (fig. 44E).

The formulas provided are complicated to the point of making absolutely no sense to the modern reader; moreover, they are fraught with errors, and the numbers are rounded off at random. Nor do the accompanying diagrams contribute much: they are not drawn to scale and often transpose three dimensions into two. For example, the illustration for the pendentive dome shows simply the plan at the base with a square inscribed in the circle, and the diagonal/diameter indicated (fig. 44A). The illustration of a barrel vault of uneven dimensions set beneath a pitched roof folds together the opposite faces of the vault, resulting in a diagram that misleadingly resembles a groin vault (fig. 44C). The drawings of the conch include the curves of both the plan and the elevation, as well as the line of the diameter (fig. 44D). The drawings most easily read—for example, determining the tiles for the roof of a house—have no practical function at all (fig. 44E).

Few, if any, of the problems and formulas given in the text could be applied to the design process; instead, established forms are presented, and practical information about them is then calculated. Understood in this way, geometry may have been used in a more pragmatic manner rather than in a theoretical sense—that is, as an aid to calculating costs and materials rather than as an element of architectural design. As such, geometry might have been more useful to a contractor overseeing a construction project than to the actual designer of a building.

Heron of Byzantium's second treatise, the *Geodesia*, includes a discussion of the application of geometric analysis to warfare—for example, calculating the height of a wall from a distance in order to construct a siege tower with the same height. Heron discusses the use of the *dioptra*, an ancient surveying device similar to a theodolite. He demonstrates its use in determining distances between points and in calculating areas and volumes, using the Hippodrome and the Cistern of Aspar in Constantinople as settings for his examples. In his introduction, Heron explains the usefulness of this information: "This examination will supply those who are eager to learn not only military knowledge, but will appear most useful for aqueducts, construction of walls, and outlines of harbors, making no small contribution to mensuration and contemplation of the heavens."[60] It is not known if the *dioptra* was used in Byzantine times, or if this is simply Heron's record of curious knowledge from Antiquity. One of the simpler exercises in the text shows the laying out of a circular area, including directions for measuring its diameter and circumference, with a rope of thirty-five *orgyiai* similar to those found in surveyors' handbooks (fig. 45).[61]

Geometry was also employed to create an underlying scheme that controlled the design and defined the primary architectural forms, as Buchwald suggests. It has frequently been posited that a simple form of quadrature was used to establish the basic dimensions of a building, and this idea is worth investigating. The explanations for laying out a military camp may give some indication of the process as practiced: the perime-

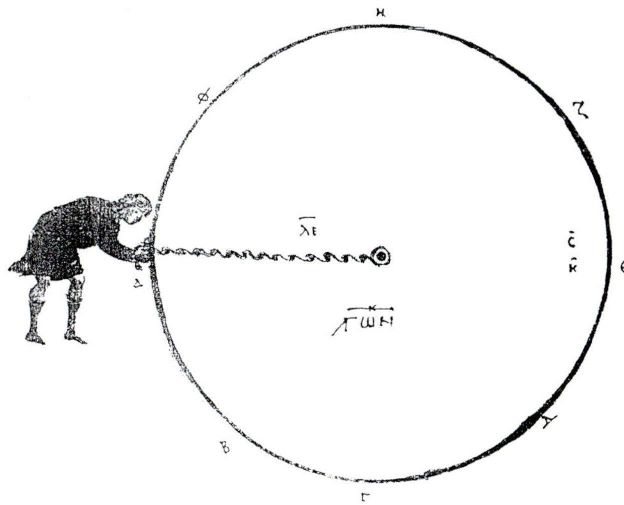

FIG. 45. Detail from a geometric treatise showing the procedure for measuring a circle. Vatican Library, Rome (MS gr. 1605)

ter of a rectangular enclosure was established by a measuring rope extended in four directions from the midpoint of the camp.[62] The military treatises do not, however, give directions for determining if the enclosure is actually square; the diagonals are not measured, and the angles go unmentioned. It is tempting to think that such a simple measuring process was used to lay out the length and width of churches like the tenth-century Theotokos at Hosios Loukas (fig. 14) or the twelfth-century Saint Panteleimon at Nerezi (fig. 46), where the plans are parallelograms, lacking right-angle corners.

The application of geometry must begin with a system of measurement. There is evidence from surviving buildings that a standard system of length was employed by Byzantine builders. Examining the buildings constructed by the architects of the imperial court in the sixth century, Paul Underwood concluded that they began with one dominant measurement that could easily be divisible by ten, and was often divided by two, to obtain important measurements in the design of a church. The dominant measurement would normally be the span of a vault or dome. Measurements were based on a foot (*pous*) of about 31.5 centimeters, which was divided into sixteen *daktyloi*.[63] The foot measure may have varied slightly, and Erich Schilbach gives the standard measurement developed after the time of Justinian as 31.23 centimeters.[64] This seems to be the approximate measurement employed in a number of later buildings. It is most clearly evident in the span of the dome, which is determined either by the internal measurement or by the distance between the center points of the supporting columns. For example, the domes of the Myrelaion and of Church H in Side (see figs. 2, 10) were approximately ten Byzantine feet in diameter, whereas the dome of the Fatih Camii in Trilye (see fig. 8) and those of several later examples were approximately fifteen feet in diameter. Often, but not al-

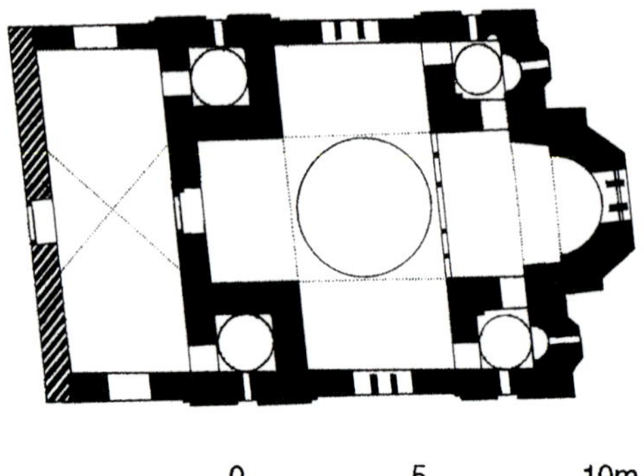

FIG. 46. Plan of the church of Saint Panteleimon, Nerezi

ways, the dome measurement was carried throughout the entire building; for example, the width of the naos was often set at twice the dome diameter.

Buchwald suggested that quadrature was, in fact, employed in a number of churches, and he tested this hypothesis with surveying equipment at the thirteenth-century Church E at Sardis.[65] Now in ruins, the church was originally a cross-in-square church topped by five domes. Buchwald started with a module of the central square and measured from the midpoints of the four columns (figs. 47–48). Although he provided no exact measurements, the module measures close to 4.7 meters on each side, or fifteen Byzantine feet. By projecting a diagonally circumscribed system of squares around the module, the internal measurements of the church could have been determined, including the square plan of the naos (two modules) and the overall length of the building (four modules). Çanlı Kilise in Cappadocia measures similarly fifteen Byzantine feet across at the base of the dome, with twice that measurement for the internal width and length of the naos (see fig. 16).[66] This system could have easily been laid out on the site with ropes. Buchwald has suggested that a similar system may have been employed in the Constantinopolitan churches of the Myrelaion (fig. 2) and the Kilise Camii, as well as in related examples at Mistra—the Hodegetria (fig. 75) and the Pantanassa churches—and in Saint John Aliturgitos at Nesebar (fig. 11A).[67] A possible flaw in his argument is that to determine the larger measurements with quadrature, it would have been necessary for the area around the building to be open and relatively level, but the Myrelaion was raised on a high platform in an urban setting, and the Mistra churches are positioned on moderately steep slopes.

Quadrature may have been used at the church of the Holy Apostles in Thessaloniki in the early fourteenth century, also apparently based on a dome module of fifteen Byzantine feet (fig. 49).[68] As Striker and Kuniholm emphasize, "The significance of [quadrature] for our purposes is not so much that the design of the plan is governed by an

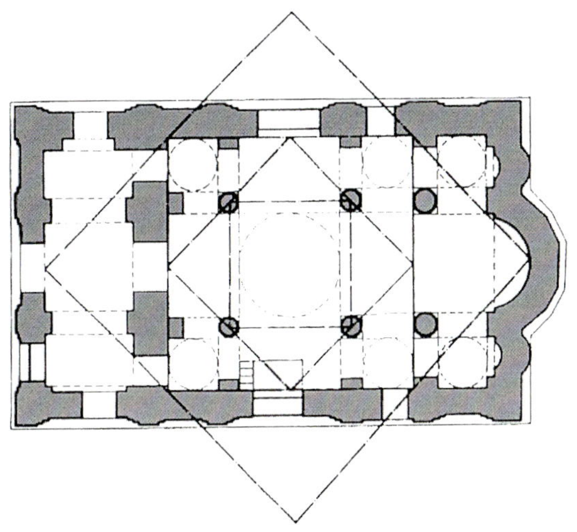

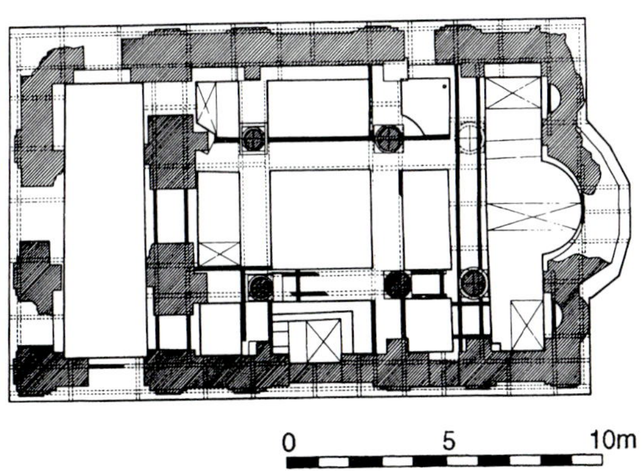

FIG. 47. Plan of Church E at Sardis showing quadrature

FIG. 48. Plan of the foundations of Church E at Sardis

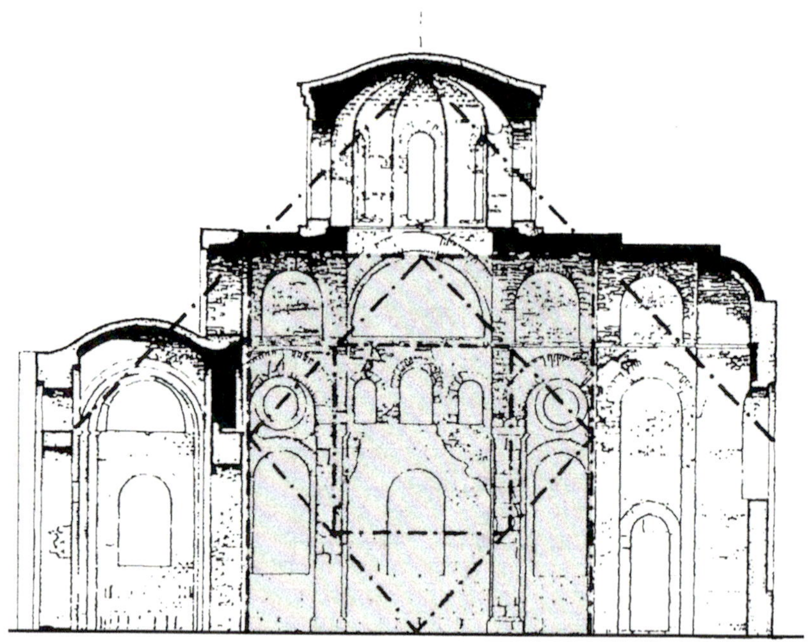

FIG. 51. Elevation of the church of the Myrelaion, Istanbul, showing geometric relationships

Either geometry or arithmetic could be used to determine the elevation of the building. Again, the proportional relationships remain relatively simple, although they may be more difficult to determine because of the settling of vaults and the raising of floor levels. Often the height to the crossarms of a cross-in-square church is equivalent to the width of the naos, or twice the basic module, as Buchwald has shown for the Myrelaion (see fig. 51).[76] The height of the dome may also be coordinated with these basic measurements, and at the Myrelaion it is three times the basic module. Striker has also demonstrated that quadrature was employed for the development of the elevation of the Holy Apostles in Thessaloniki.[77]

I have suggested that a similar system was employed at the twelfth-century church of the Chora in Constantinople (that is, the core of the present building, whose ancillary chambers date from the fourteenth century) and was adapted from a cross-in-square church to an atrophied Greek-cross plan.[78] The module in this case was the width of the naos, approximately 10 meters, or 32 Byzantine feet. The projection of the corner piers and the diameter of the dome, just under 7.5 meters, or 24 Byzantine feet, could have been determined in two different ways: either by the inscription of a circle within the square or by the basic geometric ratio of 3:4. The overall interior length, including the narthex, would have been just under 20 meters, 64 Byzantine feet, or twice the module.

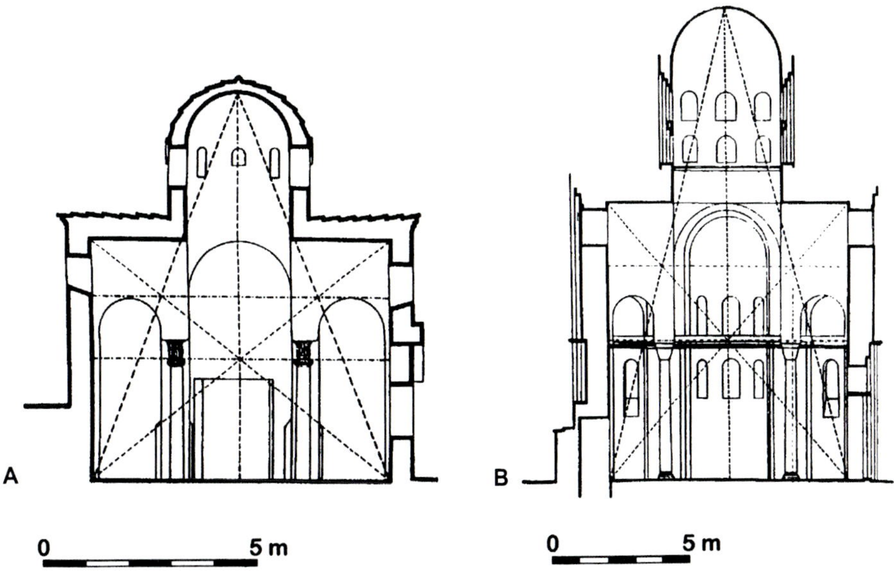

FIG. 52. Diagrams showing the "harmonic sections" in Byzantine churches:
A. Saint John the Theologian, Athens
B. Panagia Chalkeon, Thessaloniki

The same measurements could have been employed in the elevation as well. The height to the crossarms is almost the same as the module, and the height of the dome is very close to the module plus the diameter of the dome.[79]

In both the Myrelaion and the Chora churches, the relationship of the height of the dome to the overall length begins to approximate an equilateral triangle. Perhaps in some buildings, the design was controlled *both* by a system of measurements and by a system of geometric proportions. Although these relationships may be detected in *some* buildings, however, in no examples did such a system as these control *all* of the measurements in plan or in elevation. Moreover, what may have been intended according to an ideal system might now be disguised by a number of factors, including restorations, surface coverings, the raising of the floor level, the subsidence of the vaulting, and even sloppiness in the initial execution.

Mutsopulos once surveyed a variety of Greek cross-in-square churches to demonstrate that significant points in the interior elevation were controlled by an isosceles triangle, seen most clearly in the transverse section (figs. 52A–B).[80] Drawn from floor level at the lateral walls and extending to the dome, the triangle usually defines the diameter of the dome at its base. By extending a second set of diagonals from the lateral wall at the floor level to the crown of the vault along the opposite wall, a sort of star pattern forms, and the correspondences Mutsopulos discovered suggest that significant features in the elevation were controlled by the heights of the intersecting lines. Windows, column heights, cornices and other details correspond with these heights. Significantly, these relationships, particularly those determined by the isosceles triangle, were evident in churches with very different proportions in their plans and elevations. Striker applied this analysis to the churches of Constantinople, with similar results.[81] The analysis suggests that the layout of the plan and the determination of the elevation could have been two separate activities—and that the relationships within the building may be more properly termed architectural rather than geometric.

Finally, there are many buildings that employ similar plans in which no overriding system of measurements or of geometry may be discerned, and in which probably none was intended. In these examples, the builders may simply have been following the forms of an established model and approximating its proportions. Conversely, they may have been working according to an architectural logic in which such abstract geometric relationships are incidental.

In numerous examples at the highest levels of patronage, there is no evidence of an underlying grid nor of quadrature based on a square module. Buchwald has suggested several other approaches for establishing basic measurements, based on proportions of $1:\sqrt{2}$, $1:\sqrt{3}$, and $1:1+\sqrt{2}$.[82] All proportions can be achieved by extending the diagonal of a square, and $1:\sqrt{3}$ can also be easily reckoned by halving an equilateral triangle. All measurements could have been easily laid out on the site with ropes. But none of these proportional systems have yet been detected in the churches of Constantinople.[83]

Alternatives such as these, however, might help to explain some anomalies in Byzantine architecture. For example, the church of Christ Pantepoptes in Constantinople, constructed for Anna Dalassene shortly before 1087, is often regarded as the most carefully built of the later churches in the capital.[84] The church is a cross-in-square of standard design (see fig. 18). Yet neither an underlying system of measurement nor the use of quadrature is in evidence; the naos is oblong in plan, while the dome measures approximately fourteen Byzantine feet in diameter and does not seem to relate proportionally to the dimensions of the naos. On the other hand, the overall internal measurements of the building (including the narthex but excluding the curvature of the apses), approximately 32 by 56 Byzantine feet, are in the proportion of $1:\sqrt{3}$. Moreover, the diameter of the dome is one-quarter of the length.

The church of Christ Pantokrator in Constantinople, built by the Empress Eirene and her husband John II Komnenos in 1118, is a cross-in-square with a broad narthex and lateral aisles (see fig. 78). The internal length (including the narthex but excluding the apses) is identical to the overall width, about 26.7 meters, and the width of the naos, about 15.3 meters, relates to the larger measurement in a ratio of $1:\sqrt{3}$. The dome is approximately seven meters in diameter, but it does not appear to relate to either measurement, nor do these figures translate to round numbers in Byzantine feet. Perhaps the controlling measurement was the overall *external* length (including the main apse) of about thirty-one meters, or almost exactly one hundred Byzantine feet, and this could relate to the external measurement of the central domed bay (measured to the outside of the columns) of slightly greater than ten meters, or thirty-three Byzantine feet—that is, approximately one-third of the length. In any event, both the laying out of the plan and the details of construction are careless, and the irregularities increase in the second and third phases of construction. All of this is perplexing considering the imperial patronage, especially when set against the regularity of the measurements and proportions at the contemporaneous Chora, constructed by John's brother Isaak.

In contrast to the practical implications of geometrical treatises discussed earlier, the tenth-century *Poliorcetica* of Heron of Byzantium gives some hint of the theoretical underpinnings of Byzantine architecture. In chapters 30–39 of his text, Heron discusses the design of mobile siege towers, basing his information on the writings of the Hellenistic architects Diades and Charias and on Apollodorus of Damascus. In fact, the towers were fairly simple forms, constructed of a timber frame rising through several stories above a square, wheeled base. Surviving poliorcetic texts provide two different types of images for such towers: a schematic diagram, typical of the classical period (fig. 53), and the illustration of a finished device, more characteristically Byzantine (fig. 54)—the latter was perhaps first introduced into the poliorcetic genre by Heron himself.[85] In any case, the general form of the tower is relatively clear.

Curiously, Heron assigned an unusual amount of importance to harmony and proportion in the design of such siege towers. For example, he notes in chapter 30 that Diades and Charias designed towers of different sizes but with identical proportions: "On the top story they contracted [the tower] equally on all sides, in a proportion of one-fifth of the so-called 'area' of the base. . . . And they constructed [the towers] larger and smaller proportionally, increasing or decreasing the timbers for the three dimensions, that is, in length, width, and depth. Thus they partitioned the divisions of the stories commensurably with the height."[86]

The analyses provided by Heron were normally given in mathematical—that is, numerical—terms rather than based on geometry. For example, he explains at great length how to determine the contraction of the tower, and he applies the same analysis to the mobile towers designed by Apollodorus, which were apparently similar, although built to different measurements: "The 60 cubits of height and 17 cubits of the length of the base will have the same proportion in feet, and so be harmonious in ratios, because they are both measured by a common measure. For thrice 30 measures 90, and twice [30] measures 60; and again thrice eight measures 24, and twice eight measures 16. And as

CHAPTER FOUR

Buildings That Change

The adaptation or modification of existing built forms provided a significant impetus for the development of new building types and new planning arrangements in the centuries after the Transitional period. Numerous buildings were altered either during construction or immediately thereafter in response to the special requirements of the project. In addition, many buildings were reconfigured in a second construction phase, and in others the designs were copied with significant changes.

In the previous chapter, it was suggested that in most instances planning was done in situ, without the use of architectural drawings, and that the process of design continued as the building was constructed and perhaps afterwards as well. This chapter considers the latter possibility and its implications—that is, the transformation of existing buildings as a parallel to "pure" design. Although it may be impossible to reconstruct the decision making that occurred while a building was under construction, both the literary and the archaeological evidence provide some insight.

Literary Evidence for Architectural Change

Much evidence—written and otherwise—suggests that decisions concerning design continued to be made throughout the construction process. At the twelfth-century Kosmosoteira monastery, for example, the founder Isaak Komnenos relates in the *typikon* that the building was well under way before a good source of construction materials was "miraculously" discovered:

> In the beginning, the lack of building material created difficulties for me, but, as from some prearranged signal again, round about like a treasure for me there sprang forth assistance to me from the Mother of God. A discovery of the necessary material came to light—a miracle

> to see, this discovery from an unexpected source, of lime in the enclosure, and of a source of water. Thus from a previous lack I arrived at an unexpected supply, and thus saw the material for everything I needed granted by God in abundance.[1]

It is uncertain how this might have affected the design, but it is clear that not all of the preparations had been made in advance. Later in the *typikon*, Isaak noted design changes he instigated when he decided to include his own tomb in the building, at the same time requesting the fittings for it to be sent from Constantinople. The tomb was to have been "on the left side of the narthex, there where I made an extension on account of the tomb."[2] What he means by an "extension" is not clear, but the building was evidently well under way when this change occurred.

Few Byzantine churches that have survived are the result of a single period of building activity. The Byzantine buildings of Constantinople were constantly renewed, refurbished, and expanded.[3] Basil I (reigned 867–86) may have set the tone for later developments with his program of renewal.[4] The *Vita Basilii* enumerates thirty-one churches in and around Constantinople that were restored by Basil, in addition to his new constructions in the Great Palace. In fact, the text emphasizes the restoration of isolated religious foundations rather than new constructions or civic buildings or the larger concerns of urban planning: "The Christ-loving emperor Basil, by means of continuous care and the abundant supply of all necessary things, raised from ruin many holy churches that had been rent asunder by prior earthquakes or had fallen down, or were threatening immediate collapse on account of the fractures [they had sustained], and to the solidity he added [a new] beauty."[5]

The citations are all too brief for us to determine if major changes in design were effected. Among the numerous restorations recorded in the *Vita Basilii*, most buildings are claimed, somewhat vaguely, to have been "rebuilt from their foundations," "made more solid," or "made anew," although a few examples are more specific.[6] One reference may put us on a firmer archaeological footing: "He [Basil] also repaired and beautified the handsome church at the Portico of Domninus—the one that is dedicated to the Resurrection of Christ our God and to the martyr Anastasia—by substituting a stone for a wooden roof and adding other admirable adornments."[7] The writer surely meant that vaulting was introduced into the restored building.[8]

Similarly, the descriptions of several early eleventh-century churches in the *Chronographia*, written by the historian Michael Psellos, indicate changes in design and provide considerable detail. For example, Romanos III (reigned 1028–34) was "jealous of the great Solomon . . . and envious of the emperor Justinian."[9] His alleged megalomania was concentrated on the church of the Theotokos Peribleptos, on which he is said to have exhausted the treasury: "One on top of another new parts were added, and at the same time another part would be pulled down. Often, too, the work would cease and then suddenly rise up afresh, slightly bigger or with some more elaborate variety."[10] In the end, Psellos marveled at the symmetry of its walls, its encircling columns, and the lavish outfitting of the building. The description suggests that the design of the building was altered several times during the process of construction, that the plan was not fixed from the beginning, and that the masons were willing to reformulate the design as they built.

A similar situation is described in the attentions of Michael IV (reigned 1034–41) toward the monastery of the Anargyroi, Kosmas and Damian, built in an eastern suburb of Constantinople.[11] Psellos tells us that Michael's patronage arose from his hopes that the doctor-saints would heal his afflictions, and he praises the emperor's achievement:

> It was a glorious monument. Actually, not all of the foundations were laid by Michael, but he threw them over a wider area. There had been a sacred building on the spot before, although it was not noted for any magnificence, nor was it remarkable for its architectural style. This erection he now beautified, built additions onto it, and surrounded it with walls. The new chapels enhanced its glory. . . . So far as the building of sacred churches was concerned, Michael surpassed all his predecessors, both in workmanship and in splendor. The depths and heights of this edifice were given a new symmetry, and his chapels harmonized with the church to bestow on it an infinite beauty.[12]

Psellos praises the marbles and the mosaics as well as the surrounding additions, including gardens and baths. Michael's achievement corresponds to those described earlier by Basil, but here the description clearly indicates that the final product far exceeded the older structure.

Psellos reserves his greatest praise and his greatest condemnation for the church of Saint George of Mangana, built by the Emperor Constantine IX Monomachos (reigned 1042–55). What little remains of the lavish complex is buried today beneath a military installation to the east of Hagia Sophia. Excavated twice in this century, the complex is better known from Psellos's description.

> In this catalogue of the emperor's foolish excesses, I now come to the worst example of all—the building of the Church of Saint George the Martyr. Constantine pulled down and completely destroyed the original church; the present one was erected on the site of its ruins. The first builder did not plan very well, and there is no need for me to write of the old building here, but it appears that it would have been of no great dimensions if the preliminary plans had been carried out, for the foundations were moderate in extent and the rest of the building proportionate, while the height was by no means outstanding. However, as time went by, Constantine was fired by an ambition to rival all other buildings that had ever been erected and to surpass them altogether. So the area of the church and its precincts was much enlarged, and the old foundations were raised and strengthened or else sunk deeper. On these latter

> bigger and more ornate pillars were set up. Everything was done on a more artistic scale, with gold leaf on the roof and precious green stones let into the floor or encrusted in the walls. . . .
>
> The church was not yet finished, however, and once again the whole plan was altered and new ideas incorporated into its construction. The symmetrical arrangement of the stones was broken up, the walls pulled down, and everything leveled with the ground. And the reason for it? Constantine's efforts to rival other churches had not met with the complete success he had hoped for: one church above all [i.e., Hagia Sophia] remained unsurpassed. So the foundations of another wall were laid and an exact circle described with the third church in its center (I must admit that it certainly was more artistic). The whole conception was on a magnificent and lofty scale.[13]

Psellos continues to enumerate the lavish and expensive decorations of the church, the cloisters, the gardens, a second ring of buildings, fountains, and baths. "To criticize the enormous size of the church was impossible, so dazzling was its loveliness."[14]

Similar themes emerge here as in the description of the Theotokos Peribleptos, and we may justly question how much of this is rhetorical device. Moreover, two themes constantly recur in the *Vita Basilii* and in the *Chronographia*. First, an older building is renewed, and in the process it is transfigured. It is clear from the texts that both plans and elevations were altered, not simply the decorative elements. Second, the design of a building is transformed in the process of construction to enhance its impression. These themes were not merely rhetorical, and it is possible to observe the same processes in the architecture of the Middle and Late Byzantine periods.

Archaeological Evidence for Architectural Change

Several examples may be cited that parallel the renovations described in the *Vita Basilii*. Archaeologists have studied a number of sites where a basilica was transformed into a cross-domed church, with the supports strengthened so that vaulting could be introduced. For example, an Early Christian basilica at Kydna in Lycia underwent such a modification in the tenth century (fig. 55).[15] As at the church of the Resurrection and of Saint Anastasia, a stone roof replaced a wooden one. The excavations at Amorium have recently suggested a similar transformation of the large basilica there. During the ninth or tenth century, piers were introduced to support the vaulting, in a cross-domed scheme with corner compartments (fig. 56).[16] Like Hagia Eirene, it may have had a basilican plan on the ground floor, but this is conjectural. The church on Büyükada by Amasra, first published by Eyice as a cross-domed church with corner compartments, may have had a similar history.[17] Eyice had dated it to the eighth century on the basis of its plan. Another example, excavated by Fıratlı at Selçikler in Phrygia, seems to have followed the same pattern of transformation: a small Early Christian basilica was reconstructed in

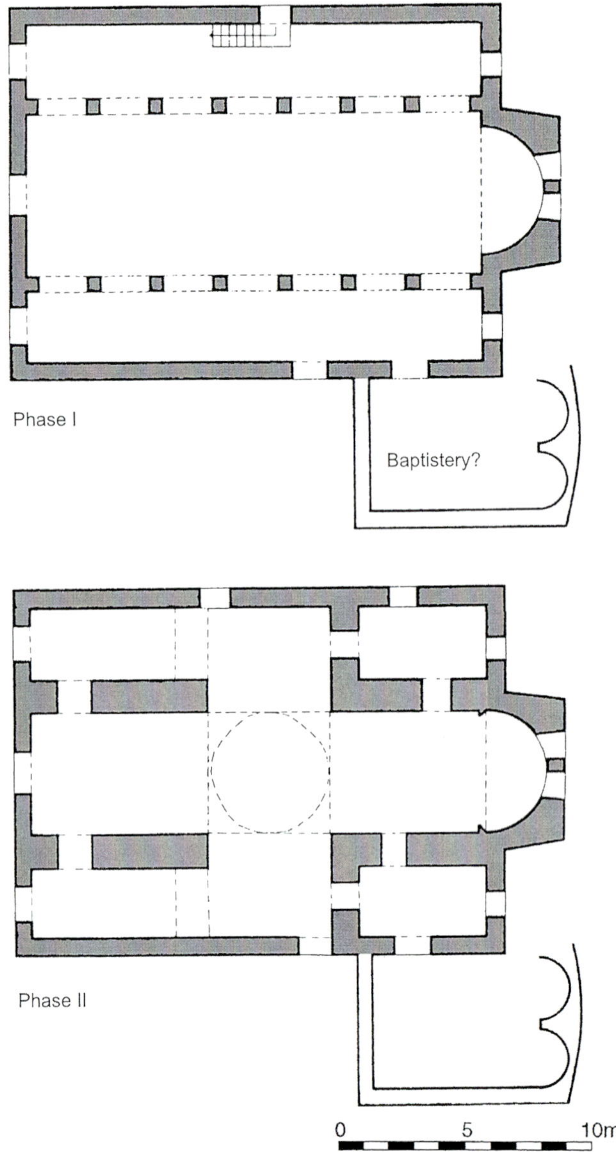

FIG. 55. Plans of the basilica at Kydna showing its transformation into a cross-domed church

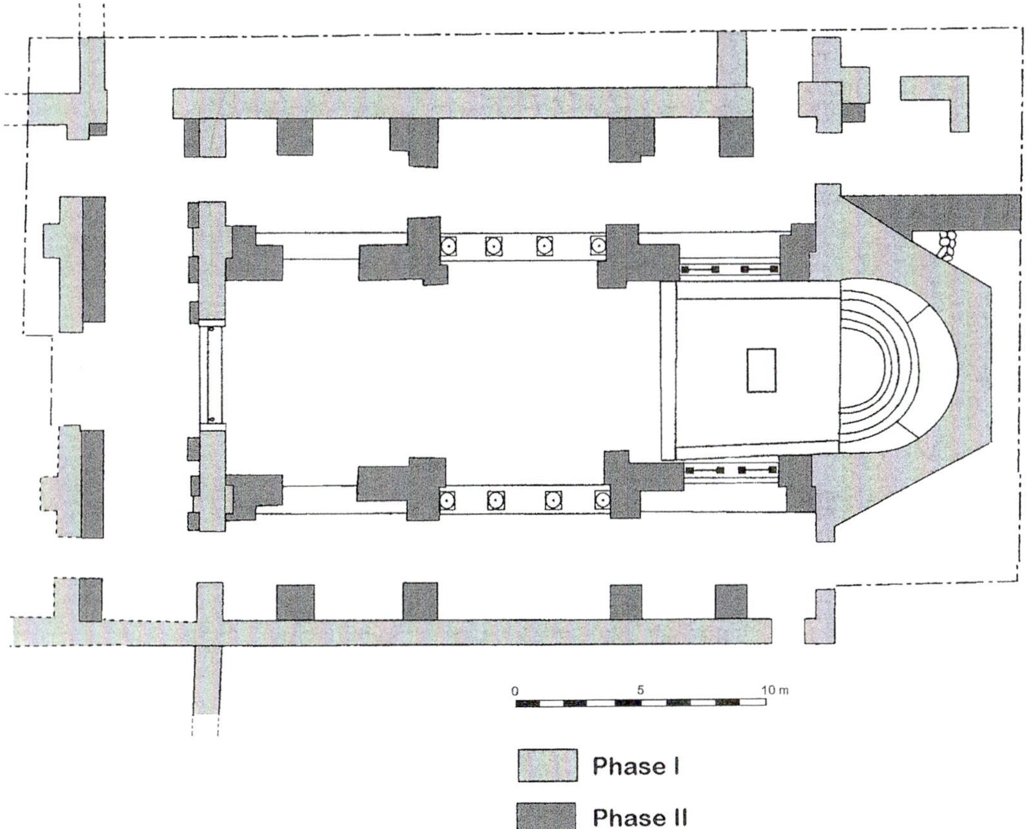

FIG. 56. Plan of the basilica at Amorium showing its transformation into a cross-domed church

the tenth century as a cross-domed church with the addition of thick walls and vaulting (fig. 57).[18]

All of these examples, in which change was clearly introduced in a later period of building activity, raise the question of what role renovations played in the development of new architectural ideas and of new building types. In the best known example, the church of Hagia Eirene in Constantinople was transformed from a domed basilica into a cross-domed church in the eighth century, following the earthquake of 740 (see fig. 22), and this fits well into the changing architectural patterns of the Transitional period.[19]

These archaeological examples provide useful parallels to the reconstructions mentioned in the *Vita Basilii*. Similarly, several surviving Middle Byzantine buildings provide parallels for the churches mentioned by Psellos. In some examples, the transformation occurred shortly after the initial construction, and in others modifications seem to have been undertaken during the process of erection. That is to say, archaeological evi-

FIG. 60. View of the Lavra katholikon from the north

The archaeological evidence from the katholikon of the Chora monastery (Kariye Camii) in Constantinople presents an example of change in response to site requirements. Excavations of the 1950s indicated not one but two phases of construction in the Middle Byzantine period, virtually identical in the details of their construction, both utilizing the recessed-brick technique (fig. 61).[25] Based on documentary evidence, the earlier phase (ca. 1077–81) was attributed to Maria Doukaina. Only the lower portions of the naos walls and the foundations of the tripartite apse could be identified, but in scale, details, and proportions, they suggest a cross-in-square church very similar in size and appearance to the contemporaneous Christ Pantepoptes (figs. 18, 62A).

The church was apparently rebuilt very shortly after this, and its plan was altered at that time. Isaak Komnenos, Maria's grandson, has been identified as the new *ktetor*, rendering a date of about 1120 or possibly in the 1140s.[26] At this time, it seems that the four columns were replaced by four stout corner piers, which in turn supported a larger dome (figs. 62B, 63). The transformation created a more unified and monumentalized interior. The excavators blamed the site for this drastic transformation, which occurred so soon after Maria Doukaina's construction.[27] The Chora was built on a slope: the terrain continues to shift downhill, and this has caused severe cracking in the surviving building.

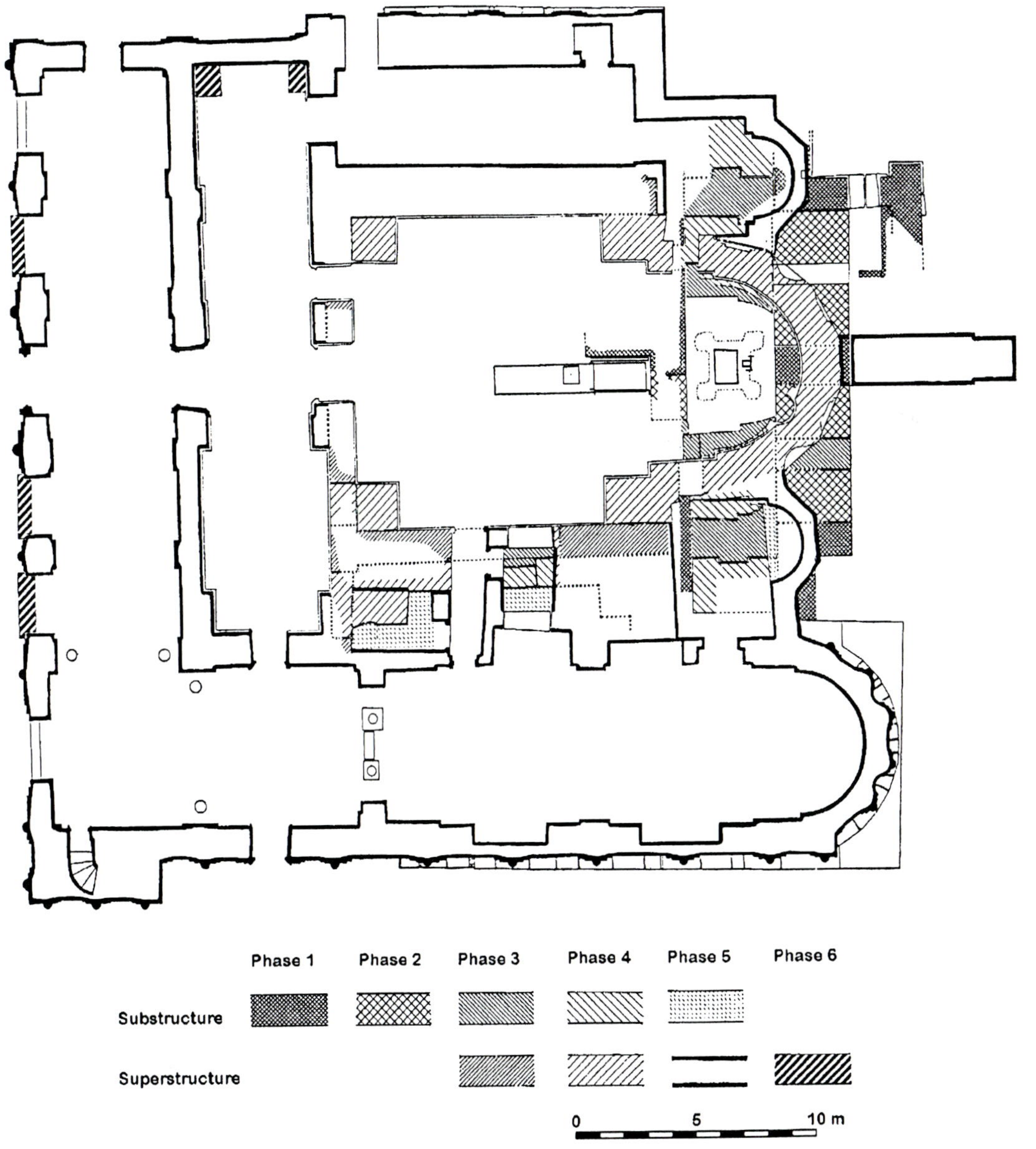

FIG. 61. Archaeological plan of the Chora, Istanbul

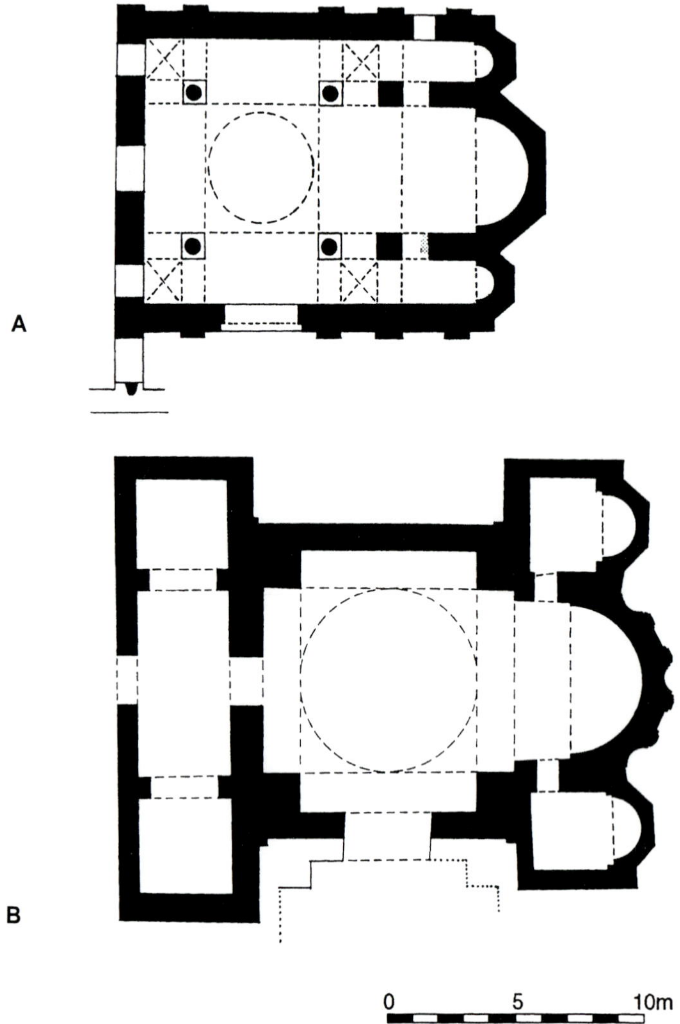

FIG. 62. Plans showing reconstructions of the (A) eleventh- and (B) twelfth-century katholikon of the Chora monastery

FIG. 63. View into the naos vaulting of the katholikon of the Chora monastery

It is possible that a large portion of the church collapsed, perhaps as a result of an earthquake, exacerbating the problems of the site. When rebuilt, a more stable structural system was introduced, utilizing piers rather than columns.

The introduction of a new plan at the Chora in the twelfth century came as a direct response to the practical necessities of the site. The resultant atrophied Greek-cross plan was not new to Byzantine architecture, but it had not appeared in mainstream architecture for at least three centuries.[28] As reintroduced at the Chora, this church type became popular in the twelfth century in Constantinople and in areas under its influence. Similar designs appear at the church of Saint Aberkios in Kurşunlu (fig. 64), located on the south shore of the Sea of Marmara, and at the church at Yuşa Tepesi on the Bosporus.[29]

In another example, the katholikon of the Nea Moni on Chios is attributed to the patronage of Constantine IX Monomachos in the 1040s.[30] The innovative vaulting of the naos superimposes an octaconch transition on a square lower level (figs. 65–68). Splendidly decorated, the conches are filled with mosaic below the tall dome.[31] In spite of the innovative form, numerous inconsistencies are evident in the design. The tower-like naos is completely out of scale with the low narthex and sanctuary. The low conch zone of the naos blocks the view of the main apse, decorated with a mosaic of the Virgin, to

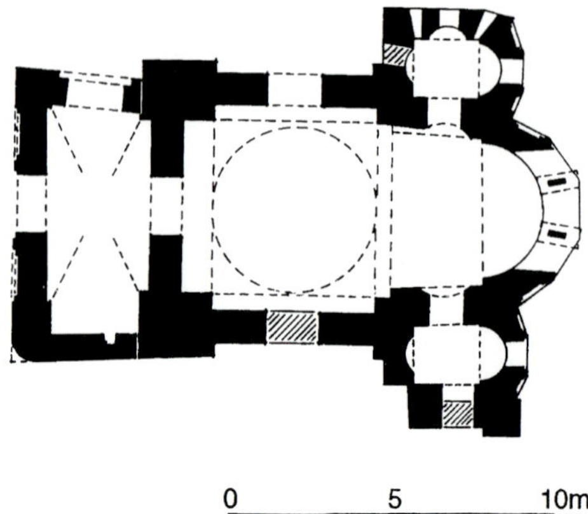

FIG. 64. Plan of the church of Saint Aberkios at Kurşunlu

whom the church was dedicated. In the section, the east wall of the naos drops far below the conch of the apse (fig. 68).[32] The marble revetments are often awkwardly adjusted to the architectural forms. The lower wall arches are flattened, and at the corners they rest on thin colonnettes rather than piers. These details appear more elegant in the reconstruction drawing than they do in reality (fig. 67).

The lower levels of the building, including the sanctuary and narthex, are identical in detail to those of a cross-in-square church. I have proposed that the church was begun as such, but that with the generous donations of Constantine, a radical new design was introduced in order to create a more exotic and impressive interior, and to create a special setting for mosaic decoration.[33] At Nea Moni, the mosaic zone begins less than six meters above the floor in the curved surfaces of the conches. This may be contrasted with the slightly earlier katholikon of Hosios Loukas, in which the mosaic zone begins about ten meters above floor level (see fig. 166), and the mosaics are consequently not as easily seen. The proposed change in the design at Nea Moni and its bold new formulation are best understood as a direct response to aesthetic concerns, to the important mosaic program with its imperial overtones.[34] Like the two examples above, Nea Moni stands at the forefront of a new building type, the so-called island octagon church, which one finds represented elsewhere on Chios—as at Panagia Krina (fig. 69)—as well as on Crete, on Cyprus, and on the mainland.[35] I have suggested that the new type had its origins in the transformation of a standard church design. In this instance, the floor plan remained virtually unchanged, whereas the elevation was altered.[36]

In the three preceding examples, only certain parts are affected in the transformation. Standard features remain, such as the longitudinal axis from narthex to sanctuary and the centralized space of the naos below a dome. Change occurs in special areas and in response to specific requirements: function, location, or decoration. Psellos's texts

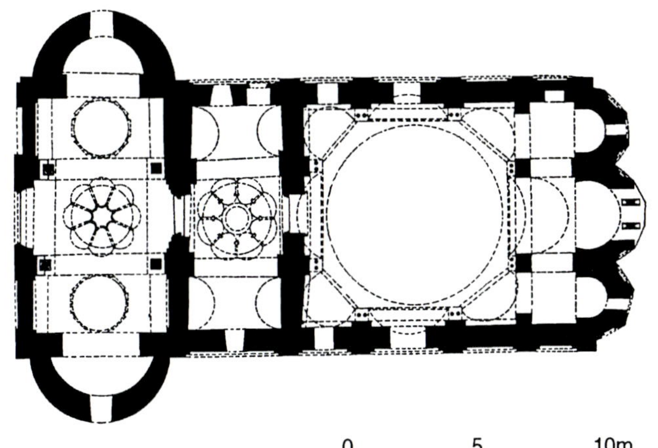

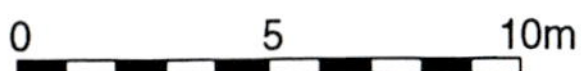

FIG. 65. Plan of the katholikon of Nea Moni on Chios

FIG. 66. View into the naos vaulting of the Nea Moni katholikon

FIG. 67. Reconstructed naos view of the Nea Moni katholikon

FIG. 68. Section of the Nea Moni katholikon

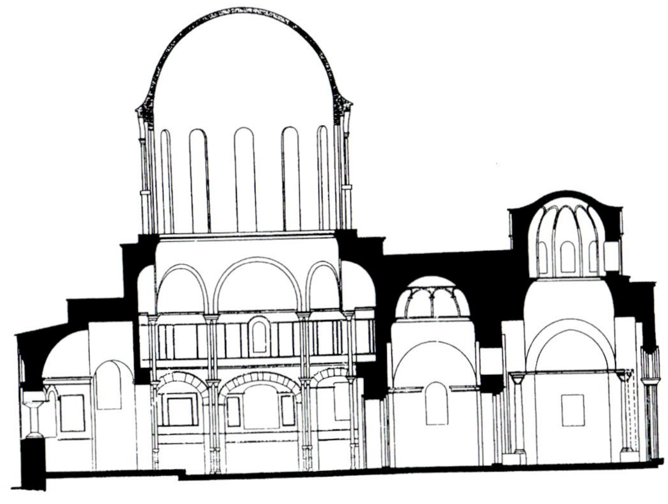

0 5 10m

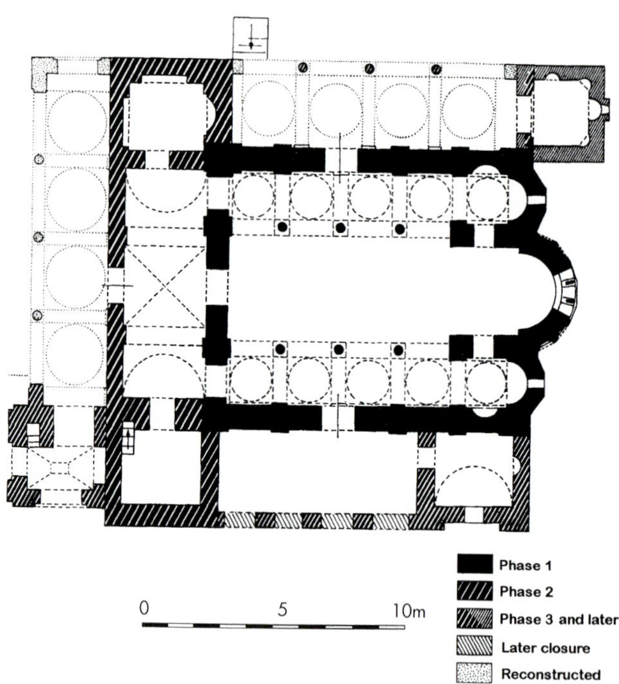

FIG. 75. Plan of the church of the Hodegetria in the Brontocheion monastery, Mistra, at ground level

At Mistra, a similar process of enlargement and elaboration occurred at several churches. The most important of these, the church of the Hodegetria in the Brontocheion monastery, constructed about 1310–22, is a curious juxtaposition of a basilica with galleries and a five-domed, cross-in-square unit (figs. 75–77). Hallensleben has examined the building and has noted sutures at the joining of the north portico, the narthex, and the flanking chapels.[42] Most instructive is the relationship of the naos and the narthex, which are not bonded to each other at the lower level, but which are bonded at the gallery level. As Hallensleben concludes, these details must indicate a change of design *after* the construction of the lower naos walls. The lateral doors, centrally positioned in each wall but now opening directly on an axis with a column, support the idea that the church was begun with a cross-in-square plan that was subsequently elaborated to include the unusual arrangement of galleries for which the extra columns were inserted.

Notable also in this context is the Pantokrator monastery (Zeyrek Camii) in Constantinople (figs. 78–79).[43] It was begun by the Empress Eirene and Emperor John II Komnenos in 1118 as a large cross-in-square church with a broad narthex and at least one lateral aisle, the present south church. When completed, the exterior surfaces were plastered. Before 1136, however, it was augmented by two separate expansions. In the second

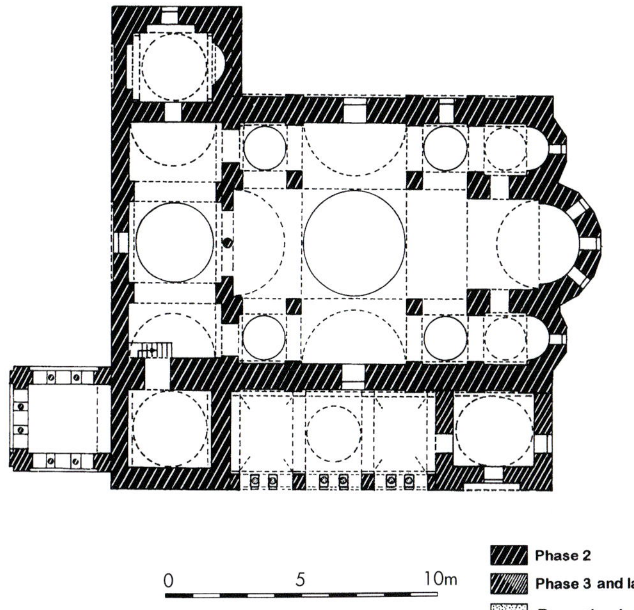

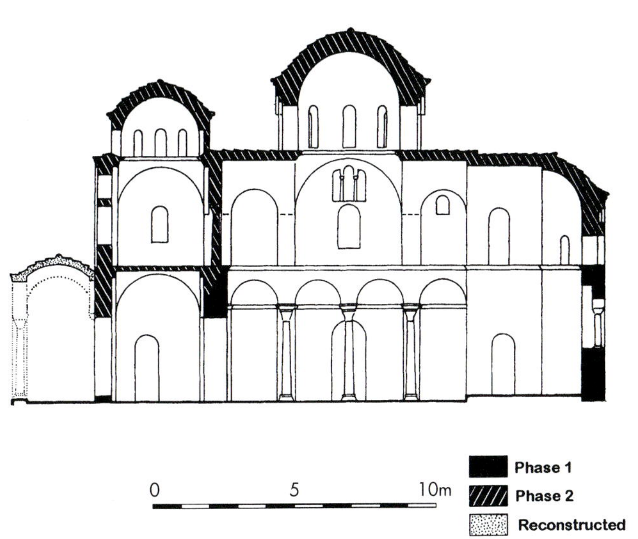

FIG. 76. Plan of the church of the Hodegetria at gallery level

FIG. 77. Section of the church of the Hodegetria

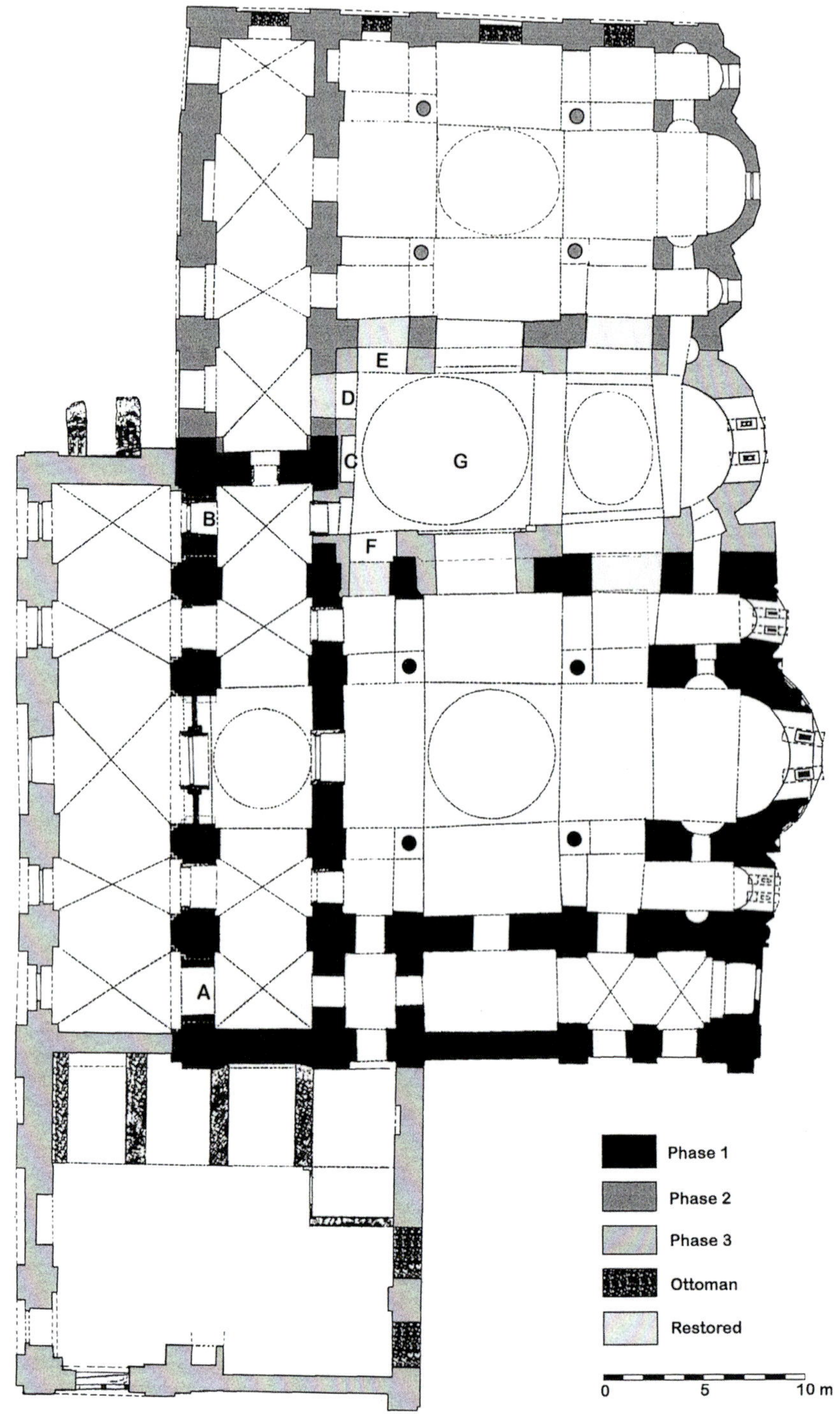

FIG. 78. Plan of the Pantokrator monastery (Zeyrek Camii), Istanbul, showing phases of construction. Letters indicate hypothetical locations of imperial tombs

FIG. 79. View of the Pantokrator churches from the east

phase, a smaller cross-in-square church was added to the north, connecting to the original church only by the narthex. In the third phase, a twin-domed funeral chapel was sandwiched between the two churches, and an outer narthex and an adjoining courtyard were added to the south church. These later additions abutted the plastered surface of the Phase I building. Both the archaeological evidence and the contemporary texts suggest that the later "phases" may represent a continuous process of construction—that is, just as soon as one part was completed, the project was expanded. Moreover, several subphases are evident. For example, the height of the exonarthex vault was raised, a dome was subsequently added above the original south narthex gallery, and the gallery floor below the dome was removed to illuminate the lower level. In the central church, the east dome was apparently an afterthought, added only after the west dome was constructed; this accounts for its curious oval shape.[44] Although the south church originally appeared monumental and symmetrical, the gradual transformation resulted in a church complex that is distinguished by its complexity—with an asymmetrical array of apses along the east facade and a hodgepodge of domes marking the functional spaces.

Similar church clusters were constructed in the following centuries through an additive process and probably in imitation of this important imperial church complex. Thus, not only new "types" could be created through the process of transformation during construction or renovation, but new systems of organization could also be developed. The ultimate form of the Pantokrator is complicated and irregular, but it is reminiscent of the descriptions of lavish palace complexes that were developed in the same period, which the texts characterize as "resembling cities in magnitude and not at all unlike imperial palaces in splendor."[45] It is perhaps significant that the Pantokrator reveals a decline in construction standards from the buildings of the previous century, but this was compensated by the complexity of form and the lavishness of the decorated surfaces.

The process of growth and expansion affected architectural style. At the Pantokrator, complexity became more important than the unity of a monumental expression or a monumental scale—as would have been the goal of a contemporary Western European architect. A sort of hierarchy of function controls the design, in which the individual liturgical spaces are easily understood from the exterior. Like the examples discussed by Michael Psellos, the building underwent a series of nearly contemporaneous transformations, resulting in something that was both novel and impressive.

Aristocratic monasteries of the Palaiologan period reflect the complexities of the Pantokrator. Here we might suspect a symbolic relationship with the past, and one that is expressed in several ways. In the monastic complexes that were developed at several sites, such as the Lips monastery (figs. 80–81), the Pammakaristos monastery (fig. 82), and the Chora monastery (fig. 83) in Constantinople, the mausoleum church of the great Komnenian emperors is reflected in complexes that were also funerary.[46] At the same time, the new additions never obscure the older edifice but are joined to it in a way that seems to respect its character. At the Chora, for example, in spite of stylistic differences, the naos and parekklesion domes are aligned and the detailing of the naos apse is reflected in that of the parekklesion (see fig. 131). Moreover, the masons seem to have been inspired by the difficulties of adding to an older building. The "mannerist" style of these Late Byzantine complexes is derived in part from the architectural response to designing around, but maintaining the integrity of, the historical core of the monastery. In these examples, the masons would appear to be responding not just to new functional considerations but also to the symbolic significance of the historical setting. It may be useful to recall Theodore Metochites' concern with the past and with his position in history.[47] The considerations reflected in the architecture are also evident in the decoration of the Chora. For example, the *Deesis* mosaic spells out his ktetoric lineage, perhaps most obviously in the "family resemblance" between Isaak Komnenos in the *Deesis* mosaic and Metochites' dedicatory image in the adjacent panel (see figs. 27, 208).[48] These two portraits establish a sort of visual dialogue with the past that corresponds with the architectural relationships.

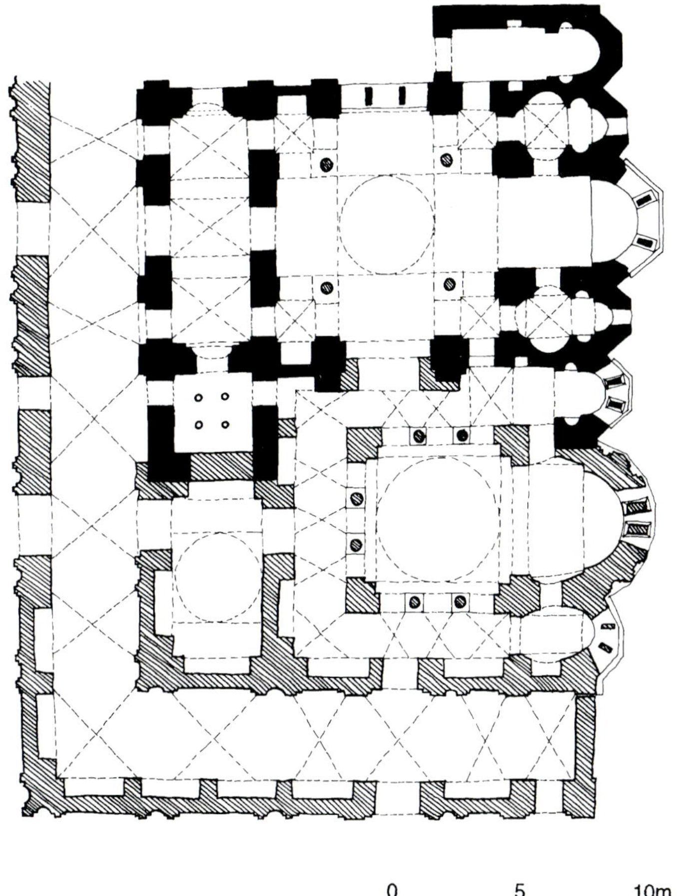

0 5 10m

FIG. 80. Plan of the Late Byzantine complex at the Lips monastery, Istanbul

FIG. 81. View of the Lips monastery from the east

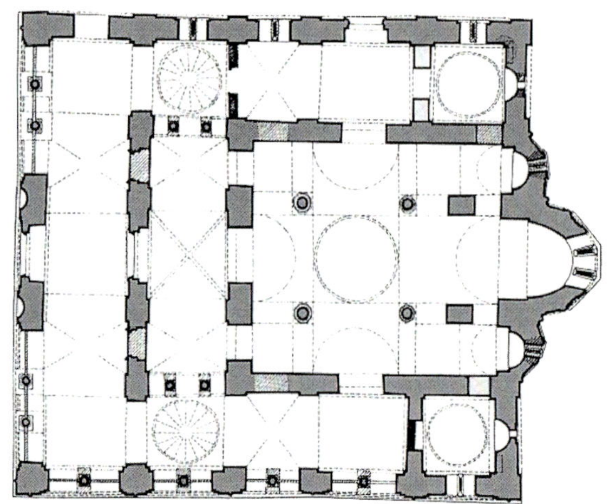

FIG. 87. Plan of the church of the Holy Apostles, Thessaloniki

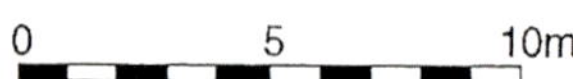

of adding to or modifying an existing structure could be conceptually quite similar. This conclusion has important implications for the interpretation of Byzantine architecture. Although many buildings are clearly the result of several periods of activity, what may look like an addition to the modern viewer may not actually represent an addition. For example, scholars have debated the construction history of the church of the Holy Apostles in Thessaloniki, which was built at least in part by the Patriarch Niphon in the early fourteenth century (figs. 87–88). S. Ćurčić noted the lack of formal integration between the cross-in-square core of the building and the domed, porticoed ambulatory that envelops it.[54] On the east facade, the juncture between the pastophoria and the ambulatory suggests two phases of construction. The construction technique and decorative details are quite similar, and both parts of the building must have been constructed by the same masons. However, the unresolved formal problems led Ćurčić to propose that there had been two phases of construction but that they were chronologically close together. C. L. Striker, however, discovered evidence of bonded masonry between the ambulatory and the pastophoria and insists from this and other evidence that the theory of a two-phase construction must be discarded.[55] The lack of formal integration at the Holy Apostles is instructive, and it may indicate how the building was understood by its masons. Although it was not built in two phases, it was clearly conceived as two distinct elements, and the separate functional components are clearly expressed and visually distinct on the exterior.

It may be significant that a similar lack of formal coherence was to be seen in the

FIG. 88. View of the Holy Apostles from the east

FIG. 90. Interior view of the Panagia Kamariotissa on Heybeliada

thirteenth centuries on which Bouras's analysis is based. Bouras suggests that instead of representing a search for new forms, the variations seek to improve the stability of the basic design.[61] We might extend the analysis to view these variations as improving and correcting a compelling but problematic design.

The problematic connection between the domed naos and the bema at Nea Moni was altered in all of the later variations. At two churches on Chios, for example—Saint George Sykousis and Panagia Krina (see figs. 69, 89B)—the bema was heightened so that the apse became the eighth recess of the octaconch zone, and the visual connection between the two spaces was more clearly established. The problem of vertical relationships was never adequately addressed, although several solutions were attempted. Only Saint George repeated the use of colonnettes to line the interior walls; in other examples, pilasters appear. In several variations, as at Panagia Krina, the corner conches were slightly reduced, but this forfeited their effectiveness in the display of mural painting. At the Holy Apostles in Pyrgoi, on Chios, and in the church of the Metamorphosis at Chortiatis, outside of Thessaloniki, arches replace the wall niches (fig. 89E). Only by extending the niches of the transitional zone to floor level are the vertical relationships resolved, as at the Theotokos Kamariotissa on Chalke and the narthex of Porta Panagia (fig. 90). The latter examples, however, may have no direct relationship to Nea Moni.

The outsized naos dome of Nea Moni is addressed in the several copies on Chios. These both raise the height of the bema vault and add a dome on a drum above the narthex. This may be seen at Panagia Krina (fig. 69) and the Holy Apostles, although the western portion of Saint George has been destroyed.[62] The interior maintains Nea Moni's sense of unity and verticality within the naos, but the other elements are brought into a better balance with it.

These variations of an experimental design give some idea of how buildings were viewed by contemporary masons. The copies of Nea Moni on the island of Chios are particularly interesting in this respect because of their proximity to the prototype. The masons noted both formal and structural problems and addressed them in subsequent buildings. This process might be regarded as another way of transforming architecture, with innovative or troublesome details reformulated from one generation of building to the next. It is possible that the same process occurred with other building types as well. On Chios, a gradual process of change is evident: the basic features of the innovative design are maintained, while the details are manipulated. Conceptually, the process is quite similar to the "buildings that change."

Functional Considerations and Architectural Change

In spite of the conservatism of architectural design after the Transitional period, there are special functional considerations that may have led to the modification of existing architectural forms or even to the development of new ones. For example, the architectural commemoration of church and monastic founders was a concern of increasing importance in the Middle and Late Byzantine periods. Although no imperial, royal, or noble burial has survived intact in Constantinople, numerous texts testify to the impressiveness of the tombs and their settings.[63] According to Byzantine custom, burials were almost never allowed in the naos, but the faithful wanted to place the tomb as close as possible to the naos to gain spiritual benefit from the regular performance of the mass and the saying of special prayers.[64] In several twelfth-century royal burials, the presence of the tomb was of such significance that it affected the design of the building that housed it.

During the Middle Byzantine period, the most common settings for burial were the narthex and annexed chapels. At the tenth-century church of the Theotokos of Lips in Constantinople, for example, numerous sarcophagi have been excavated beneath the floor of the narthex.[65] At Saint John of Troullo, perhaps twelfth-century in date, arcosolia were provided in the narthex, apparently for burial.[66] Funeral chapels were often connected to the narthex and could be understood as functional extensions to it.[67] At Saint Panteleimon at Nerezi, dated 1164, for example, four tiny domed chapels appear

FIG. 91. View of Saint Panteleimon at Nerezi from the southeast

at the corners of the naos; the western two are accessible only from the narthex (figs. 46, 91).[68] Both of these may have been funerary in function, and the north chapel included an arcosolium tomb. As the provincial foundation of Alexios Angelos-Komnenos, a Komnenian prince, the church certainly reflects Constantinopolitan architectural concerns.[69] If, as is often suggested, its five-domed design is based on that of the Nea Ekklesia, Saint Panteleimon would represent the adaptation of an existing church type for funerary purposes.[70]

In several churches associated with the Komnenian family, special accommodation was made for burials. The standards for imperial and noble burials may have been established by the construction of Eirene and John Komnenos at the Pantokrator monastery in Constantinople, which was begun in 1118 and was enlarged twice before 1136, when its *typikon* was written.[71] The south church was equipped with a broad narthex that may have originally been intended to receive imperial burials in arcosolia in the outer bays (see fig. 78); Megaw suggested that the southern bay (A) may have been where Eirene was first laid to rest in 1134.[72] However, by 1136 the original Pantokrator church had been augmented by the addition of a second church to the north, a funeral chapel sandwiched between the two, as well as an outer narthex in front of the original narthex. Whatever the original function of the arcosolia in question, the northern one (B) was eliminated in the later expansion of the building.

The funeral chapel, dedicated to Saint Michael and said to be "in the form of a *heroon*"—that is, comparable to the imperial mausolea at the church of Holy Apostles—was added only in the third phase of construction, between the two cross-in-square churches.[73] To some extent this accounts for its unusual and irregular form—a long space topped by two oval domes, terminating in a broad apse. However, its design clearly took into account the desire to associate the funeral setting with the performance of the liturgy.

The imperial tombs were clustered beneath the western dome. One arcosolium survives in the western wall; to its south is an entrance to the chapel from the narthex. To the north the rough masonry of the second entrance indicates that it was originally closed and functioned as an arcosolium. The arch in the south wall was also closed, offering a third arcosolium, and the similar treatment of the north arch suggests that it was also closed (see fig. 78).[74] These were probably set aside for distinguished members of the family. The western two may have been intended for the tombs of John II (died 1143) and Eirene.[75] There were other burials in the Pantokrator: John had requested that he and his son and heir Alexios (died 1142), who actually predeceased him, be buried in the same tomb.[76] Of the many people whose commemoration was requested in the *typikon*, only John Arbantenos, a nephew by marriage who made significant donations to the monastery, was given permission to be buried there, although the location of his tomb is not specified.[77]

John's son and successor, Manuel I, had his first wife Eirene (Bertha of Sulzbach) buried at the Pantokrator in 1160.[78] Manuel was subsequently buried there in 1180 in a lavish tomb that incorporated an *opus sectile* floor, the relic of the Stone of the Unction, and a tomb marker of dark stone topped by seven domes.[79] The latter may have been freestanding beneath the western dome of the chapel.

The eastern dome of the *heroon* is called the "dome of the Incorporeal" in the *typikon*.[80] Beneath it were the templon and bema of the chapel, equipping it for the liturgy.[81] The western part of the chapel is referred to as the "*heroon* of the exterior," indicating its separation from the liturgical space.[82] Where was the division? In Middle Byzantine architecture, domes normally indicated separate functional spaces. It may be that much of the area under the eastern dome was set aside for the liturgy, which was celebrated here three days each week, with the area under the western dome for burial. Both areas were connected to the churches on either side, and all were unified in the commemorative celebrations in the church.[83] But it is clear from the *typikon* that the chapel was understood as composed of two distinct functional spaces.

masked through the application of mortar. When mortar was used in large quantities, its drying time would have been a critical factor in the construction process, and even for a small building the construction time would be dependent on the stability of the mortar. The fatal collapse of scaffolding that killed Saint Athanasios of Athos may be blamed on the not yet rigid mortar (*titanos*) of the wall under construction.[47] Lime mortars take weeks to dry, particularly if laid thickly, and builders would have to add additional stabilizers if they were to proceed quickly. Tests of early Byzantine mortars indicate that deformation caused by creep action and shrinkage may be high at first, but after about thirty days the mortar becomes relatively stable.[48]

Stone and Quarrying

The region around the Sea of Marmara offered a rich variety of natural stones for which numerous quarries are known from antiquity. Because of the continued importance of Constantinople as a center, a great variety of imported stones appear in its buildings as well. For standard construction, however, the stone most commonly used was a tertiary limestone or occasionally a sandstone, both of which were quarried locally near Hebdomon (modern Bakırköy), and which vary in color from cream or buff to a silvery gray.[49] Available in an area of perhaps one hundred square kilometers immediately west and northwest of the city, between Bakırköy and Safraköy, a mactra limestone belonging to the Upper Miocene period provided an excellent source of building material throughout the Byzantine period. Found in stratiform deposits, the thicker layers (about twenty-five to fifty centimeters thick) that provided the best building material were at a depth of six to seven meters.[50] At the end of the nineteenth century, the hollows and mounds created by quarrying were still visible around Bakırköy.[51] During the last century, however, this area has been entirely built over with the modern expansion of Istanbul, and the quarries no longer function.

There is little information about quarrying operations in the Middle and Late Byzantine periods. Presumably, local quarrying of limestone continued in Constantinople, as evidenced by the fine construction materials employed as late as the early fourteenth century at the Chora and at the Pammakaristos. But only a few texts from the later periods refer specifically to quarrying: the term *lithoxoos* is used for both the stonecutter and the quarryman; *marmararios* refers to the marble worker.[52] In the eleventh century, Michael Psellos indicated the continuation of quarrying in reference to the extravagant building program of Romanos III; for the construction of the Peribleptos monastery, he wrote that "Every mountain was hollowed for material, and the miner's art esteemed higher than philosophy itself. Of the stones thus obtained, some were split, others polished, others

FIG. 100. View of the quarry at the Çanlı Kilise settlement, near Akhisar

turned for the sculptures."[53] It is a commonplace in the literature that stones were brought from afar for an important construction project. At Nea Moni on Chios, it was claimed that the marbles were brought from Constantinople, but much of the stone was actually quarried locally. Most marbles in the naos revetments and door frames are of Chian origin.[54] Moreover, the marble quarries on Chios seem to have been functioning in the mid-eleventh century, at least in a limited capacity for local use. Within the city limits of Constantinople itself, it was probably impossible to quarry building stone, and much had to be transported from the Thracian hinterland. But for isolated building projects outside the capital, local sources of stone were essential. For the construction of a fort in Dacia by John Tzimiskes in the latter part of the tenth century, older quarries were reused and new sources of stone were found.[55] Archaeologists have identified fifteen different types of stone—mostly limestone—used in the fortress at Pacuiul lui Soare (in modern Romania), from possibly twenty or twenty-five different quarries.[56]

At the settlement of Çanlı Kilise in Cappadocia, we have identified the quarries from which building material was taken for the construction of several masonry churches. To remove the blocks of stone, a series of steps was cut into a plateau of hard tuff.[57] Although the plateau immediately above the site could have provided a good source of limestone, the builders preferred the softer and more easily manipulated tuff, which was quarried a bit farther away but still less than a kilometer from the churches (fig. 100). Evidence of another method of quarrying was found in several unfinished rock-cut rooms of the same settlement; spaces were formed by isolating projecting blocks of stone, which then could have been removed in one large piece (fig. 101).

Except for the use of more sophisticated tools, quarrying practices have not changed

FIG. 111. Exterior view of the prothesis dome of the Theotokos Kosmosoteira at Pherrai

the roof, which he had appropriated from the imperial arsenal.[104] In medieval Dubrovnik, documents record the existence of a workshop specializing in the construction of lead-sheathed roofs.[105]

At the Pantokrator, the recent reroofing required sixty metric tons of two-millimeter-thick lead sheeting. Undoubtedly the church was originally covered with lead, but this was likely removed in the thirteenth century. During the Latin Occupation, Baldwin II, the last Latin ruler, used the Pantokrator as his residence but was compelled out of poverty to sell the lead from the roofs of monastic buildings.[106] Remains of ceramic tiles were found on the apses of the north and south churches, but they were similar to examples from Pergamon and probably represent the reroofing of the building in the Late Byzantine period.[107]

The early churches of Kievan Rus' were also roofed with lead, and this seems to have been the standard roofing material. Only at the Tithe Church in Kiev have ceramic tiles been found, though in limited amounts, and these may have been used as cornices.[108] The provision of a lead roof is frequently mentioned in the Old Russian Chronicles. For example, in 1151, Archbishop Nifont roofed the church of Saint Sophia of Novgorod with lead.[109] Not available in Rus', the lead seems to have been imported from Poland.

The Byzantine love of curvilinear surfaces and undulating forms was well served—and perhaps encouraged—by the use of lead sheeting on the roof. This is particularly true of the architecture in and around Constantinople. In fact, it is difficult to imagine

FIG. 112. View of the Chora, Istanbul, from the west, ca. 1860

some of the more elaborate roof forms with any other type of covering. These forms were not as popular with the masons during the Ottoman period, when many roof and domes were leveled; the picturesque undulations were eliminated with an infill of rubble.[110]

Windows

The forms of Byzantine windows were dependent on glass technology, which was limited to the production of small pieces of window glass.[111] These had to be set into a framework of wood, stone, or stucco. Few windows have survived, but the evidence clearly indicates that the window openings we see today are considerably larger than the area that would have been devoted to glazing—sometimes up to three times as large. This is an important consideration in understanding the effect of natural light on the Byzantine interior.

Glass was produced in a variety of locations, and archaeological evidence indicates that makers of glass vessels also produced window glass. However, finds of window glass from the Middle and Late Byzantine periods are rare.[112] Most commonly, Byzantine window glass was blown into round pieces, or oculi, often with a folded outer edge and a thickening toward the center, frequently called "crown" glass. Two Middle Byzantine glass kilns have been excavated in Corinth, and fragments of window glass were found in association with them.[113] At Sardis, many panes of colored glass were found in association

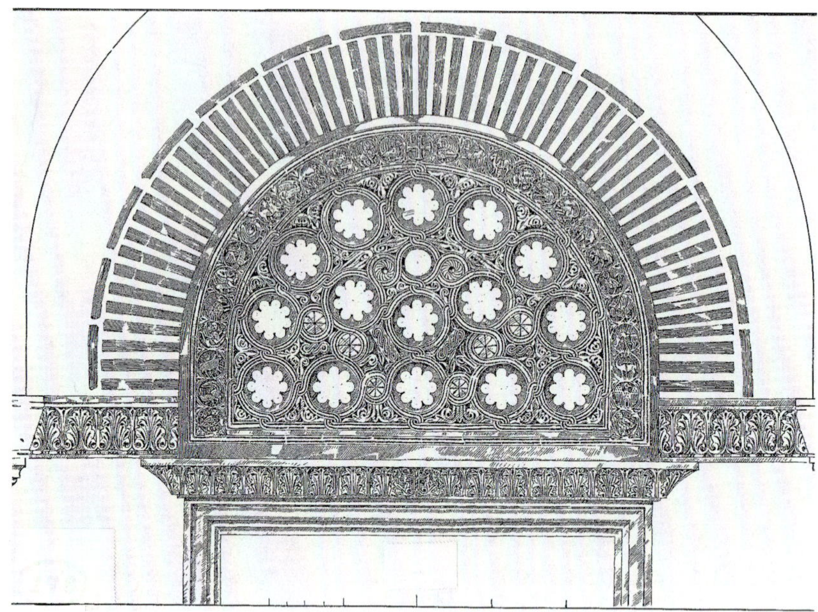

FIG. 113. Drawing of the window in the west doorway of the katholikon of Hosios Loukas monastery

with Church E. They are believed to be of local production, datable to the thirteenth century.[114] In Constantinople, from which few physical remains have been discovered, textual evidence indicates that the shops of glassmakers were located near the church of the Chalkoprateia, on a street called Dikymbalos. The Middle Byzantine v*ita* of Saint Photeine records that an urban fire started there in a workshop of glass smelting.[115]

Pieces of window glass were often organized into geometric patterns, as had been the practice in the Early Christian period, when the window screens could be quite elaborate.[116] A perforated marble window grille, measuring seventy-nine by seventy-five centimeters, divided into square panels, was found in the excavations at the South church at the Lips monastery in Constantinople.[117] Its original location is not known, and it may be considerably older than the church where it was found. It certainly does not represent a typical Byzantine window insofar as the evidence survives. A similar window grille was found at the early sixth-century church of Saint Polyeuktos in Constantinople.

Most commonly, windows consisted of a series of oculi set into an armature, or transenna. Examples are known from Middle Byzantine Greece with molded or carved stucco frames for small oculi. During the restorations at Hosios Loukas in Greece, elaborately molded stucco grilles were uncovered and others were recorded in situ (fig. 113). The carved ornament corresponded with the eleventh-century sculpture elsewhere in

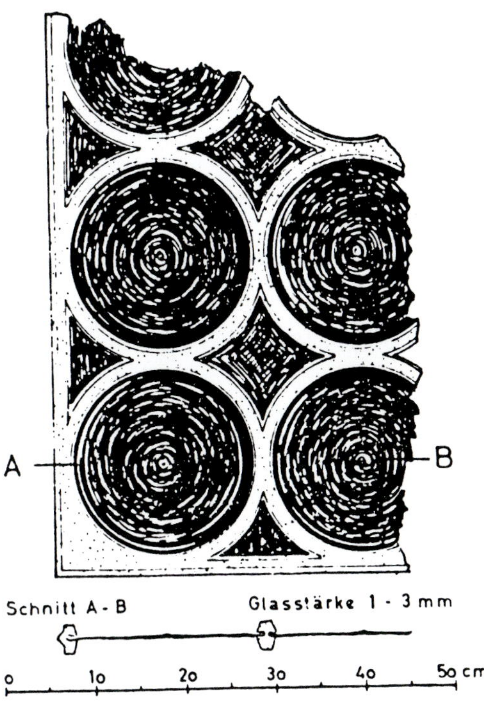

FIG. 114. Reconstruction of a window from the Pammakaristos, Istanbul

the church, and the transennae were subsequently used as models for the present, restored windows (see fig. 167).[118]

In Constantinople, fragments of oculi and their stucco frames were found in a Palaiologan context at the Pammakaristos, in a small grave crypt below the exonarthex.[119] The reconstructed oculi measured about twenty centimeters in diameter and were fixed into the stucco frame with mortar on both sides. In addition to the round pieces, triangular pieces were set around the edge, and additional square pieces are hypothesized in the reconstructed design (fig. 114). Hallensleben reported that the oculi had folded edges and thickened toward the center.[120]

Fragments of glass oculi were also found in the bema excavations at the Chora.[121] Elsewhere at the Chora, pieces of the stucco frames of windows have been preserved, sometimes secured in place with iron pins.[122] Although the Chora's Byzantine windows have all disappeared, one of the dome windows may have survived until the nineteenth century and is visible in a photograph of about 1860 (see fig. 112). It had two rows of oculi filling the opening. One intriguing painted element at the Chora is a false window in the lunette of an internal passage. It consists of one large oculus and pieces of several others, set into a frame.[123]

Similar glass discs in stucco frames were found in situ in the early fourteenth-century church at Gračanica.[124] The diameters of the discs varied between six and sixteen centimeters. In addition, several original windows are preserved in the church at Lesnovo, built in 1341.[125] A lead window frame removed from the naos dome is now in the National Museum in Belgrade (fig. 115), but the original frames are seen in situ in a prerestoration photograph. Each window contained about twenty oculi, organized into two staggered rows. Several panes were overlaid with decorative patterns in lead that would have helped to secure them in place. In addition, three complete windows made with stucco frames survive in the wall between the naos and narthex of the same church. These consist of a single row of oculi with triangular pieces around the edges and a half-oculus at the top.

In Kievan Rus', window frames were normally of oak or pine but similar in form to the Byzantine examples. One from the eleventh century was found in situ at Saint Sophia in Kiev. It measured 92 by 145 centimeters, divided into three rows of openings with oculi 22 centimeters in diameter.[126]

Limited evidence indicates that stained glass was also used in the churches of Constantinople. The excavations at the Chora and at the Pantokrator uncovered quantities of painted stained glass and the lead cames with which it was set, indicating that a technique so strongly associated with Western Europe also appeared in Byzantium. The glass from the Pantokrator can be dated to about 1125 and seems to have come from the bema window.[127] The glass was cast in pans rather than blown, as was the practice in Western Europe. In addition to painted geometric and floral patterns, one piece showed details of a human face, and Megaw proposed a reconstruction of the apse windows with large standing figures represented (fig. 116).

At the Chora, two batches of stained glass were discovered. A variety of colored fragments with painted vegetal and ornamental patterns were found in the bema, and the H-shaped cames with which the glass was set were found in the excavation of the parekklesion. These are believed to have come from the early twelfth-century bema window.[128] Pieces of unpainted glass were also found in the parekklesion, with portions of the stucco frame still in situ in the east window.[129] The east window of the fourteenth-century parekklesion was apparently filled with colored glass set in simple geometric patterns.

Recent technical analysis of the glass from the Chora and Pantokrator indicates a different chemical composition than that of Western glass.[130] The unusually high level of boron in the Byzantine glass may be indicative of a local source of sand. Although it is sometimes suggested that the Byzantine stained glass represents an independent development and a local production—the early date and mature form of the Pantokrator glass might suggest that the Byzantine development preceded and influenced the Western European tradition—this hypothesis is hotly contested by Western medievalists.[131] In

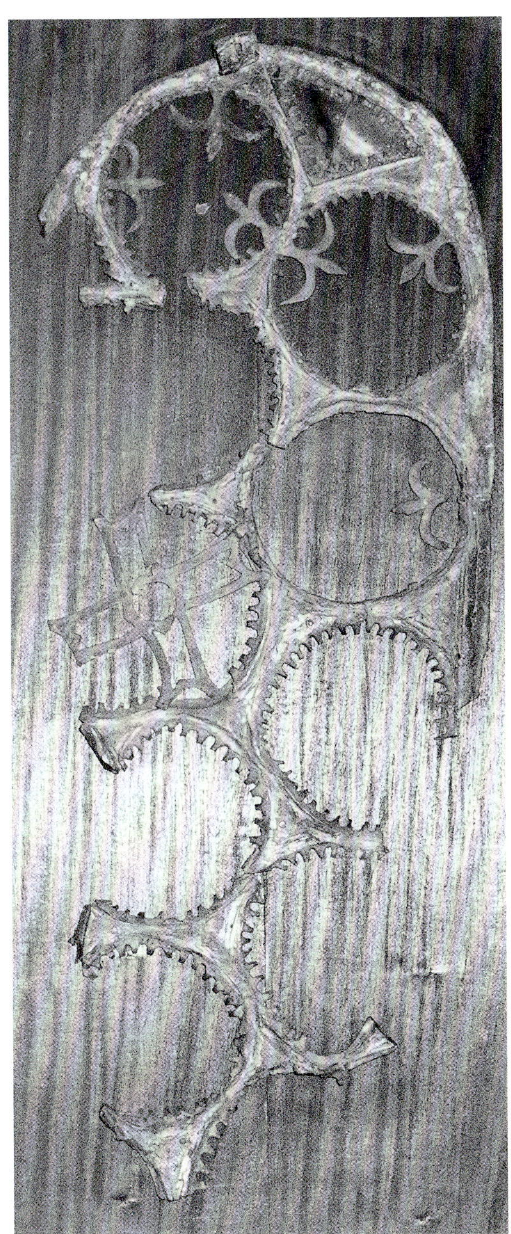

FIG. 115. Lead window frame from the naos dome of the church of the Archangels at Lesnovo, now in the National Museum, Belgrade

FIG. 116. Hypothetical reconstruction of the stained-glass windows in the bema of the south church of the Pantokrator, Istanbul

fact, although colored glass was commonly used in Byzantium, the evidence for painted stained glass is thus far limited to these two closely related examples. The patrons of the two buildings in question, an emperor and a crown prince, were brothers.

The limitations of glass production meant that Byzantine windows remained small, with the areas given over to glazing smaller still. It may indeed be the response to the available technology that led to the development of distinctive window forms. Typically the Byzantines favored tall, thin windows or windows divided into two or three tall, thin lights, and these would have been most suitable for supporting a frame of oculi.

An examination of building technology amplifies the picture of architectural production during the Byzantine period. Masons did not exist in isolation, but relied on suppliers of brick, stone, mortar, glass, and other building materials. The technological possibilities and limitations of materials would have influenced both the design and scale of a building project.

CHAPTER SIX

The Construction of Foundations and Walls

Byzantine workshops made significant contributions to the standardization of construction practices and to the transmission of architectural knowledge. This chapter will examine the construction methods of foundations and walls, including the use of scaffolding. Foundations were certainly an important consideration in any building project, and although they are usually the best surviving portion of medieval buildings, they are often the least studied.[1] For wall construction, the technical aspects will be emphasized in an attempt to identify the distinguishing characteristics of a workshop. Facade articulation and decorative details will be discussed briefly, since more attention has been given to them by other scholars. Because buildings with identical wall systems often have very different plans and types of vaults there was more flexibility concerning design within a given workshop than has been assumed.

Foundation Systems

Byzantine foundations were constructed of brick or stone. They were dug to bedrock if possible and occasionally cut from the bedrock. At Çanlı Kilise in Cappadocia and at the church near Seben in Bithynia, stepped foundations were cut directly from the bedrock, augmented by masonry to create a level platform for the construction of the naos (figs. 17, 117).[2] Similarly stepped foundations may be observed occasionally in Constantinople, as in the fourteenth-century exonarthex foundation at the Chora.[3]

The detailed examination of the foundations of the tenth-century Theotokos church at the Lips monastery indicates the degree of sophistication in their design. A level platform was created at a depth of 1.4 meters below the naos floor and covered with a layer of lime and crushed brick, which the excavator mistakenly took to be the floor of an older building.[4] Above this rose the masonry foundations for the walls, as well as two transverse foundation walls that secured the bases of the four freestanding columns to the

FIG. 117. View of the church at Seben-Çeltikdere from the east, showing stepped foundations

outer walls (fig. 118). The intervening spaces were packed with rough stones, without mortar, above which the tenth-century floor was laid.

Church E at Sardis employed a grid system for its foundations, in which the nine-bay plan of the church is reflected (figs. 48, 119). Foundation walls, without footings, extended to a depth varying between 1.3 and 2.0 meters below the floor of the church.[5] As broad as 1.7 meters below the superstructure walls, the foundations actually rise above the foundations of an older basilica that, according to its excavators, was in use until the construction of the smaller Church E.[6] The interior lines of foundations are not completely bonded to the perimeter, perhaps to counter possible unequal settling. At the top of the foundation walls, timber beams were laid with two parallel beams set within each wall. Where they met, the beams were connected by iron spikes, and they were covered with a protective layer of high-quality, hard mortar. These would have provided additional stability. Although regarded as unusual by the excavators, wooden reinforcement may actually be standard Byzantine practice in foundation construction.[7]

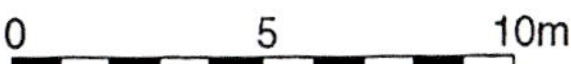

FIG. 118. Longitudinal section cut through the north aisle of the Theotokos of Lips, Istanbul, looking north, showing the foundations and the positions of burials

FIG. 119. View of the foundations of Church E at Sardis

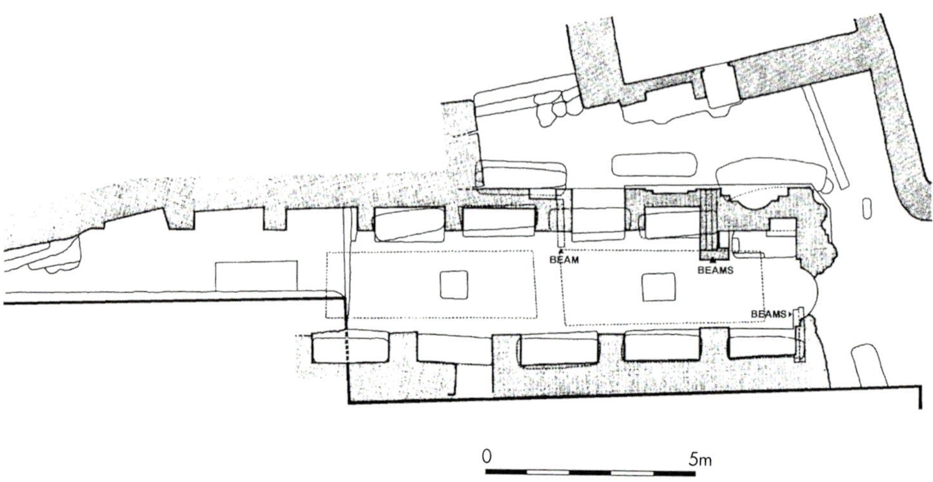

FIG. 122. Plan of the funerary chapel near Hagios Athanasios, Didymoteicho, showing the positions of rock-cut tombs and of cavities for wooden beams in the foundations of the walls

reinforcements are known from many locations. At the tenth-century Tithe Church in Kiev, the bases of the foundation trenches were strengthened with wooden reinforcements—layers of groundsels secured into position with wooden stakes. This was covered by a layer of lime and crushed brick, above which the foundations were constructed.[15] Identical systems were employed at several early masonry buildings elsewhere in Kiev, as well as at Saint Sophia in Novgorod, often with spikes joining a system of beams that ran parallel with the walls. Wooden reinforcements have been found only in these early buildings and have not been observed in foundations in Kievan Rus' after about 1080. This is significant, because the architecture of Kievan Rus' was most closely connected with Byzantium before 1080, when Byzantine masters were at work at many sites in this region. As Rappoport emphasizes, the use of wooden reinforcements surely represents a Byzantine foundation system.[16]

If different components of a building were not of the same weight and would have settled differently, unbonded foundations were included. This was the case at the Fatih Camii at Enez, where the lightweight, wooden-roofed exonarthex was not bonded to the heavier main block of the building, although both were constructed at the same time (figs. 123–24).[17] The same may have occurred at the Pantepoptes, where the deep foundations form a cistern that extends below the naos and narthex but not below the exonarthex (see figs. 18, 120). Recent investigations suggest that the original Middle Byzantine exonarthex had the form of a portico; it was either contemporaneous or nearly contemporaneous with the main block of the building, but it was constructed above lighter foundations and was not bonded.[18] The settling of these lighter foundations

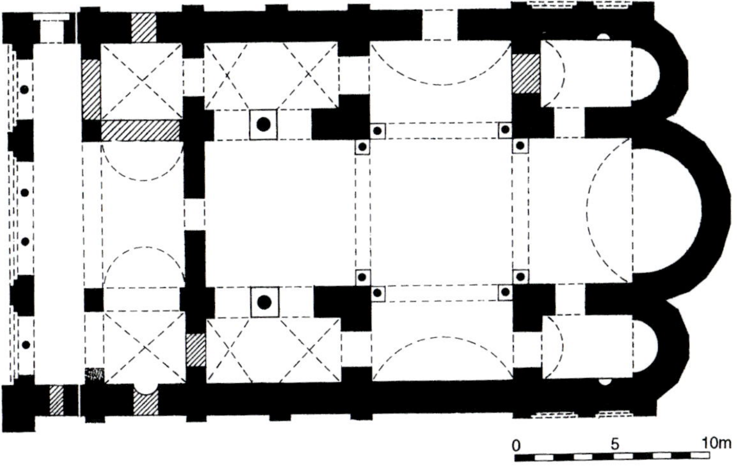

FIG. 123. Plan of the Fatih Camii at Enez

FIG. 124. View of the Fatih Camii from the west

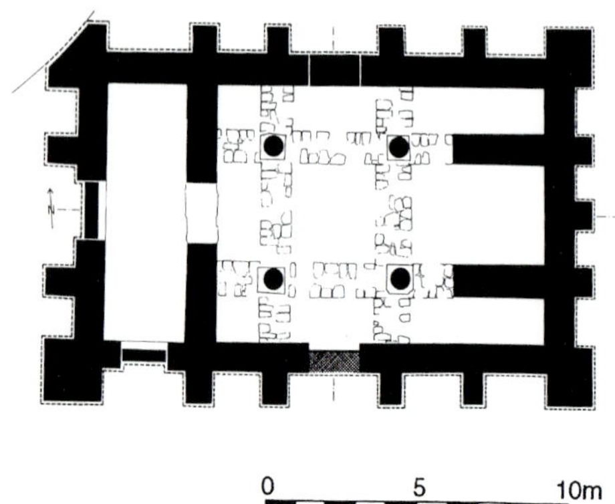

FIG. 125. Plan of substructures of the Myrelaion, Istanbul

eventually led to the collapse of the original exonarthex and necessitated its reconstruction in the Late Byzantine period.

Older foundations could be reused if they were deemed strong enough for the new construction. Paul Magdalino has recently emphasized the continuity of site occupation in medieval Constantinople, and this extends to the remains of buildings as well.[19] Just as bricks and columns could be reused, so could foundation systems. The eleventh- and twelfth-century naos of the Chora, for example, rests on a series of vaulted substructures that date from the sixth to ninth centuries.[20] The early site history of the Kalenderhane Camii is equally complex (see fig. 133).[21] At the so-called Apokaukos church in Selymbria, dated 1327, the large church was constructed above an older cistern, and the plans of the two are not related.[22] The ninth-century church known as Ayasofya in Vize was constructed on the foundations of an Early Christian basilica of which the apse is still visible to the east.[23] Similarly, the Middle Byzantine churches of Side all seem to have been built on older foundations.[24] Recent excavations at the twelfth-century church of Saint Aberkios at Kurşunlu demonstrate that it was also built on older foundations.[25] In many instances, the reuse of the site was more clearly related to its sanctity than to the foundations. The existence of older foundations could also affect the design of the new church, as the "buildings that change" discussed in chapter 4 suggest.

Because of the irregular terrain of Constantinople, artificial terracing was often necessary to create a level platform for the construction of the building proper. In the most extreme example, the tenth-century Myrelaion required a duplicate building at the lower level to bring the church to the height of the adjacent palace (figs. 1–4, 125). Although it virtually replicated the four-column plan of the church above, the substructure was initially functionless and was only converted to a funerary chapel in the fourteenth century.[26] The substructure was provided with its own foundation system, which formed a grid pattern below the internal supports.[27]

Although a complex system of substructures was often necessary, functional spaces were seldom included. There are only rare (and problematic) examples in and around Constantinople of a chapel or a functioning crypt being incorporated into the foundations of a church. The so-called Odalar Camii, perhaps twelfth century in date, included a series of burial chambers in its lower level. Set into the slope, the lower level also created a level platform for the naos. The building is now overbuilt and all but destroyed; it was never properly examined, so it is not known if the lower level was intended from the beginning as a burial crypt.[28] The Bogdan Saray, probably built in the fourteenth century as a private chapel, also included a burial crypt (see fig. 152).[29] Another example is the church of the Savior at the Chalke, known only from descriptions.[30] At Hosios Loukas in Greece, a unique funerary crypt lies below the katholikon, but its inclusion is due in large part to the sloping topography of the site and the unusual circumstances of its foundation.[31] The same may be true for the funerary chapels at Asenovgrad and at Bačkovo in Bulgaria, both of which are set dramatically on sloping ground.[32]

At the twelfth-century church known as the Gül Camii in Istanbul, a substantial masonry platform provides the base for the building.[33] It includes a series of small chambers and passageways that bear little relationship to the plan of the building above it. These extend under the bema, naos, and narthexes and protrude further to the west and southwest. Although these were once thought to be reused from an older building, the masonry construction is identical to that of the church, and therefore the two must be contemporaneous (fig. 126).

In most Constantinopolitan buildings, the foundations included cisterns. Although the Myrelaion church did not include cisterns in its substructures, the interior of the adjacent Early Christian rotunda was subdivided by columns and converted to a vaulted cistern that also formed the substructure for the palace of Romanos Lekapenos (see fig. 12).[34] In the area of Topkapı Palace alone, a recent study has counted more than forty cisterns—all of which were contained within the substructures of buildings.[35] The twelfth-century naos of the Pammakaristos included a large colonnaded and vaulted cistern somewhat similar in plan to the church above it. The cistern extends under the naos and parts of the ambulatory, with the columns of the cistern set directly below the columns of the naos (fig. 127).[36] At the Pantepoptes, the plan of the vaulted cistern relates more directly to the plan of the church (see figs. 18, 120). In several instances where only the cisterns have been preserved, scholars have suggested the plan of the vanished building above them based on their substructures. Many of these clearly must have been churches, with a curvature resembling an apse along the east side, but the lack of direct correspondence leaves many details unclear. A cistern near the Fatih Camii is a good example (fig. 128).[37]

At the Mangana area of Istanbul, impressively extensive but very confusing substruc-

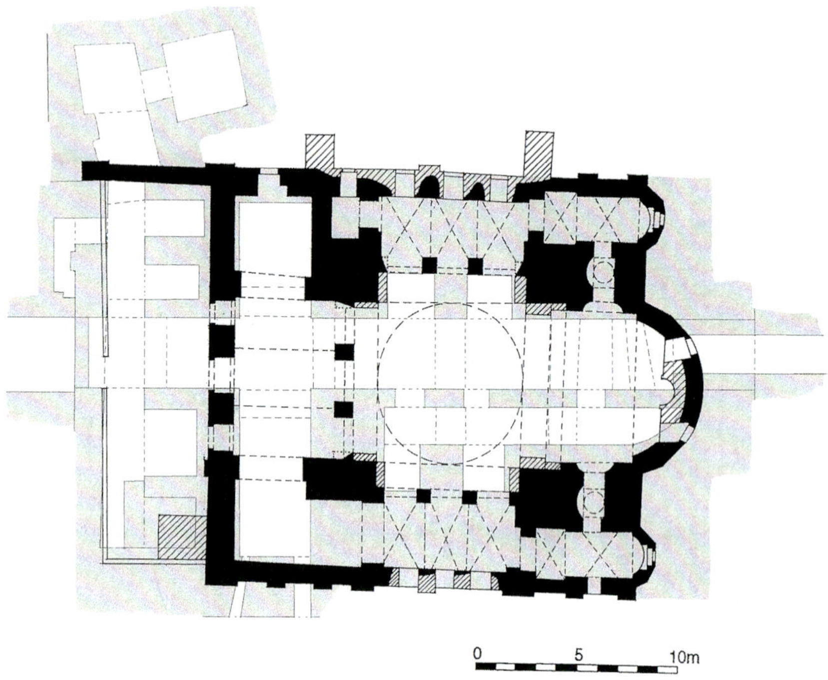

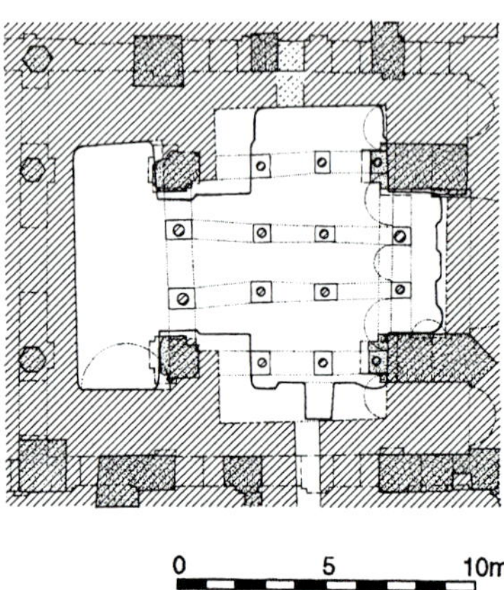

FIG. 126. Plan of the Gül Camii, Istanbul, indicating ground level in black and the substructures in gray

FIG. 127. Plan of the cistern under the naos of the Pammakaristos, Istanbul

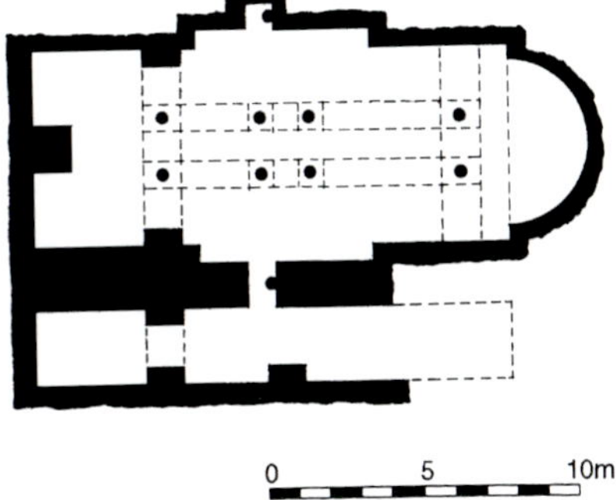

FIG. 128. Plan of a cistern near the Fatih Camii, Istanbul, probably the substructure of a church

tures extended beneath the church and monastery of Saint George, the Mangana Palace, and possibly the Philanthropos monastery and church of the Panachrantos (fig. 129).[38] These provided a level terrace where the ground drops away immediately before the seawall to the east. Several periods of foundation walls have been identified, with the majority from the eleventh century. A detailed interpretation of them is hindered owing to their partial destruction at the time the railway line was built. The meager remains of the superstructure of the church of Saint George indicate a general relationship between the substructure and the form of the church. The substructure is divided into a grid of vaulted compartments, with four domical vaults below the area of the naos, and the areas below the ambulatory are similarly subdivided. To the south, some walls of a large building, presumably the palace, are preserved.

The danger of reconstructing the plan of a building based on its substructures was recently demonstrated by the resurveying of the site of the so-called Bryas Palace, built by the emperor Theophilos in an Asian suburb of Constantinople. Alessandra Ricci has shown that what was once interpreted as a domed audience hall of a palace in the Arab style was in fact the substructure of a church; its apses could be traced on the upper level. The plan of the church may have been similar to that of Saint George of Mangana. What was interpreted as the colonnaded hall to the west seems to have been instead a cistern below the atrium of the church.[39]

In some of the better preserved examples of substructures containing cisterns, such as those below the fourteenth-century funeral chapel at the Chora monastery, one can observe conduits that led from the roof to collect rainwater (fig. 130). The barrel-vaulted cisterns were once interpreted as burial crypts related to the funeral chapel above them, but the presence of conduits and the lining of hydraulic mortar indicates that these were cisterns.[40] With the demise of the ancient aqueduct system of Constantinople—that is, the *public* system of waterworks—private institutions included their own systems for the collection and storage of water. One can only wonder about the healthiness of water

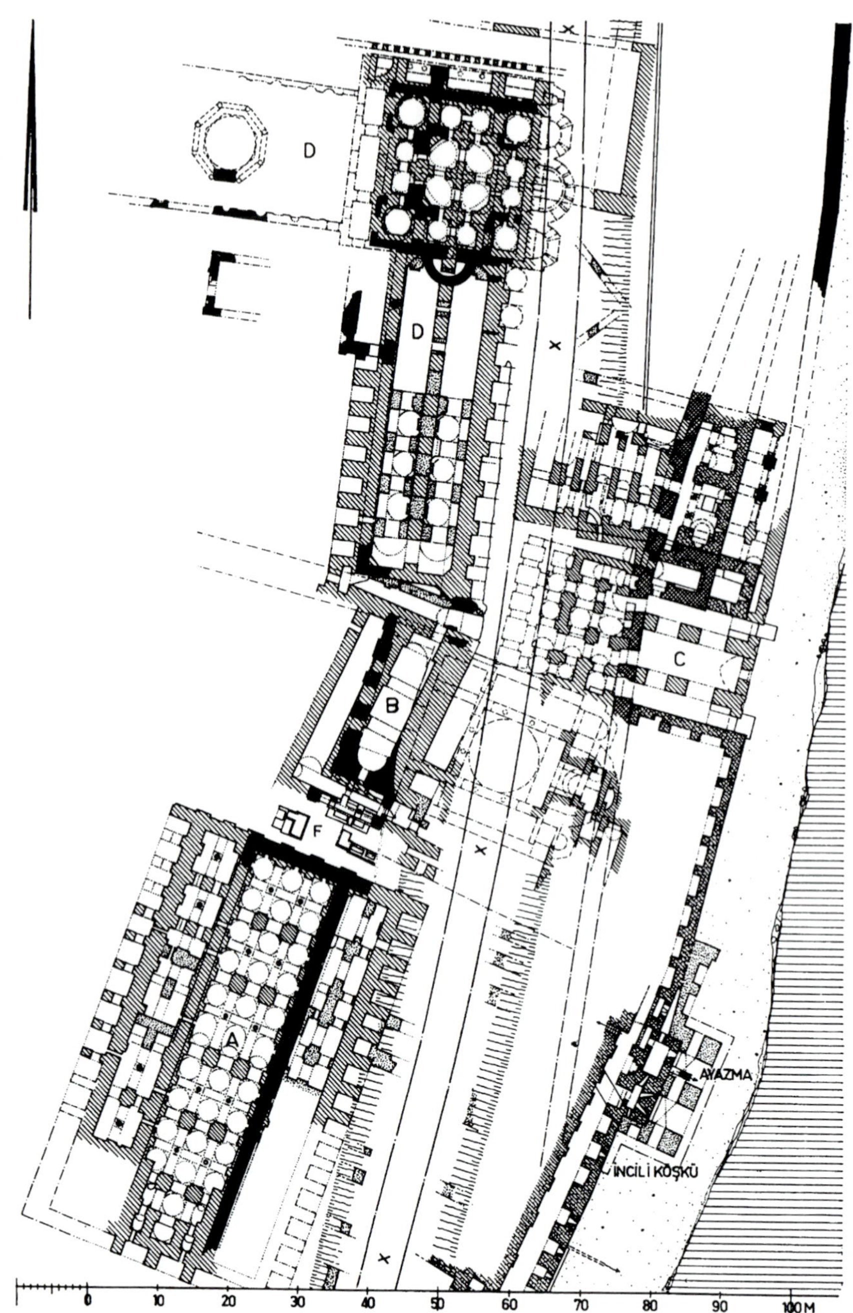

FIG. 129. Plan of foundations and substructures in the Mangana region:

A. Palace

B. So-called monastery of the Theotokos Panachrantos

C. Monastery of Christ Philanthropos

D. Monastery of Saint George

FIG. 130. Conduits draining into a cistern below the parekklesion of the Chora, Istanbul

stored beneath tombs. Moreover, in an area plagued by earthquakes, any tremor would have cracked the waterproof lining of the cisterns. Consequently, most buildings suffered, and continue to suffer, from dampness.

Wall Construction

The most characteristic wall construction in Byzantine buildings was formed by alternating bands of brick and stone, following the example of Late Roman *opus mixtum*. Squared stone faced both the inner and outer surfaces of the wall, and mortared rubble filled the space between the facings. The bricks would normally form a leveling course, extending through the thickness of the wall and binding the two faces together. In a standard pattern of repetition there are three to five courses of stone, with a total height of two-thirds of a meter or less, and three to five courses of brick, with a height of about one-third of a meter or slightly more. A typical example is the early fourteenth-century Chora, which has four courses of stone, measuring 64 to 68 centimeters high, alternating with four courses of brick, measuring 42 to 46 centimeters high (fig. 131). The bricks measure 4 to 5 centimeters thick and are laid close together, whereas the mortar joints measure 5 to 7 centimeters thick.[41]

FIG. 131. View of the Chora from the southeast

Numerous variations of this wall system occur. The tenth-century Myrelaion is constructed almost entirely of brick, although solid brick is rare in surviving buildings and was probably more costly (see fig. 3). Some buildings alternate a single course of stone with one or more courses of brick. This is seen in the Late Byzantine portions of the monastery of Lips, where the pattern of repetition is one stone to one brick, but with occasional bands of five or six bricks (figs. 81, 132). Similar masonry appeared at the end of the twelfth century at the church now known as the Kalenderhane Camii (fig. 133). Both the Middle and Late Byzantine portions of the Kilise Camii employ a repeat pattern of two or three brick courses to one course of stone.[42] But there do not appear to be easily defined chronological parameters for the appearance of broad bands and narrow bands in the wall construction. Both systems appear, with numerous variations, throughout the period under discussion. Although basic systems of wall construction may have been established by workshop practices, they cannot be taken by themselves as the identifying features of a specific workshop.

In spite of the numerous variations of the system, there is almost always integrity in the wall construction of Constantinople. In standard practice, both the inner and the outer surfaces of a wall correspond: where a brick course appears on the exterior, the same

FIG. 132. South facade of Saint John of Lips, Istanbul, before restoration

FIG. 133. View of the Kalenderhane Camii, Istanbul, from the southwest

FIG. 134. Broken wall at the Tekfur Saray, Istanbul, showing continuous coursing

will appear on the interior (fig. 134). The interior and exterior cornices also will normally correspond, and arcading on the exterior normally coincides with the springing of arches and vaults on the interior. The wall was regarded as a solid element, not simply as facings on a rubble core.

Although this may not sound unusual, it is the integrity of the wall that distinguishes Constantinopolitan construction from that of many other areas of the empire.[43] For example, the eleventh-century Çanlı Kilise in Cappadocia utilizes alternating bands of brick and stone on its main external facades in a manner that resembles Constantinopolitan construction. The brick is used only as a facing material, however, and the interior wall surface is entirely of stone (see fig. 17).[44] In areas of damage, it is evident that mortared rubble fill was layered to correspond to the exterior coursing. Thus, in spite of the brick-banded exterior and the Constantinopolitan decorative features, technically the building is closer to the standard, all stone construction of Asia Minor, in which a rubble core was faced with neatly squared stone on both surfaces. The same contrast between a banded brick and stone exterior and an all stone interior facing has been observed in a tenth- or eleventh-century church near Seben in Bithynia (see fig. 117).[45] In the chapel of Saint Catherine at Didymoteicho in Thrace, the exterior facades have broad, alternating

FIG. 135. View of the chapel of Saint Catherine at Didymoteicho from the north

bands of brick and stone, but the internal system is completely different, and the banding does not correspond to that of the exterior (fig. 135).[46] All of these buildings must be attributed to local workshops in spite of their Constantinopolitan outward appearance. In such examples as these, a clear differentiation between construction technique and architectural style helps us to localize the builders.

A variety of other techniques of wall construction have been observed throughout Byzantine territory, and these are also useful indicators for the presence of regional workshops. For example, the tenth-century Theotokos church at Hosios Loukas is the earliest cross-in-square church in Greece, and it is normally suggested that its plan was imported from the region of Constantinople.[47] On the other hand, the masonry tells a very different story, with brick and stone mixed in a very dissimilar way from that of the capital (see fig. 15). Bricks are frequently positioned vertically, for example, with the individual stones surrounded by brick on four sides, in a system that is called *cloisonné*, borrowing a term from enamelwork. In addition, decorative bands of dogtooth—that is, bricks set at a 45-degree angle—add depth and shadow to the surface, forming both horizontal bands and the outlining of arches. When similar dogtooth bands appear in the monuments of Constantinople, they invariably form a cornice at the top of the wall, but never appear in the middle. Nor do they surround arches, except when the arches are at

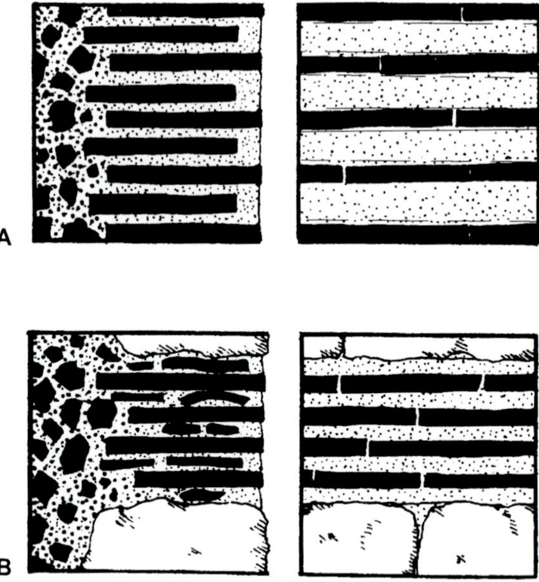

FIG. 136. Diagrams of the recessed-brick technique:
A. Wall section and facade detail of standard construction
B. Wall section and facade detail of the "brick-filled mortar joints" variation

the top of the wall. Similarly, the Late Byzantine monuments of Thessaloniki are seen in close relationship to the architecture of Constantinople. This may be true in terms of principles of design and certain decorative details, but the wall construction is distinctive, with rough fieldstone and cloisonné (see fig. 88).[48]

Sometime in the second half of the tenth century, a second method of wall construction seems to have originated in Constantinople. The so-called recessed-brick or concealed-course technique has been the subject of much discussion.[49] In standard practice, the technique is characterized by the recessing of alternate courses of brick from the wall surface. These are consequently concealed within the mortar bed, and the joints appear to be considerably wider than the brick (figs. 136A, 137). Normally, recessed brick was used in walls in conjunction with stone courses, alternating a single stone course with broad bands of recessed brick.

Both aesthetic and structural reasons have been suggested for the development of the technique.[50] The characteristic striped effect, created by thin bricks and wide mortar beds, seems to have been appreciated, and the technique was often continued into the arches. Moreover, it was consciously imitated. For example, the exceptionally broad mortar joints appear in the eleventh-century additions to the Koimesis church in Nicaea

FIG. 137. View of the Mangana substructures, Istanbul, showing construction in the recessed-brick technique

as well as in the Çanlı Kilise in Cappadocia (see fig. 17), but neither example employs recessed brick.[51]

In other examples, the technique is used for structural reasons. For example, at the Panagia Chalkeon in Thessaloniki, dated 1028, the mortar joints are thin, and recessed bricks appear only at the critical points of the construction—the corners and on the apses—apparently as stabilizers (fig. 138).[52] The same limited use may have occurred at the Pantepoptes, although the recessed-brick technique is much more visible in areas of repair.[53] In many examples, however, the technique appears where the brick is used only as a facing on a rubble core. In these examples, the alternating positions of the bricks created an irregular inner surface that allowed the facing to bond more easily with the core. The logic of this method is comparable to that of ancient Roman wall construction, in which the facing bricks were triangular-shaped and laid so that the exterior surface was smooth but the inner surface was jagged, to bond with the concrete core.[54]

The appearance of the recessed-brick technique also corresponds with formal changes in wall treatment that occurred in this period, as it became standard to articulate surfaces with arcading, stepped pilasters, and niches. As surfaces became more three-dimensional, it would have been increasingly difficult to coordinate bricks of regular

FIG. 138. Detail of the east facade of the Panagia Chalkeon showing exposed courses of recessed brick

measure with walls of varying thickness.[55] This may explain the use of the technique in buildings at the highest levels of patronage, such as at the eleventh-century church of Saint George of Mangana and at the twelfth-century churches of the Pantokrator, the Chora, and the Kosmosoteira, all of which have highly elaborated walls (see fig. 93).

Most likely there is not one single explanation for the appearance and popularity of the technique. Either structural or aesthetic reasons may have dominated in different circumstances. But in Byzantine architecture, structure and decoration were closely related. External arcading, for example, could both strengthen the building at critical points and articulate the facade. Similarly, recessed brick may have been employed to satisfy structural and aesthetic considerations simultaneously.

Another explanation may also apply to a number of examples of the recessed-brick technique, primarily in the thirteenth and fourteenth centuries. This variation, which we may distinguish as "brick-filled mortar joints," may derive from standard recessed-brick construction, but the motivation for its use appears to differ.[56] This technique seems have been employed to take maximum advantage of reused materials. Reused bricks or tiles could be employed as facing, as long as they were in good condition, and damaged materials could be employed as filler (fig. 136B). At the Pantokrator in Constantinople, the exonarthex construction alternates large bricks in the exposed courses and smaller, thinner tiles in the recessed courses (fig. 139). All were apparently reused. The fill at the Panagia Chalkeon in Thessaloniki was also of reused tiles (see fig. 138).[57]

After the end of the twelfth century, presumably as new materials became harder to

FIG. 139. Detail of the south facade of exonarthex of the Pantokrator, Istanbul, showing recessed-brick construction and the remains of painted plaster

obtain, almost all examples of brick-filled mortar joints resulted from the reuse of materials. In addition, the quality of the mortar deteriorated in the later period, and the recessed courses would have acted as stabilizers. The thirteenth-century churches of Latmos, for example, employ this technique, and the buildings are constructed entirely of *spolia* from the ancient city of Herakleia. Recessed bricks are used as spacers in the brick courses, and this seems to have preserved the buildings; the mortar has almost entirely fallen away (fig. 140).[58] A similar technique was used in a few modest Late Byzantine churches in Constantinople, such as the Bogdan Saray and the İsa Kapı Mescidi (fig. 141).

This explanation does not apply to all examples of the recessed-brick technique. For example, although the technique was taken to Kievan Rus' by Constantinopolitan masons at an early date, that region lacked a preceding Roman or Early Christian architecture to provide a supply of building materials, and it lacked a tradition of masonry architecture. Consequently, the bricks must have been produced at the time of construction.[59] However, archaeologists have noted the large proportion of misfired bricks, and the recessed-brick technique may have been employed to take maximum advantage of this material, which could be concealed within the thickness of the walls.[60]

The recessed-brick technique is also significant to our discussion of workshops and workshop practices. There are some general chronological boundaries for the appearance of recessed brick. The standard technique, with broad mortar joints, appears primarily in the late tenth through twelfth centuries in Constantinople and in areas associated

FIG. 140. East facade of the church on Kahve Asar Ada, Bafa Gölü (Latmos), showing brick-filled mortar joints

FIG. 141. Interior view of the İsa Kapı Mescidi, Istanbul, looking east

with the capital. Brick-filled mortar joints are found primarily in the later centuries over a more diffused area. Significantly, it would have been necessary for masons to learn both variations of the technique within the context of a workshop. They could *not* have been learned purely from later observation. After a building was completed, the characteristic recessed courses of brick would have been invisible. The outer appearance could have been copied, as it apparently was at the Koimesis of Nicaea and at Çanlı Kilise, but without the structural advantage of the recessed courses. Thus, at least in the Middle Byzantine period, the use of recessed brick can be associated with one or more Constantinopolitan workshops. Combined with other technical details, the presence of recessed brick has helped to identify masons from Constantinople at work in Kiev, Chernigov, Jerusalem, and elsewhere.[61] The technique stands as a useful indicator of the movements of Constantinopolitan workshops—at least until the twelfth century, by which time the technique had become widely disseminated.

In numerous examples where the construction technique was not very fine, the exterior of the church would have been plastered and perhaps painted on the exterior. The exterior of the south church of the Pantokrator was covered with plaster, which was at least in part painted. On the south facade of the exonarthex, a frescoed rinceau survives around a blocked window (see fig. 139). The regular nicking of the mortar beds on other facades was meant for the adherence of a plastered surface, which is partially preserved below the Ottoman roof.[62] At Veljusa, the entire church was plastered and painted to resemble brick and stone construction, repeating in a more regular way the details of the actual construction (fig. 142).[63] A similar example was excavated at Abdera-Polystelon, where a rubble surface was plastered and painted in patterns that suggest masonry.[64] Fictive masonry became much more common in the later centuries when good building materials were in short supply. By the second half of the fourteenth century, it had become a standard procedure in Serbia.[65]

Exterior plastering could have been used on buildings of careful construction as well. At the Pantepoptes, for example, the exterior surfaces may have also been plastered and painted. Van Millingen suggested that the exterior was revetted with marble; he could find no other explanation for the projection of the cornices.[66] With the recent removal of the early Ottoman minaret, however, significant portions of a Middle Byzantine exonarthex were uncovered, on which some of the Byzantine plastering remains (fig. 143).[67] A recently uncovered foundation wall in the Unkapanı district of Istanbul was constructed in the recessed-brick technique, and part of its wall surface was decorated with an elaborate meander pattern in brick. This was covered with a thin layer of white plaster, and the brick courses were regularized by etching along the edges and highlighted with red paint. In the final analysis, exterior plastering may have been simply a matter of aesthetic choice.

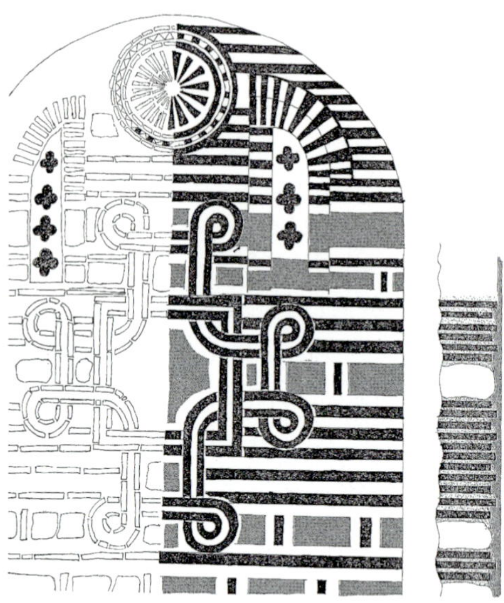

FIG. 142. Drawing of a facade detail from the church of the Virgin Eleousa, Veljusa

FIG. 143. Detail of the south facade of the exonarthex of Christ Pantepoptes, Istanbul

FIG. 144. Detail of the masonry on the west facade of the church at Seben-Çeltikdere

Treatment of Mortar Beds

Because of the irregularities in the brick and stone of Byzantine construction, the application of mortar became an important consideration in the outward appearance of a building. In standard construction, mortar beds were either finished flush with the surface or beveled downwards. Sometimes an outer layer of finer mortar would be applied as a finish material. This has been observed in the churches at Nerezi and at Chortiates, near Thessaloniki, from the twelfth century, as well as at the eleventh-century Pantepoptes in Constantinople and the church near Çeltikdere (figs. 143–44).[68]

The edges of the mortar beds were often scored using a sharp instrument, sometimes employing a straightedge as well. In numerous examples a cord was stretched along the edges and impressed into the mortar, leaving a ropelike pattern. The latter detail may derive from the masons' practice of stretching a cord to denote the horizontal line along which the course of bricks was to be laid. Marking the mortar bed with both methods was common in Constantinople and areas under its influence.[69] In both variations—incised or marked with a cord—the builders seem to have wanted to give a clean impression to the construction, particularly when the materials were irregular. These details appear even when the wall was intended to be covered with plaster, as well as on surfaces that were not meant to be seen. Unfortunately, these technical details were lost in many buildings when the masonry was repointed.

FIG. 145. Detail of the masonry on the south naos wall of the Fatih Camii, Enez

Some details are a bit whimsical and have no logical explanation. At the Fatih Camii of Enez, cords were impressed into the mortar beds, including occasionally the loops at the ends of the cords (fig. 145).[70] Similar cord impressions appear in the mortar beds of the early Kievan churches as well and should be associated with the presence of Byzantine masons.[71] Incised mortar beds appear over a very broad area, however, and are not specifically limited to Constantinople, or to Byzantine architecture for that matter. One finds incisions and cord impressions in Hellenistic and Roman architecture.[72] Incisions and cord impressions are also found in plaster imitation marble interiors.[73] Ötüken has noted numerous Early Christian examples of the practice, and Schäfer has observed cord impressions in the mortar finish of Islamic buildings as well, as at the Ribat at Monastir in Tunisia.[74]

Combined with other technical details, incised mortar beds help to identify workshops of masons, as is suggested for the early Kievan monuments. In the eleventh-century substructures of Saint George of Mangana, the construction is in the recessed-brick technique, and the mortar beds are etched along the brick courses (see fig. 181). However, at intervals, coupled vertical incisions appear. Sometimes these incisions correspond to the divisions between the bricks, but not always. There may be a good technical explanation for them, but, then again, they may reflect nothing more than the whim of the mason. Combined with other technical details, distinctive etchings may help to identify a workshop. For example, the foundations that are normally ascribed to the nearby Philanthropos monastery (see fig. 129), and for which a Palaiologan dating is sometimes suggested, look suspiciously like those of the Mangana. Both are built in the recessed-brick technique; both had clusters of semicircular and triangular responds and extravagantly decorated surfaces (see fig. 157). These similarities can be augmented by

FIG. 146. Detail of the eleventh-century masonry at the Holy Sepulcher, Jerusalem

similar etchings in the mortar beds, with parallel vertical incisions. It is possible that either what is called the Philanthropos was actually part of the Mangana complex, or the dating of the Philanthropos is incorrect, or else there was a very strong continuity in the workshop tradition of the Mangana region. On the other hand, similar coupled vertical incisions appear in the prothesis of the Fatih Camii at Enez, which may be securely dated to the second half of the twelfth century. Consequently, this detail may be more common, and thus less indicative of a specific workshop, than it might first appear.

An additional example of etched mortar beds is instructive. The eleventh-century portions of the Holy Sepulcher in Jerusalem were built in the recessed-brick technique, and the broad mortar beds were both scored along the edges and marked with sets of parallel vertical incisions, comparable to those at the Mangana (fig. 146).[75] Rebuilt by Constantine Monomachos, the same patron as the Mangana, the eleventh-century Holy Sepulcher shares many technical similarities in its brick construction, including decorative patterns and triangular and semicircular responds. I suggested several years ago that masons from Constantinople worked at the Holy Sepulcher.[76] They may have, in fact, been part of or closely related to the Mangana workshop.

At the Pantokrator, similar incisions appear in the mortar beds on the apse of the south church, in spite of the fact that its exterior was plastered upon completion. The incisions are a bit sloppy, and the horizontal lines are often at a slight angle and are set up to 1.5 centimeters from the brick (fig. 147). These are combined with coupled vertical incisions that extend between the horizontals; in the upper part of the apse, these include inscribed X's. As at the Mangana, there is no good technical explanation for the incised patterning, which would have been covered almost immediately when the facade was plastered. The exterior surfaces of the other two churches at the Pantokrator are not as

FIG. 147. Detail of the masonry on the apse of the south church of the Pantokrator, Istanbul

well preserved, but there is evidence of the same pattern of incisions, including the inscribed X's, on the apse of the middle church. Constructed in the third and final building phase, the middle church was begun perhaps a decade after the south church was completed. Thus, its masons could not have copied the technical details from the adjacent building. The similarities must indicate that the same workshop was responsible for both churches—and probably for the north church as well.

Scaffolding and Putlog Holes

To construct high walls and vaults, it was necessary to provide platforms for the workers at different levels. In Byzantine construction, scaffolding was often built into the walls of a building or anchored to it. It is still possible to detect vestiges of the beams' attachment to the wall in the surviving pattern of putlog holes. A system of protruding beams was built into the courses of masonry as the building rose. Beams could have extended through the wall, projecting out of both facades (fig. 148).[77] Two or more beams at the same height supported the platform on which the masons worked. As the wall rose, additional putlogs were required for platforms at higher levels. When the building was completed, workmen removed the scaffolding and filled the putlog holes. The scaffolding could be used again by the plasterers and painters who could work from the top of the building downward, removing the putlogs as they went. The positioning and filling of putlog holes were tied to localized building practices, and Giorgos Velenis has demonstrated that they may be used as evidence for the identification of workshops.[78]

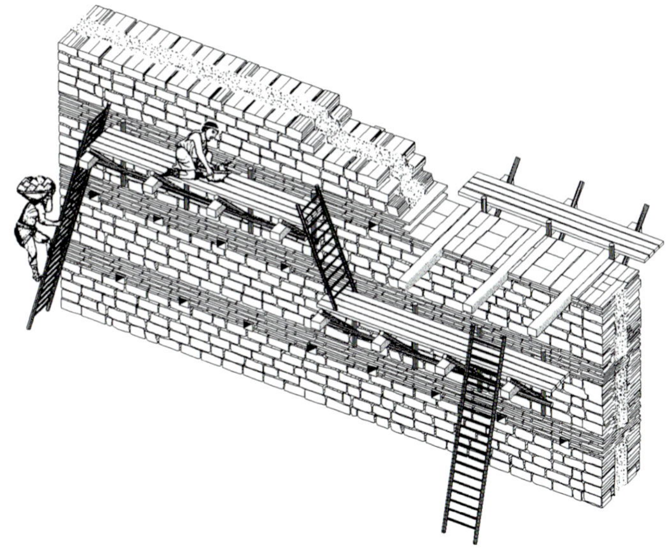

FIG. 148. Drawing showing scaffolding system with putlogs

Scaffoldings are frequently mentioned in Byzantine literature. Construction accidents are a commonplace in hagiographical literature, with the saint often intervening to save or resuscitate a victim after a fall or after the collapse of the scaffolding. Some accidents are blamed on demons: the *vita* of the ninth-century saint Euthemios the Younger relates that during the construction of the church at Peristerai (near Thessaloniki), demons twisted the timbers at the top of the building—apparently the scaffolding—causing a workman to fall, although he was not injured.[79]

Varied types of scaffolding supported the builders on high. This work was particularly dangerous, and a number of accidents are recorded as resulting from the collapse of scaffolding. But from the texts it is often difficult to determine exactly what has collapsed. The *vita* of Euthemios refers simply to *ta xyla* (the wood). The word most frequently used is *klimax*, which normally means a ladder. There is often little difference between a ladder and a scaffold. The same is apparent in medieval illustrations, as in a mosaic from San Marco in Venice showing the construction of the Tower of Babel (see fig. 29), or in the illustrations to Psalm 95 in the marginal psalters (see fig. 28). Based on the texts, it is possible to identify three different types of scaffoldings: hung, freestanding, and built-in.

At the church of Saint Photeine in Constantinople, for example, the painters "were embellishing the ceiling with their art when the plank of wood on which the weight of the entire ladder (*klimax*) was supported broke—and this ladder was skillfully made of many pieces of wood; it suddenly collapsed, bringing the artisans down with it. And surely they would have been stabbed by these [pieces of wood] and crushed to death, had

FIG. 152. View of the Bogdan Saray from the northwest, ca. 1910

FIG. 153. North facade of the Tekfur Saray, Istanbul

FIG. 154. Interior view of the substructures of the Gül Camii, Istanbul

33). The similarity of the construction techniques in these two buildings, separated by almost a century as well as by the Latin Occupation, may indicate the continuity in the workshop practices of the Byzantine capital.

Some variations occur in buildings constructed in the recessed-brick technique. At the Pantokrator and in the substructures of the Gül Camii, many putlog holes are aligned with the exposed brick course, set between two recessed courses (fig. 154). The same may have occurred in the superstructure of the Gül Camii, although the recent, heavy-handed application of mortar has destroyed the evidence.[89]

In some buildings that are related to Constantinople, such as the tenth- or eleventh-century Karagedik Kilise in the Ihlara Valley, the putlog holes are useful indicators of distinctions in workshops. At the Karagedik Kilise, some of the putlog holes appear in the stone courses with a notch cut into the stone, a detail that is not found in Constantinopolitan construction (fig. 155).[90] Similar putlog holes appear in a single course on the south facade of Çanlı Kilise (see fig. 17).[91]

Wooden Reinforcement

As masons constructed walls, they built tie beams into the thickness of walls and nailed or toggled them together at the corners to aid in stabilizing the construction until the mortar could set to its ultimate hardness (fig. 156). This practice has already been noted

FIG. 155. North facade of the Karagedik Kilise in the Ihlara Valley

in relationship to the foundations of buildings. Wood was also used as tie beams in arches, vaults, and domes for the same reason, as will be discussed in the next chapter. In recent times, surviving elements of wood have been studied by dendrochronologists, and they have provided some assistance in dating the monuments.[92] However, within the majority of examples, particularly in damp climates like that of Constantinople, the wood has deteriorated, leaving only a system of cavities and holes as evidence of its role in construction. Nevertheless, the positioning of wooden beams within the walls is another factor that may be tied to workshop practices, as Velenis has discussed.[93]

In Constantinople, wooden beams commonly appear within the stone courses, but they are virtually impossible to detect from the exterior unless the building has fallen into ruins. In other areas, the position of beams may be indicated by changes in materials on the facades.[94] In the fourteenth-century additions to the Chora and the Pammakaristos, wooden beams were positioned at the level of the cornices, which were in turn connected to the exposed tie beams spanning the arches, as was probably common practice (see fig. 83). In the late thirteenth-century additions to the Theotokos of Lips, wooden beams were built into the stone courses at various levels, and these beams can be observed through breaks in the inner wall of the south ambulatory.[95] At the İsa Kapı Mescidi, now in ruins, tie beams are apparent in both the brick and stone courses.[96] At the ruined Sinan Paşa Mescidi, a tie beam appears just below the meander course, faced with brick on the facade.[97]

FIG. 163. West facade of Hagia Theodora, Arta

The way in which decorative patterns are integrated into the architectural framework differs from region to region. In many areas of Greece and Macedonia, broad bands of decoration extend over large wall surfaces, as may be seen on the east facade of the Holy Apostles in Thessaloniki (fig. 88) or on the west facade of Hagia Theodora in Arta (fig. 163), to note two extreme examples.[120] Such carpet-like patterning is not to be found in Constantinople, where even the most lavish decoration is subordinated to the architectural framework. Even when confined to a niche, the brick decorations of Constantinople are relatively restrained. Only the niche head is patterned, while the remainder of the niche follows the standard system of wall construction. In Epiros and Macedonia, on the other hand, decorative patterns fill the niches, as for example at the Paregoretissa at Arta (fig. 74) or the Holy Apostles in Thessaloniki (fig. 88).[121]

Architectural historians are fascinated by ruins, in part because many details can only be properly observed in ruined buildings. If a building is complete, many technical details are invisible; only when the wall is broken is its section revealed. The fact that many technical details were only visible while the building was under construction emphasizes the importance of the workshop for the transmission of architectural knowledge. Scholars today often confuse architectural style and workshop practices.[122] When analyzing the details of Byzantine architecture, it is useful to remember that style is something that could be learned through observation: the outward appearance of a building could be imitated years after it was completed. On the other hand, workshop practices could only have been learned through direct participation in the construction process. These technical details represent the signature of the workshop.

CHAPTER SEVEN

Structural Design, Structural Expression, and the Construction of Arches and Vaults

Because of its small scale, Byzantine architecture of the Middle and Late periods has not elicited a great deal of interest in terms of structural systems or vault construction. The only book on the subject—that of Auguste Choisy—is now more than a century old.[1] Byzantine structural systems lack the bravura of scale and technical mastery that is associated with contemporaneous Romanesque and Gothic developments or with the earlier monuments from the period of Justinian. Much attention has been given recently to the statics of large-scale vaults—specifically that of Hagia Sophia.[2] Certainly the scale of Hagia Sophia demanded that structural concerns were of the first priority, but structure in later Byzantine architecture has not been considered. After the Transitional period, the scale of buildings was dramatically reduced. A typical dome of the period of the tenth to the fourteenth centuries measured less than 6 meters in diameter, compared to the 31.2 meter span of Hagia Sophia's dome. Thus, structural concerns no longer demanded preference in architectural design.[3]

It may actually be more appropriate to talk about Byzantine vaulting in terms of *construction* rather than in terms of structure. Byzantine masons would have been more concerned with the process of vault construction than with principles of statics. Consequently, the masons created a variety of structural systems that were appropriate for the scale of their buildings and that could be built quickly and simply—methods that were efficient, expeditious, and ideally suited to the small scale of the monuments. In addition, construction practices after the Transitional period may have had a direct effect on architectural design, with the development of new solutions that were functional and aesthetically pleasing on the one hand, but that responded to the available building technology on the other.

In addition to a concern for the pragmatics of vault construction, Byzantine masons also considered the integration of the vaulting into the overall design of the building. Although small, the vaults of a Byzantine church were nevertheless heavy enough to re-

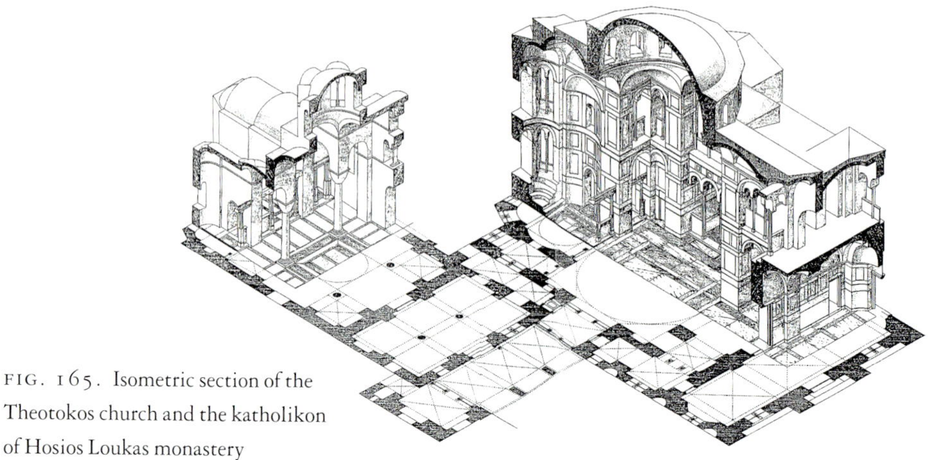

FIG. 165. Isometric section of the Theotokos church and the katholikon of Hosios Loukas monastery

rests above eight piers (see figs. 14, 165–66).[10] The masons here chose to employ squinches, or corbeled arches, rather than pendentives, to make the transition from the rising walls to the dome. This allowed the weight of the dome to be more evenly distributed over eight points of support rather than four. Instead of concentrating the loading at the corners, as a pendentive would, the corbeled arch of a squinch adjusts the weight to the sides.[11] At the same time, the tall naos is enveloped by subsidiary spaces on two levels, which help to brace against the outward thrust of the hemispherical dome. Although the development of the dome on squinches before the time of Hosios Loukas is unclear, the design of the katholikon is remarkably sophisticated, and its origin remains one of the great mysteries of Byzantine architecture. An exotic Eastern origin—Arab, Sasanian, or Caucasian—is frequently suggested. In any case, the design has been reinterpreted and constructed in a Byzantine manner.[12]

Whatever his ultimate inspiration, the builder who designed the katholikon of Hosios Loukas clearly understood structure. He created a remarkably open design.[13] Throughout the building, the bearing wall is virtually eliminated in favor of a system of point support. Groin vaults appear consistently in the secondary spaces, and these adjusted the weight to key points of support rather than relying on wall support. The main facades of the building are composed of arches in series that express the structural system, but within the arches, the wall is merely a curtain wall primarily composed of non-structural windows and closure slabs (fig. 167). The katholikon of Hosios Loukas is arguably the most sophisticated achievement in structural design since Hagia Sophia.

The precedents for the sophisticated understanding of structure evident at Hosios Loukas are Byzantine. A similar structural clarity and openness are evident in several

FIG. 166. Interior view of the Hosios Loukas katholikon looking east

have required any special carving, and it was light enough to be easily raised to its ultimate destination without special equipment. Although illustrations often show hoisting mechanisms for the erection of columns, bricks and mortar are normally carried in hods by workers (see figs. 28–29, 99). All told, a Byzantine vault was far simpler to construct than a Roman, Romanesque, or Gothic vault.

There is a great variety in the choice of vaulting forms in Byzantine architecture. Barrel vaults, groin vaults, and domical vaults were used individually or in series. Moreover, they could be used interchangeably. In a cross-in-square church, for example, the corner compartments could be covered by any of the three types of vault, and the crossarms could be covered by either barrel vaults or groin vaults—any number of variations exist. The Myrelaion has groin vaults in both locations (see figs. 1–4). The Pantepoptes has groin vaults in the corner compartments and barrel vaults in the crossarms (see fig. 18). The south church at the Pantokrator has domical vaults in the corners and barrel vaults in the crossarms (see fig. 78). The parekklesion in the Pammakaristos has domical vaults in the corners and groin vaults in the crossarms (see fig. 193). In other respects, the plans of the buildings are similar, and on a small scale, the selection of vaulting type may have resulted primarily from aesthetic choice rather than from structural considerations.

A similar variety is found in domes, which were normally hemispherical and raised on windowed drums. The interior of a dome could be left as an unarticulated surface, but more commonly it was divided into segments corresponding to the number of windows in the drum. In Constantinople, all surviving Byzantine domes have articulated surfaces. Divisions into eight, twelve, and sixteen were common. Other divisions were rare, as for example at the Nea Moni on Chios, which originally had a unique, nine-sided dome.[19] The interior surface of a dome could be divided by ribs, which extended into the drum between the windows (fig. 169), or treated as a so-called "pumpkin dome" with fluted segments that billow outward (fig. 170). No single type would have had a structural advantage, and they appear interchangeably. For example, the south church at the Pantokrator had both a ribbed dome above the naos and a pumpkin dome above the narthex gallery; in the middle church at the Pantokrator, the two types appear side by side. Both unarticulated domes and pumpkin domes appear in the Holy Apostles in Thessaloniki. At the church known as the Vefa Kilise Camii in Istanbul, ribbed and pumpkin domes appear side by side in the exonarthex. Occasionally, hemispherical domes were constructed without drums, as in the domed octagon churches at Daphni and at Hosios Loukas (see figs. 5, 166). Both have unarticulated inner surfaces.

Arches were normally semicircular. Ogival arches appear rarely in Late Byzantine architecture and only in a decorative capacity, as at the Chora and Pammakaristos (see figs. 131, 151).[20] And although slightly pointed arches had appeared already in the sixth century, at Qasr Ibn Wardan in Syria and in the eighth-century reconstruction of Hagia

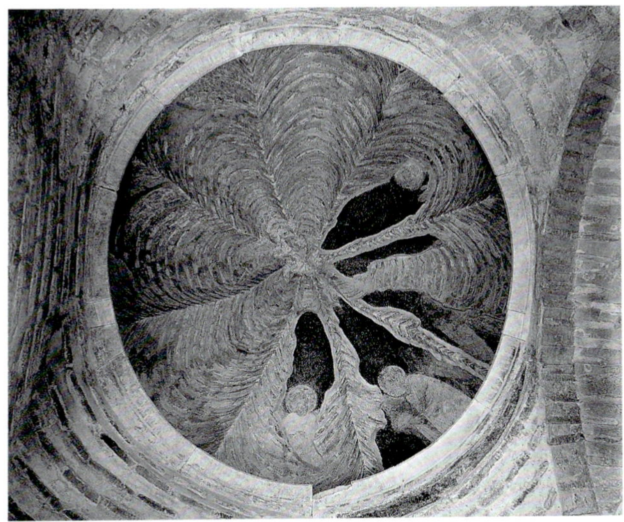

FIG. 169. View into the dome above the north aisle of the Pammakaristos, Istanbul

FIG. 170. View into the dome of the prothesis of the Chora, Istanbul

FIG. 171. Detail of an arch in the naos of Ayasofya Camii, Vize

Eirene in Constantinople, they were not used in the later periods.[21] Horseshoe-shaped arches were common in central Anatolia but not in Constantinople.[22] Flattened or segmental arches sometimes appear, as in the naos of Nea Moni on Chios (fig. 67), but in general the masons of Constantinople were conservative in their use of the arch.

Sometimes steps were taken to simplify the construction by reducing the span of the arch. In the ninth-century church at Vize, for example, the arches of the naos are not entirely voussoir arches. They are built in horizontal courses at the imposts, and the proper voussoir construction only begins high on the haunches (fig. 171). Oddly, almost the opposite occurs in some arches of the eleventh and possibly twelfth centuries. At the Mangana, for example, the angle of the brick voussoirs rises dramatically through the haunches, so that the radiating lines of the voussoirs do not converge on a single center point (see figs. 137, 162B).[23] At the same time, the shape of the arches tends slightly toward a catenary curve. The motivation for this form is not clear, nor is its construction logical. It may have simply resulted from rapid but careless construction.

Wooden Reinforcement of Arches and Vaults

Copious quantities of mortar were used to expedite wall construction, with the mortar joints sometimes as thick as the bricks. The same practice extended into the vaulting. This had both advantages and disadvantages. Although it eliminated the necessity of

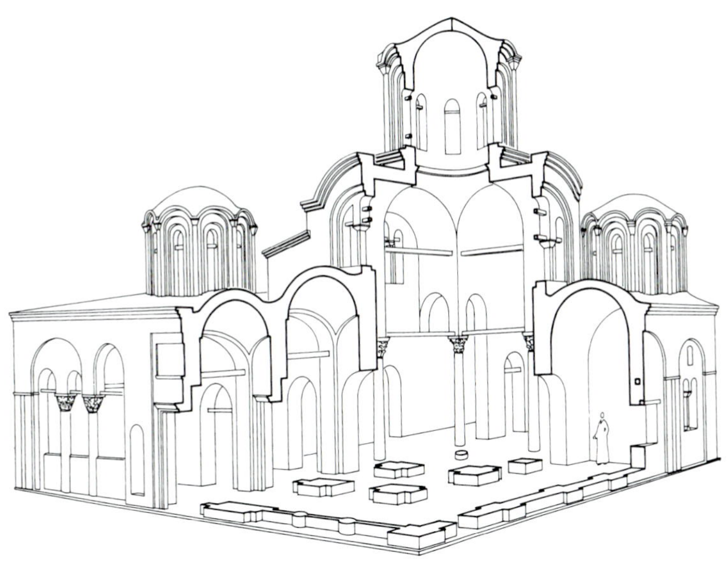

FIG. 172. Perspective section of the church of the Holy Apostles, Thessaloniki

specially cut voussoirs, lime mortar was subject to plastic flow. The wall was often reinforced at critical points with pilasters that articulated the structural system. More importantly, as the wall rose, wooden beams were inserted at various levels to stabilize the construction until the mortar set to its ultimate hardness. Nailed or toggled to one another, the wooden beams created a series of tension rings that secured the building against deformation, thus allowing construction to proceed at a rapid rate.

The system of wooden ties, begun in the walls, continued into the level of the vaulting, where it became visible in the form of tie beams that extend across the springings of arches and barrel vaults.[24] Although the tie beams no longer played a significant structural role after the mortar hardened, they were commonly left in place and decorated. In the fourteenth-century church of the Holy Apostles at Thessaloniki (fig. 172), for example, the attenuated naos required two sets of tie beams at different levels. One set appeared just above the columns, at the springing of the lower vaults, with a second set at the springing of the barrel vaults of the crossarms.[25] A similar system survives in the katholikon of Chilandar monastery on Mount Athos, dated 1303, with beams at two levels. In the early churches of Kievan Rus', the emphasis on attenuated forms sometimes required as many as five tiers of tie beams, as at the twelfth-century Cathedral of the Archangel Michael at Smolensk (fig. 173).[26] Clearly, the system of wooden reinforcement was inherited from Byzantine architecture.

Although most of the beams deteriorated, at the Chora in Constantinople the cavities

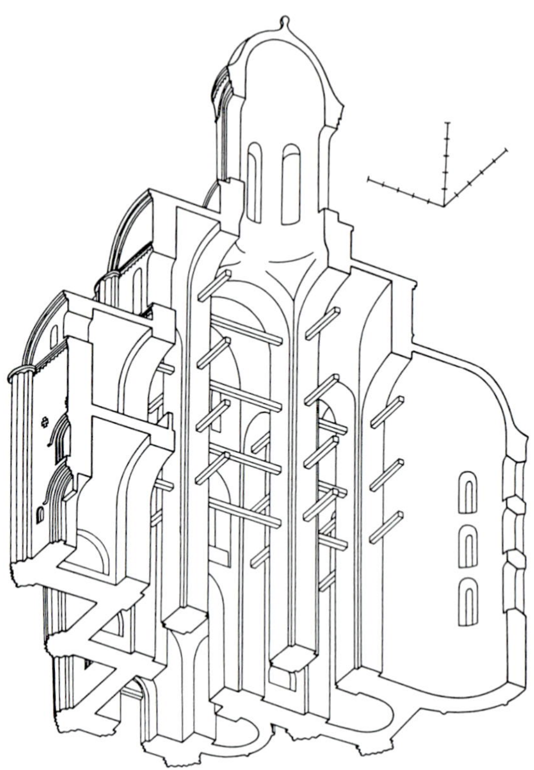

FIG. 173. Axonometric section of the Cathedral of the Archangel Michael, Smolensk

and beam holes for the original twelfth- and fourteenth-century systems of tie beams and wall beams were preserved (see figs. 63, 83). These provided twentieth-century archaeologists with the guidelines for the structural reinforcement of the building, which was necessary as a part of the restoration carried out in the 1950s. A series of cavities measuring approximately fifteen by fifteen centimeters was found in the thickness of the walls, positioned directly behind and slightly higher than the marble cornices. Square openings in the wall surface at the same height—that is, at the springings of the arches and vaults—connected directly to the beam cavities and extended slightly beyond, into the thickness of the wall. Set at the same level, the tie beams must have been anchored by toggles to the wall beams. Metal rods were introduced in the 1950s, duplicating the original wooden system.[27]

The blocks forming the marble cornices at the springings of the vaults were either fastened together by metal pins or secured by a system of wooden beams immediately behind them. The structural significance of the cornices of Hagia Sophia in Constantinople has been emphasized by L. Butler, who suggests that they be understood as a combination of tension chains—pinned together, they would help to contain the outward thrust

FIG. 174. View into the naos dome of the Chora, Istanbul, showing the stubs of tie beams in the windows and iron cramps in the cornice

of the vaulting at the critical points—and leveling courses, forming a base for the springing of the vault.[28] Butler has also observed a similar structural role for the cornices of other vaulted sixth-century churches, such as Basilica B in Philippi and Saint John in Ephesus.[29] These contained the outward thrust of the vaulting at the most critical points in the buildings. Scholars sometimes assume that cornices were pinned together, but the evidence is limited.[30] In a standing building, these details may be covered by the masonry of the vault above the cornice, and in a damaged building, the level of the cornices may be inaccessible. Moreover, too often when architectural sculpture is published, only the decorated surface is illustrated. Still, there is some evidence to suggest that marble cornice blocks were cramped together in later Byzantine churches. Some iron cramps appear in the cornice of the naos dome of the Chora (fig. 174).[31] Cramps were also used in the dome cornice of the Fatih Camii at Enez, where the individual blocks are *spolia*, with some still preserving ancient inscriptions (fig. 175). The dome cornice blocks at the Kalenderhane were also joined by cramps.[32] The cornices were thus not simply decorative features but may best be understood as visual expressions of the structural system.

Whether or not metal connectors were employed, a chain of wooden beams was usually positioned within the thickness of the wall immediately behind the cornice. At the Chora, the system described above extended throughout the building and was connected to the system of tie beams (see fig. 83). Cavities appear in the same position at the thirteenth-century church of Saint John of Lips. Megaw made similar observations in the tenth-century Theotokos church, noting that the wooden reinforcement ringed the entire building and was visible at the same levels in the window openings.[33] The beam cavities varied in size, with a maximum thickness of twenty-two centimeters for the wooden beams. These beams formed a tension ring, but they also served as anchors for the tie beams that extended across the vaults. Moreover, they helped to stabilize the columns and internal supports in a cross-in-square church by connecting them with the outer walls. Where a tie beam extended across an arch or a vault, it intersected another beam set within the thickness of the wall. Such an integrated system of wooden reinforcement was also studied in areas of Hagia Eirene and must have existed in almost all Byzantine churches (fig. 176).[34] Similar systems of wooden reinforcement were common in early churches in Kievan Rus' as well.[35]

Byzantine domes were normally raised on windowed drums in which wooden reinforcement was employed. In addition to tie beams at the springing points, wooden chains that formed tension rings were built into virtually every Byzantine dome at several levels. These may be seen in the windows of the drums of most surviving domes. Stubs of the beams appear in the windows of the Chora (see fig. 174), and two rows of beams are visible in the windows of the attenuated naos dome at the katholikon of Chilandar monastery. A standard element in Byzantine construction practices, the wooden tension ring was not simply the Renaissance invention of Filippo Brunelleschi for the dome of Florence Cathedral, as it is often said to be.[36]

In addition to metal cramps joining cornice blocks, there are a few examples of Byzantine buildings in which metal was employed in a structural capacity. At the tenth-century Theotokos of Lips, for example, a wrought iron collar was set into the masonry of the apse, just below the exterior cornice (fig. 177).[37] This height corresponds with the upper interior cornice as well as with the floor level of the flanking roof chapels. The collar was formed by lengths of rod 2.5 centimeters in diameter joined to form a chain. Another section of chain was discovered at the same height in the north facade, just below the sill of the lunette window.[38] This suggests that the chain was continuous, extending around the entire naos.

At the twelfth-century Theotokos Kosmosoteira at Pherrai, the unusual design called for innovative structural measures. The church has two domed corner compartments flanking the western entrance. The reused columns here were doubled, no doubt because of their thinness (see figs. 92–94). But the stability of the corners was still questionable, and thus the master mason included metal tie rods, rather than wooden tie beams, to

FIG. 175. Detail of the dome cornice of the Fatih Camii, Enez, showing iron cramps

FIG. 176. Diagram showing the system of wooden reinforcement in Hagia Eirene, Istanbul

FIG. 177. Detail of the east facade of the Theotokos of Lips, Istanbul, showing the iron collar in the apse

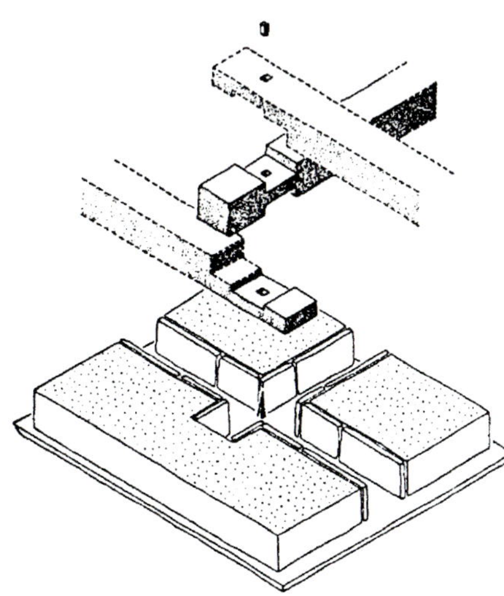

secure the supports to the outer walls of the building (see fig. 94). The rods are set at a slight angle, apparently to connect them from the upper surface of the marble capital—that is, between the capital and the impost, rather than above the impost—to a stabilizing course within the wall.[39] The antiquity of the tie rods is confirmed by the southwest capitals, which were reworked and enlarged with sculpted plaster that envelops the tie rods as they join the capitals.[40] The rods meet the outer wall at a height that corresponds with the springing of the lower vaults and the sills of the lower range of windows. Although there is no cornice at this level, it is a logical point to have set a stabilizing beam within the wall.

Flying Buttresses

One structural curiosity of Late Byzantine architecture is the flying buttress. Flying buttresses make occasional appearances in the Late Byzantine architecture of Istanbul, apparently under the influence of Gothic forms, following the Latin Occupation in the thirteenth century. However, they were never fully understood, and they were never utilized as integrated parts of a structural system, as they had been in Western Europe. Flying buttresses were added to the western gallery of Hagia Sophia either during the Latin Occupation of the thirteenth century or possibly in a restoration of 1317. Of uneven construction, they may have been part of the same project that added a belfry to the west facade (fig. 178). The masonry in the large north and south buttresses is similar, and these may have originally been flying buttresses that were later blocked. Part of the process of shoring up the Great Church over time, the western buttresses are positioned at points where they are practically useless, without a proper relationship to the structural system of the building.[41]

A single flying buttress was added to the apse of the Chora as a part of a major reconstruction in the early fourteenth century, designed to brace the twelfth-century apse on unstable terrain (see fig. 131). Like the buttresses at Hagia Sophia, this offered no more than the appearance of security; over the centuries it shifted away from the building, and the lower flyer collapsed. Before the restoration of the 1950s, a scaffolding was necessary to support the remainder of the buttress.[42]

Vault Construction with and without Centering

The use of centering—and the lack of its use—is an important but overlooked consideration in Byzantine construction. Byzantine vaults were constructed with or without centering, depending on their scale.[43] A large barrel vault, for example, would have re-

FIG. 178. View of the flying buttresses on the west facade of Hagia Sophia, Istanbul, looking north

quired substantial wooden formwork in order to maintain a regular curvature (fig. 179). The complexities of construction with centering are frequently discussed in handbooks on Roman architecture.[44] Sometimes the impression of the formwork was left in the damp plaster, and this can help to reconstruct its form. This is common in Roman architecture, as in the substructures of the Domus Aurea, but similar evidence is only occasionally found in Byzantine architecture. In the substructures of the Myrelaion, for example, the barrel vaults were constructed above semicylindrical wooden centering onto which a layer of mortar was laid before the bricks were put into place (fig. 180).[45] In a fourteenth-century funeral crypt at Didymoteicho, the haunches of the barrel vault were constructed without additional support, but wooden centering was used for the crown of the vault, which was formed above a layer of mortar that preserves the pattern of the planking.[46] Similar impressions are found in the barrel vaults of the Gül Camii substructures (see fig. 154). In these examples, however, the pattern of the formwork was left because none of the spaces was ever decorated or meant to be seen.

In the substructures of Saint George of Mangana, the broad arches were constructed over rough centering, beginning just above the springing point, where beam holes appear, and the centering was probably supported on the tiebeams (fig. 181). The arches were then neatly built in the recessed-brick technique. But the bricks were probably hurriedly dropped into position, and, as elsewhere in the Mangana, the voussoirs are not concentric (see fig. 137). Although the edges of the soffits are finished, the central surface was left rough, leaving a thick covering of rough mortar that bears the impressions of the wooden centering.

A centering constructed of wood, even for a simple arch, was by necessity a complicated work of carpentry. It had to form the shape of the vault and hold the form under varying loads; the larger and heavier the vault, the more complex the formwork required. Wood can support great loads for short durations, but it will deflect over time. The centering would also have to be removed without damaging the building or causing sudden cracking of the vault.[47] In addition, the centering required support from below, either on scaffolding that extended to floor level or, like the workers' scaffolding, was hung on cornices, corbels, or ledges within the building. The centering could also have been anchored into the masonry by putlogs or simply connected to the tie beams, as apparently occurred at the Mangana.

In surviving exposed vaulting, there may be nothing to indicate the use of centering. Often we simply assume that centering was employed, but in an important, broadly based study, Sanpaolesi suggests that a remarkable number of large Ancient, Early Christian, and Islamic domes may have been self-supported—that is, constructed without centering—and he notes various methods of laying interlocking webs of masonry.[48] This possibility should also be considered for much of Byzantine architecture. Byzantine masons often preferred smaller vaults that could be constructed of pitched and corbeled bricks without formwork. Numerous small, unsupported vaults required less skilled labor and possibly less construction time than a single large supported vault covering the same area.

There were advantages and disadvantages to both systems. A supported vault required the expert skills of a carpenter to prepare the formwork, but the subsequent construction of the vaulting could have progressed rapidly and without the use of skilled laborers because the shape was fixed by the formwork. Perhaps more important, there was no need to wait for the mortar in the lower masonry to harden before completing the vault. This meant that the actual construction could proceed rapidly. If the formwork could be reused for multiple vaults of the same shape and size, this was also an advantage. In sub-

FIG. 179. Hypothetical reconstruction of the wooden formwork necessary for the construction of a large barrel vault

FIG. 180. Interior view of the Myrelaion church substructure, Istanbul, looking north, showing the impression of formwork in the vaults

FIG. 181. Interior view of the Mangana substructure, Istanbul, showing the impression of formwork in the arch

structures like the Myrelaion and Mangana, the formwork may have been left in place to insure the stability of the vaults as the superstructure was built. In the construction of unsupported vaults, it was always necessary to take into consideration the drying time of the mortar, but the skills of the trained carpenter would not have been necessary.[49]

In fact, most vaults in secondary spaces were clearly constructed without centering, and it is easiest to begin with these to understand the methods of vault construction. The masons faced two challenges in uncentered construction. The first was to define the shape of the vault, which could be done either by visual inspection or by using a cord or measuring rod. For example, a fixed length of cord anchored at the centerpoint could be used regularly to check the radius of a curved surface as it was constructed. The second challenge was what is known as "moment"—the tendency of an incomplete arch or vault to fall inward. The masons had to build in such a way that the bricks would stay in place until the mortar hardened. This was accomplished by using a mortar of stiff consistency. If the bricks were scored with finger marks, this also increased the adhesion. In addition, bricks could be laid in horizontal courses, or in pitched courses, or they could be keyed together. All of these methods were used in Byzantine vaults.

A tunnel in the ruined Byzantine monastery on Sivriada (Oxya) shows the simplest form of a pitched brick barrel vault (fig. 182). Instead of voussoir construction, the bricks were set on end and at a slight angle, with each succeeding course leaned against the previous one. Construction thus proceeded from one end of the vault to the other. More complex examples of pitched brick vaults cover two cisterns at the south church of the Pantokrator monastery (fig. 183).[50] Here the courses of brick are set at an angle and leaned against each other. Construction began at opposite ends of each crypt; at the intersection, horizontal courses were laid at either side, and the system continued upward to form awkward barrel vaults. The spaces narrow toward the east and would have necessitated complicated formwork to fit the space. Similarly, in a functionless gallery at the Chora, the space is trapezoidal, and the bricks were pitched from both ends, with an irregular area of fill where they meet.[51] The irregular barrel vaults that cover the cistern below the naos of the Pammakaristos are also of pitched brick, set without formwork (see fig. 127).[52]

Occasionally the masons chose to construct vaults of pitched brick in the major spaces of the building as well. At Saint Panteleimon in Thessaloniki, both the north and south chapels were covered by uncentered barrel vaults (fig. 184). Braced by the wall to the east and a centered arch to the west, the vault of the north chapel was built in successive stages by alternating bands of pitched brick arches from the east and west with vault segments on the north and south flanks. The construction process was similar to that of the Pantokrator substructure.

Groin vaults with a domical profile could also be constructed without centering, as

FIG. 182. View into a tunnel at the monastery on Sivriada (Oxya), showing the barrel vault constructed of pitched brick without formwork

FIG. 183. View of a vault below the bema of the south church of the Pantokrator, Istanbul, showing sectioned construction of pitched brick without formwork

FIG. 184. View of a vault in a lateral chapel at Saint Panteleimon, Thessaloniki, showing sectioned construction of pitched brick without formwork

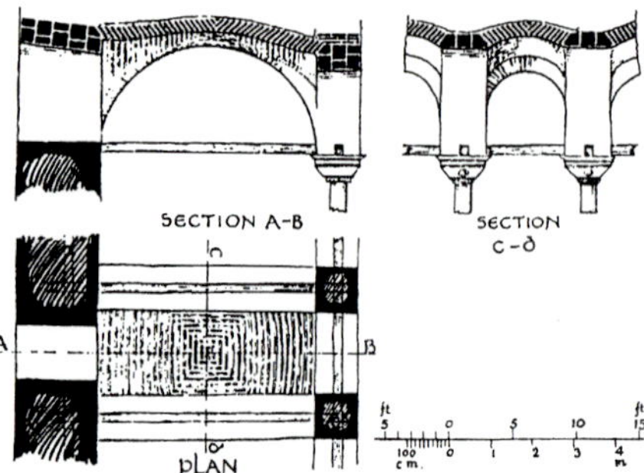

FIG. 185. Diagrams of the side aisle vaulting of Hagia Eirene, Istanbul

was the case in the aisle vaults of Hagia Eirene (fig. 185).[53] Here the bricks were not laid radially—that is, they do not follow the curvature of the vault as it billows upward. Rather, the bricks were leaned against each other in successive courses, built up from four sides. The intersections at the corners helped to stabilize the construction until the mortar set. The substructures of Gül Camii have similar domical groin vaults (see fig. 154). Although in both examples the final form is domical, the vaults were constructed as groin vaults; they were built up in triangular segments above four arches.[54] Groin vaults constructed without centering are also found in some of the back rooms of the Chora.[55] The same may be seen in an odd vault at the Kalenderhane Camii. A long, rectangular bay of the outer narthex is bounded by arches, and the vault was built up from these in wedge-shaped segments, apparently without centering. To either side, however, the courses of brick curve outward, and in its final form the vault seems to be a combination of a groin vault and a domical vault.[56] Similar uncentered, domical groin vaults are still constructed today in Iran.[57]

Half-domes and conches were also built without formwork, as for example, in the apse of the church of Saint Aberkios at Kurşunlu, dated 1162 (fig. 186).[58] The conch was constructed in wedge-shaped sections, beginning with the triangular areas of the flanks; the horizontal rows were then placed across the center, and the process was repeated. A similar system is found in the main apse of the church of Saint John of Troullo in Istanbul, perhaps of the twelfth century (fig. 187). Here the conch is formed by triangular segments of brick courses to either side, laid at an angle, with bricks forming an arch at the center of the vault. Above these defining elements, the remainder of the conch was constructed in a manner that resembles an uncentered groin vault, built up successively from three sides.[59]

Unsupported construction was common in niches and small conches. In the simplest form, as in the chapels of the Theotokos of Lips, a chevron pattern is formed and the conch was built up from the sides (fig. 188).[60] The same is evident in the shallow, lateral

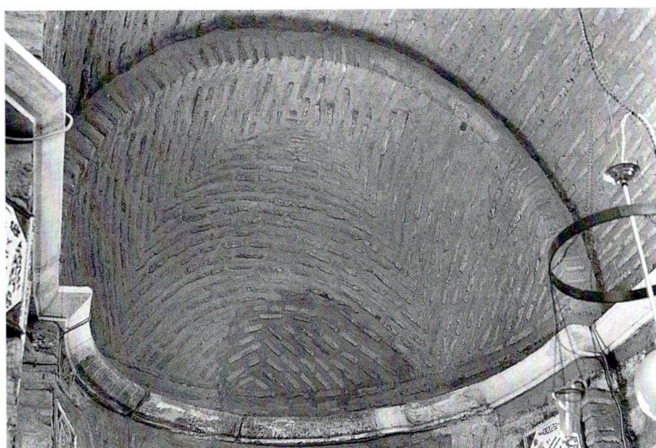

FIG. 186. View into the apse of Saint Aberkios at Kurşunlu

FIG. 187. View into the apse of Saint John of Troullo, Istanbul

FIG. 188. Detail of the vaulting in a gallery chapel at the Theotokos of Lips, Istanbul

FIG. 189. View into the bema of Saint John of Lips, Istanbul, looking southeast

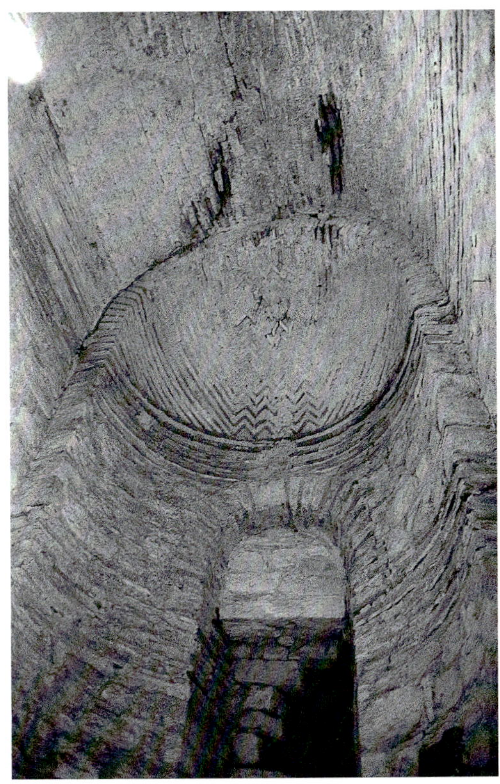

FIG. 190. View into the prothesis apse of the Fatih Camii, Enez

apses in the bema of Saint John of Lips (fig. 189).[61] In a lateral apse of the İsa Kapı Mescidi (fig. 141) and in the niches of the northwest gallery of the Kalenderhane Camii, triangular segments were built up on the sides, with horizontal layers across the center of the conch.[62]

More complex chevron patterns often appear, with the chevrons forming a W at the center. This is a common feature in the niches on apse facades, as at the Pantokrator (see fig. 79) and at Gül Camii. They also appear in interior conch construction, as in the lateral apses of the Fatih Camii at Enez (fig. 190).[63] Similarly, in an eleventh-century Byzantine chapel at the Holy Sepulcher in Jerusalem, both V-chevrons and W-chevrons appear in the squinches.[64] The Enez vault would appear to be a variation of apse construction without formwork, and the interlocking pitched bricks were held together rigidly during construction. A similar zigzag pattern was sometimes used in uncentered medieval Persian vaults, apparently for the same constructional reasons.[65] Although these chevron patterns are attractive and are often discussed as "decorative brickwork," their origins in construction practices, as well as their structural logic, must be emphasized. Clearly, the lateral apses at Enez were originally covered with fresco plaster, so call-

FIG. 193. View into the vaulting of the Pammakaristos parekklesion, Istanbul

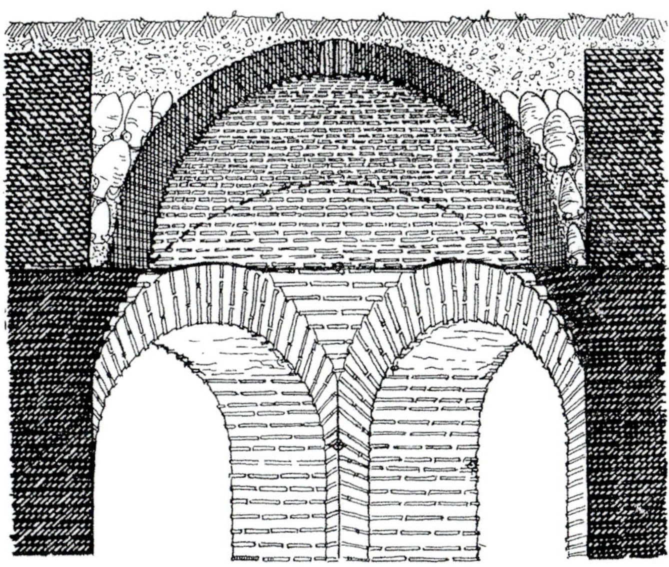

FIG. 194. Section drawing of the Mangana substructures, Istanbul, showing a vault packed with amphorae

Pendentives mark a transition in the elevation of the building, and on the exterior one usually finds corresponding large blocks of masonry, either square or octagonal, immediately below the dome. During construction, these presented problems of excess weight at the upper level of the building. The large masses of masonry required an excessive period of time to dry, and improper drying could lead eventually to structural failure. The problem was frequently met by filling the dead spaces with empty amphorae, as was done at the Lips and Chora monasteries, in the substructures of the Mangana (fig. 194), and elsewhere.[72] However, these amphorae did not have a direct connection to the inner surface of the pendentive. The visible tubes were most likely intended to facilitate drying during the construction process and to prevent a subsequent buildup of moisture in the dead space behind the pendentive. In modern masonry construction, "weep holes" are left periodically in the mortar beds for the same purpose.

Similar features appear in early Russian architecture as well, where they are called *golosniki*, or "resonators."[73] From the eleventh century onward, masons in Kievan Rus' included ceramic pots in the vaulting, following the Byzantine example, but they added pots in wall surfaces as well. At Saint Nicholas of the Dry Spot in Pskov, begun in 1371, for example, the upper walls of the naos are lined with the mouths of imbedded pots. The multiple pots created a hollowness that increased the resonance of the interior. Thus, a single priest chanting the liturgy would sound like a multitude.[74] But nothing like this

FIG. 195. View of the apse of Saint John of Lips, Istanbul, during restoration, showing amphorae packed between the vault and the east facade

is found in the Byzantine buildings, and the resonators must represent development specific to Rus'. It may be that the increased height of the churches of Rus' diminished their acoustical properties, and that resonators were developed in response.

The use of amphorae to lighten Byzantine vaults was not limited to the pendentives. During the repairs to the roof of the south church of Lips, amphorae used to level the roof were found in the spaces between adjoining vaults. Similarly, at both the Lips and the Pantokrator, amphorae were found between the rising wall of the apse and the curvature of the conch (fig. 195). Invariably, the amphorae were packed with their mouths pointed downward, to prevent the buildup of moisture. Pots have also been found in similar positions behind the vaults of the Kalenderhane.[75]

Because the scale of most Byzantine churches was small, most of the vaults required little or no formwork. Often formwork was limited to the arches that divided the space into smaller bays, where bricks were laid in a radiating pattern of voussoirs. In the groin or domical vaults, the courses of brick were laid close to horizontally—in effect, corbeled. The difference is evident in the eleventh-century vaults at the Mangana (see figs. 181, 194), between the radiating voussoir construction of the arches, which was built over centering, and the nearly horizontal courses of the vaults, which were uncentered.[76] The same type of vault construction was observed in the eleventh-century narthex dome of Nea Moni on Chios during the recent repairs to the roof.[77] The domes of Saint Sophia in Kiev, of similar date, were constructed in the same manner.[78] Pasadaios once noted

FIG. 196. View into the diakonikon dome of the Chora, Istanbul

that in a Middle Byzantine cistern in the Beyazid district of Istanbul, the domical vaults must have been laid without support because the courses of brick were nearly horizontal.[79] Although he regarded this as unusual, I believe this must be regarded as standard construction practice.

Many domes could have been constructed without formwork or with minimal formwork. A ribbed dome, as for example at the Pantokrator or at the Pammakaristos (fig. 169), could have been laid with a light formwork only for the ribs. Normally these are precise in their geometry, whereas the webs between them may be less carefully defined. Ribs and webs were bonded, and the ribs thus acted as stiffeners for the web construction. A ribbed dome in the Chora is similar; on the exterior, the nearly horizontal laying of the brick courses was observed during its repair (figs. 196–97).

In contrast, a pumpkin dome—formed by a series of interlocking curved surfaces—could have been built without any centering. Actually, the geometry of a pumpkin dome created a uniquely rigid form, with each segment having an arched shape but positioned horizontally or nearly horizontally (fig. 198). The interlocking of the flat arches concentrated the load at the ridges, but it also prevented them from shifting inward before the mortar set. This added the stability necessary for unsupported construction. Once each course was completed around the circumference, it became self-supporting. The sloppiness evident in a twelfth-century example from Saint Aberkios at Kurşunlu and in a fourteenth-century example from the Chora (fig. 170) is a good indicator of the absence

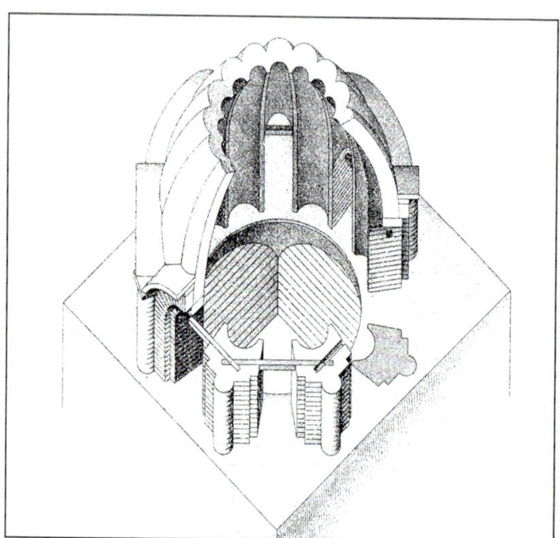

FIG. 197. Exterior view of the diakonikon dome of the Chora during restoration

FIG. 198. Diagram of a pumpkin dome

FIG. 199. Aerial view of the katholikon of Chilandar monastery on Mount Athos

of centering. Such irregularities would have been disguised when covered with mosaic or fresco plaster, however, as is evident in the Chora's narthex domes (see fig. 191).[80] Often the pumpkin form was expressed on the exterior as well; it may still be seen in the unrepaired areas of the minor domes of the Kosmosoteira (see fig. 111) or at the katholikon of Chilandar monastery (fig. 199).[81]

Both ribbed and pumpkin domes—and, indeed, Byzantine vaulting forms in general—may also be discussed in *aesthetic* terms. That is, they are often examined primarily in relationship to the manipulation of space or to the interior program of mosaic or fresco decoration. Clearly, these domes satisfied both the constructional and the decorative concerns of the builder.

With the decrease in building scale from the sixth century onward, there is a parallel shift of emphasis in the practical concerns of building from structure to construction. Byzantine masons created effective and efficient building methods that were best suited for the small buildings that characterize the architecture of the later periods. They were also able to develop integrated systems of reinforcement capable of withstanding tensile forces during the setting process. Finally, the preference for small, subdivided interiors may have developed in part as a response to the practicalities of construction.

CHAPTER EIGHT

Builders and Artists: Creating the Decorated Interior

A Byzantine church was not regarded as complete until its interior surfaces were embellished. Some form of wall covering and a painting program were integral to its final form. A Byzantine patron had several choices when it came to interior decoration; most were directly related to the budget and to the availability of materials. The vaults and upper walls of a church interior could be covered with mosaic or fresco, or with a combination of the two media. The lower walls could be paneled with marble revetments or covered with painted plaster. How was the interior decoration of a building coordinated with its design and construction? It is likely that the masons responsible for the architecture had a good idea of how the interior was to be ornamented and that they planned accordingly. The selection of vaulting forms and the articulation of wall surfaces may have been related to the nature of the decorative program that was to cover them. But there were other, more pragmatic concerns; for example, if the interior surfaces were to be revetted, the cornices would have to project further than they would if the walls were to be frescoed. And from a practical point of view, if the construction and adornment were coordinated, builders and artists could use the same scaffolding. At the same time, the selection of finish materials might affect the building's design, or unusual elements in the decoration might require a special architectural framework.

In some instances, however, it is evident that the builders had only a general sense of the decorative program, or that there was a time lag between the completion of the construction and the initiation of the painting. In Cappadocia, for example, some rock-cut interiors were marked with simple, linear crosses upon the completion of the carving and were only later frescoed. Moreover, some of the rock-cut churches were painted only in part; the apse conch and a few significant icons were completed, but nothing else.[1] Many of the churches may have been painted only gradually over time, and as a result, the coordination of the decorative program and the architectural framework was minimal. One might expect the same limitations in any region where there were not active workshops of both painters and masons—that is, when the building was constructed before the arrival of the painters.

Despite the often impressive qualities of Byzantine architectural design and construction, it was the finish materials and the venerated images that elicited the recorded responses of the Byzantine viewers, and these were critical elements to the appreciation of the final product. Writers lovingly described the marbles and mosaics; these proclaimed the message of the building through the impression of luxury on the one hand and through the iconographic program on the other.

A Byzantine church was more than just an abstract form in brick and stone. Its forms were recognizable and carried a variety of general meanings, such as the economy of salvation and the system of the universe. But the church was also a framework for a complex, multilevel program of figural decoration in mosaic or fresco, through which more specific meanings could be expressed. The selection and placement of images interacted with the services celebrated in the church to emphasize the message of the liturgy and to express the order within the Christian cosmos. It is no coincidence that the standard Middle Byzantine church types were developed simultaneously with a standardized program of interior decoration, and both aspects should be examined together.

Revetments

Following the Roman example, a Byzantine wall was like a sandwich, composed of the wall itself and the finish materials. The brick and stone of the construction may have been visible on the exterior, but they were never left exposed on the interior. Both the interior and exterior facades were covered with plaster or with marble revetments. The west facade of Hagia Sophia preserves some of its external revetments, but other examples are rare. The church of the Virgin of the Pharos, known from the *ekphrasis* discussed in Chapter One, was also revetted on its atrium facade. Cramps for supporting external revetments survive on part of the lateral facades of the Nea Moni on Chios, the Theotokos of Lips, and the Chora in Constantinople, but the interpretation of this evidence is not clear.[2]

In the interior, the most lavish system of wall covering was made with book-matched panels of patterned marbles. Cut from the same block and unfolded across a stretch of wall, the marbles present an impression something like a Rorschach test (see fig. 103). Different colors and types of marbles were used side by side to create field and frame. The rich impression of several different colored and patterned stones side by side may appear garish today, but this was the preferred system in Byzantium. The visual abundance of the interior was heightened with the use of paint and gilding. In effect, any surface that was not in itself decorative was decorated. Capitals, cornices, and tie beams were nor-

FIG. 203. View into the parekklesion of the Chora, Istanbul, looking east

Neredica was constructed and painted in rapid succession in 1198. As a result, its frescoed surfaces are quite irregular. These could have been smoothed over if the masonry had been allowed to settle before the interior was plastered and painted.[31]

Mosaic and fresco were sometimes employed in the same building, with mosaic in the main spaces and fresco in the subsidiary spaces. At the Hosios Loukas katholikon, for example, the naos and narthex are decorated in mosaic, while the subsidiary chapels and the crypt are frescoed.[32] Stylistically, the two are similar, and considering the close technical relationship of the two media, they could have been executed by the same artists. At the Chora, the naos and narthexes have mosaic decoration, but the parekklesion and the minor spaces have frescoes.[33] Distinctive stylistic similarities and even a slight overlap at the juncture of the exonarthex and parekklesion indicate that the same painters worked in both areas.[34]

There are some notable exceptions to the coordinated systems of mosaic and revetments. At the early fourteenth-century Hodegetria church in the Brontocheion monastery at Mistra, the walls were revetted with marbles, but the upper walls and vaults were covered with fresco.[35] This might be explained by the lack of materials or perhaps by the lack of trained artisans in the Peloponnese. Certainly, mosaics are rare outside the capital in the Late Byzantine period.

More curious and more difficult to explain is the situation at the nearly contemporaneous Holy Apostles in Thessaloniki, where the vaults and upper walls were covered with mosaics, but the lower walls, below the cornice, were frescoed. Xyngopoulos proposed that this represented a change in the program of the interior decoration. Originally, he suggested, marble revetments were intended for the lower walls, but these proved to be too expensive, and subsequently the walls were frescoed.[36] Recent scholars have emphasized the stylistic similarities of the mosaics and frescoes, as well as the iconographic unity of the two.[37] Nevertheless, following standard practices, revetments would make more sense than fresco below the mosaic decoration.

Iconographic Programs

Otto Demus suggested three systems of interpretation for the decorative programs of Middle Byzantine churches: the hierarchical-cosmic, in which the church represents the ordering of the Christian universe; the topographical, in which "the building is conceived as an image of (and so magically identified with) the places sanctified by Christ's earthly life"; and the liturgical-chronological, in which the icons are arranged according to the sequence of church festivals.[38] Demus believed that the standard decorative program must have been elaborated for a cross-in-square church, because the three schemes are so closely accommodated to the building type.[39] The fact that most of the important

FIG. 205. Detail of the fresco decoration on the south wall of the naos of Çanlı Kilise, near Akhisar, in 1907

FIG. 206. View into the prothesis of Çanlı Kilise, looking east

FIG. 207. View into an exonarthex dome of the Vefa Kilise Camii, Istanbul

painted with a frieze of white spades and crosses. The artist extended this pattern onto the flat wall surface to either side, creating a painted cornice where none existed in the architecture.

In the lateral apses, small cornices mark the springing of the conch (fig. 206). However, the artist evidently found the area of the conch too restricted for his subject matter, and in both apses, the painting overlaps the cornices. In the north apse, the bust of an archangel is represented with wings spread, and his left wing is awkwardly overlapped by the projecting cornice. These many details should indicate that although both the artist and mason responsible for Çanlı Kilise were skilled and aware of the styles of the major centers, they did not work together, and the artist experienced some difficulty in adapting his "program" to the preestablished architectural framework.

Among the few surviving and understudied examples of Late Byzantine art in Constantinople are the dome mosaics in the exonarthex of the Vefa Kilise Camii. The three domes of the exonarthex are distinct in their architectural forms—both ribbed and pumpkin domes are used, and the compartments of the drums were apparently decorated with a program of the ancestors of Christ (fig. 207). The only serious examination of the mosaics to consider the chronology dated them to between 1295 and 1300, based on stylistic analysis.[53] Grape saw the mosaics as representative of the so-called "cubist" style popular at the end of the thirteenth century. This stands at odds with the architecture, which is normally, albeit tentatively, dated to about 1320.[54] A closer examination of the paintings may resolve this problem. The artist responsible lacked the skill of his contemporary at the Chora, and rather than interacting with the architectural framework, the figures instead appear imprisoned by it. The "cubist" impression of the figures is emphasized precisely because they are boxed into the compartments of the vaults. Moreover, the restoration filled in missing areas with a grid pattern that also encourages the cubistic impression.

In contrast to these examples, the Constantinopolitan artist responsible for the lavish mosaic program of the Cathedral of Monreale in Norman Sicily, dating to the 1180s, found himself contending with unfamiliar architectural forms.[55] In this instance, a sense of unity was created, but at the expense of the original architectural framework. The recent restorations at Monreale indicate that during the initial mosaic decoration, windows were suppressed and decorative columns were removed to create uninterrupted mural surfaces.[56] Thus, the standard view that one master was responsible for overseeing the construction of a church, as well as its decoration, must be modified.[57] The impression of continuity and harmony in the interior was primarily the contribution of the mosaicist, who was willing to sacrifice features of the spatial articulation and to subordinate the architecture to the well-defined decorative program.[58]

In contrast, at the Chora in Constantinople, the relationship appears so close that the master mason and the artist may have been the same person, or else the two worked in a close association (see figs. 107, 203, 208).[59] We might also credit the dynamic interrelationship of architecture and art at the Chora to its learned and involved patron, Theodore Metochites. The founder's presence is evident in the iconographic program.[60] At the same time, the innovative "mannerist" style of the art and architecture of the Chora finds significant parallels in the self-conscious literary style of Metochites' many writings.[61] He clearly provided the builders and artists with "hothouse conditions" to create something new, and the intellectual content of both the style and the iconography of the building point back to Metochites' inspiration and possibly also to his supervision.

In the narthexes, a type of sail vault was introduced, rather than the more common groin vault (see fig. 107). The form of the vault is odd: the bays were normally rectangular and their size varied from one to the next. In order to regularize them, additional arches were added, springing from the lateral arches, to frame a square central panel that was topped by a domical vault.[62] The additional arches provided a setting for portraits of saints in roundels or patterned borders, whereas the domical vault provided a flat surface for the extensive narrative program of the narthexes. The surface was certainly more adaptable for narrative than a groin vault would have been, but the bowing of the surface caused the artist to stretch and contort the scenes. The selection of the particular type of sail vault, then, was not entirely successful, representing a compromise between the artist and the mason.

On the other hand, the process of adapting the narrative scenes to the curve of the vault seems to have profoundly influenced the development of the artist's distinctive style.[63] Unlike the painters of Çanlı Kilise or of Vefa Kilise Camii, the artist of the Chora was not limited by the architecture but was able to work with it in a dynamic way. And in contrast to Monreale, where the setting was altered to suit the decorative concept, at the Chora both the style and the program of the art were fitted to the setting.

In the major spaces of the Chora, the vaulting types were carefully selected to suit the decorative medium.[64] The domes that were designed for mosaic are pumpkin domes, with an undulating, faceted surface that was ideal for mosaic (see fig. 191). The multiple curves of the domes would capture light entering the dome from all angles, creating a shimmering surface and suffusing the interior with a golden glow. The frescoed domes of the parekklesion and of the diakonikon were articulated with ribs, whose surfaces were better suited to the flat impression of fresco (fig. 196). The only exception is the pumpkin dome of the prothesis, which was decorated with fresco (fig. 170). However, it is a blind dome, without fenestration, and it was not subject to the lighting effects of the other pumpkin domes in the building. Most likely, it was used here to visually enhance the confined, low space of the prothesis.

Of course, the selection of dome form and decoration seen at the Chora was not universal. At Vefa Kilise Camii, both ribbed and pumpkin domes were covered with mosaic (see fig. 207). At the Pammakaristos parekklesion, the dome is ribbed and decorated with mosaic, but the thick plaster coating creates an undulating surface resembling that of a pumpkin dome (see fig. 193). At the Holy Apostles in Thessaloniki, two of the ambulatory domes are pumpkin domes, but they are decorated with fresco, and the flatness of the medium emphasizes the irregularities of the surface. Because the naos of the Holy Apostles was decorated with mosaic, one wonders if these other domes were originally intended for mosaic. On the other hand, the naos dome—decorated with mosaic—was left plain and unribbed. The eastern two ambulatory domes were similar, and at least the northeast dome was frescoed.

Returning to the Chora, there is more to understanding the decoration than simply noting how the architectural framework influenced the artist. Irregularities in the architectural forms seem to have resulted from a direct response to the necessities of the complex decorative program, suggesting that the mason, too, adjusted his designs to suit the decorative program. For example, the oversized south bay of the inner narthex seems to have been intended as a sort of founders' chapel, where the deceased benefactors of the

building materials and available technology affected architectural design. Masons took into consideration the limitations and possibilities presented by construction in brick and stone, as well as by the glazing technology, the use of *spolia*, and the availability of roofing materials. Innovations are evident in the formulation of a system of tensile reinforcement with wood and metal and in the development of vaulting and of integrated structural systems that were perfectly suited to the scale and types of buildings common in the Middle and Late Byzantine periods. Although standard construction techniques were learned and transmitted within the conservative environment of the workshop, we frequently witness the modification of these, for example to create attractive decorated surfaces or to allow the construction of uncentered vaults. In either case, the overall form of the building was not altered, but certain details were manipulated, either to facilitate construction or to present a more pleasing outward appearance.

Analysis of the decorated church interior raises questions about the degree of interaction between artists and masons. In most monuments, the masons must have understood the necessity of the interior decoration, and they must have planned accordingly, even if they did not know the specifics of the decorative program. In some of our finest surviving monuments, however, the careful interrelationship of architectural form, decorative surface, and iconographic program suggests a close working relationship between artist and mason and leaves open the question of whether certain *protomaistores* might have been both painters and masons.

It is clear that the workshop played a role in both the innovative and the conservative aspects of Byzantine architectural development. Architectural knowledge was transmitted from one generation to the next through a program of apprenticeship. Masons learned construction systems that worked, but they also learned where variations might be introduced into a building. An emphasis on detail is evident in Byzantine descriptions of buildings, but it is also apparent in the process of design; innovation appears on a small scale, affecting specific features of a building but not the basic schema. It is not simply the luxurious surface that gives a Byzantine building its special character. Recalling the words of Leo VI, the details "have a beauty that corresponds exactly to that of the rest of the church";[13] the appreciation of detail clearly informs our assessment of Byzantine architectural production. Able to address the special needs of a particular site or the wishes of a particular patron, Byzantine church architecture is best viewed as a responsive architecture—of endless "variations on a theme." Byzantine builders knew the theme, but, more importantly, they were aware of a range of possible variations.

ABBREVIATIONS

AASS *Acta Sanctorum*, 71 vols. (Paris, 1863–1940)

AB *Analecta Bollandiana*

AD *Archaiologikon Deltion*

AJA *American Journal of Archaeology*

ANCIENT STRUCTURES *Studies in Ancient Structures. Proceedings of the International Conference*, ed. G. Özşen (Istanbul, 1997)

AST *Araştırma Sonuçları Toplantısı*

BHG *Bibliotheca hagiographica Graeca*, ed. F. Halkin, 5 vols. (Brussels, 1965–84)

BMFD *Byzantine Monastic Foundation Documents*, ed. J. P. Thomas and A. Hero (Washington D.C., forthcoming)

BMGS *Byzantine and Modern Greek Studies*

BSCA *Byzantine Studies Conference, Abstracts*

BZ *Byzantinische Zeitschrift*

CA *Cahiers archéologiques*

CSHB *Corpus scriptorum historiae byzantinae*

DCHAE *Deltion tes Christianikes Archailogikes Etaireias*

DMA *Dictionary of the Middle Ages*, 13 vols. (New York, 1982–89)

DOP *Dumbarton Oaks Papers*

FESTSCHRIFT HALLENSLEBEN *Studien zur byzantinischen Kunstgeschichte. Festshcrift für H. Hallensleben zum 65. Geburtstag*, ed. B. Birkopp, B. Schellewald, and L. Theis (Amsterdam, 1995)

GOTR *Greek Orthodox Theological Review*

GRBS *Greek, Roman and Byzantine Studies*

IM *Istanbuler Mitteilungen*

IRAIK *Izvestiia Russkago Arkheologicheskago Instituta v Konstantinopole*

JÖB *Jahrbuch der österreichischen Byzantinistik*

JSAH *Journal of the Society of Architectural Historians*

ODB *Oxford Dictionary of Byzantium*, ed. A. Kazhdan, 3 vols. (Oxford, 1991)

PG *Patriologiae cursus completus, Series graeca*, ed. J.-P. Migne, 161 vols. (Paris, 1857–66)

RBK *Reallexikon zur byzantinischen Kunst*

REB *Revue des études byzantines*

TTKB *Türk Tarih Kurumu Belleten*

VIZVREM *Vizantijskij vremennik*

ZRVI *Zbornik radova vizantološkog instituta*

NOTES

Chapter One

1. See P. A. Hollingsworth, "Byzantium, History of: "Dark Ages," *ODB* 1:350–52, for a convenient summary and bibliography.

2. P. A. Hollingsworth and A. Cutler, "Iconoclasm," *ODB* 2:975–77, with further bibliography.

3. T. F. Mathews, *The Early Churches of Constantinople: Architecture and Liturgy* (University Park, Pa., 1977), 177–79.

4. R. Krautheimer, *Early Christian and Byzantine Architecture*, 4th rev. ed., with S. Ćurčić (Harmondsworth, 1986), 103–6 passim.

5. See O. Demus, *Byzantine Mosaic Decoration* (London, 1948); and further comments by E. Kitzinger, "Reflections on the Feast Cycle in Byzantine Art," *CA* 36 (1988): 51–73. T. F. Mathews, "The Sequel to Nicaea II in Byzantine Church Decoration," *Perkins Journal* 41, no. 3 (1988): 11–23, questions the Demus interpretation. See also below, Chapter 8.

6. Demus, *Byzantine Mosaic Decoration*, 11.

7. Mathews, "Sequel to Nicaea II," 11–23.

8. Demus, *Byzantine Mosaic Decoration*, 11. His words find a resonance in Byzantine *ekphraseis*, such as that of the Nea Church.

9. See comments by S. Kostof, *A History of Architecture: Settings and Rituals* (Oxford, 1985), 18–19.

10. *Historia mystagogica*, ed. F. E. Brightman, *Journal of Theological Studies* 9 (1908): 257; trans. in C. Mango, *Art of the Byzantine Empire 312–1453: Sources and Documents* (Englewood Cliffs, N.J., 1972), 143 (hereafter cited as *Sources*).

11. For the changes in the liturgy as they affected architecture, see Mathews, *Early Churches*, 177–80; see also H. Wybrew, *The Orthodox Liturgy: The Development of the Eucharistic Liturgy in the Byzantine Rite* (London, 1989).

12. See, among others, R. Ousterhout, *The Architecture of the Kariye Camii in Istanbul* (Washington, D.C., 1987), 96–106 (hereafter cited as *Kariye*); S. Ćurčić, "The Twin-Domed Narthex in Palaeologan Architecture," *ZRVI* 13 (1971): 333–44; P. A. Mylonas, "Armenika Gkavit kai Byzantines Lites," *Archaiologia* 32 (1989): 52–68 (with English summary).

13. Mathews, *Early Churches*, 177–80. For evidence on Middle Byzantine ambos, see M. Dennert, "Mittelbyzantinische Ambone in Kleinasien," *IM* 45 (1995): 137–47; U. Peschlow, "Die mittelbyzantinischen Ambo aus archäologischer Sicht," in *Thymiama ste mneme tes Laskarinas Boura* (Athens, 1994), 255–60; and J.-P. Sodini, "Les ambons médiévaux à Byzance: Vestiges et problèmes," in ibid., 303–7.

14. Mathews, "Sequel to Nicaea II," 11–23; also R. Taft, "The Frequency of the Eucharist throughout History," *Concilium* 172 (1982): 13–24.

15. C. L. Striker, *The Myrelaion (Bodrum Camii) in Istanbul* (Princeton, 1981).

16. See, among others, G. Babić, *Les chapelles annexes des églises byzantines* (Paris, 1969); S. Ćurčić, "Architectural Significance of Subsidiary Chapels in Middle Byzantine Churches," *JSAH* 36 (1977): 94–110; Ousterhout, *Kariye*, 110–14.

17. L. Theis, "Die Flankenräume im mittelbyzantinischen Kirchenbau" (Habilitation thesis, University of Bonn, 1996).

18. See the recent suggestions by S. Ćurčić, "What Was the Real Function of Late Byzantine *Katechoumena?*" *BSCA* 19 (1993): 8–9.

19. Ousterhout, *Kariye*, 106–10.

20. Krautheimer, *Early Christian*, 340–43, 520; also N. Schmuck, "Kreuzkuppelkirche," *RBK* 5 (1991): 356–74.

21. Among the more recent literature, see comments by C. Mango, *Byzantine Architecture* (New York, 1976), 249; Schmuck, "Kreuzkuppelkirche"; and I. D. Lange, "Theorien und Entstehung der byzantinischen Kreuzkuppelkirche," *Architectura* 16 (1986): 93–113.

22. Mango, *Byzantine Architecture*, 178–80; developed by V. Ruggieri, *Byzantine Religious Architecture (582–867): Its History and Structural Elements* (Rome, 1991), esp. 139–41.

23. C. Mango and I. Ševčenko, "Some Churches and Monasteries on the South Shore of the Sea of Marmara," *DOP* 18 (1964): 279–98. For the chronology, see P. I. Kuniholm, "First Millenium A.D. Oak Chronologies" (Wiener Lab, Cornell University, Ithaca, N.Y., typescript, 14 March 1995), 5.

24. M. S. Pekak, "Zeytinbağı/Trilye Bizans Döneme Kiliseleri," in *XIII. AST* (Ankara, 1995), 1:307–38, based on the author's unpublished dissertation, "Zeytinbağı (Trigleia) Bizans Döneme Kiliseleri ve "Fatih Camii" (Tarih ve Mimarisi)" (Hacettepe University, Ankara, 1991).

25. S. Eyice, "L'église cruciforme de Side en Pamphylie," *Anatolia* 3 (1958): 35–42, discusses the evidence for the abandonment of the city by the ninth century, thus dating the church before then; he believes this to be the oldest example of the cross-in-square type. See also A. Mansel, *Die Ruinen von Side* (Berlin, 1963), 168–69; and more recent comments by H. Buchwald, "Western Asia Minor as a Generator of Architectural Forms in the Byzantine Period: Provincial Back-Wash or Dynamic Center of Production," *JöB* 34 (1984): 200–234, esp. 206.

26. For Bulgaria, see K. Mijatev, *Die mittelalterliche Baukunst in Bulgarien* (Sofia, 1974); for Cappadocia, see L. Rodley, *Cave Monasteries of Byzantine Cappadocia* (Cambridge, 1985), fig. 44; For Bithynia, see Y. Ötüken and R. Ousterhout, "The Byzantine Church at Çeltikdere," in *Festschrift Hallensleben*, 85–92, esp. nn. 9–10.

27. Striker, *Myrelaion*, 30–31.

28. Many of the Myrelaion's unusual features, as well its the all-brick construction, appear

in early Islamic architecture as well; the decorative tiles from the interior are Sasanian in flavor. Considering the fashion for Arab architecture in the preceding century, this would not be surprising; see Mango, *Byzantine Architecture*, 194.

29. Striker, *Myrelaion,* 24–25.

30. Demus, *Byzantine Mosaic Decoration*, passim; see also below, Chapter 8.

31. Photios, *Homily 10;* trans. in Mango, *Sources*, 185–86.

32. For the term, see J. T. Matthews, "The Byzantine Use of the Title Pantocrator," *Orientalia Christiana Periodica* 44 (1978): 442–62.

33. Photios, *Homily 10;* trans. in Mango, *Sources*, 186.

34. See S. Kostof, *Caves of God*, 2nd ed. (Oxford, 1989), for a general introduction to the architecture of the region.

35. *Historia mystagogica*, ed. F. E. Brightman, *Journal of Theological Studies* 9 (1908), 248–67 and 387–97; significant portions are translated in Mango, *Sources*, 141–43.

36. See the discussion in Wybrew, *Orthodox Liturgy*, esp. 139–44.

37. Ibid., 140.

38. C. Mango, "Approaches to Byzantine Architecture," *Muqarnas* 8 (1991): 41.

39. Krautheimer, *Early Christian*, 390–93 and fig. 354B.

40. The church described at the so-called Botaniates Palace in Constantinople may have been a triconch, but it could also have had two lateral chapels; see M. Angold, "Inventory of the So-called Palace of Botaniates," in *The Byzantine Aristocracy IX to XIII Centuries*, BAR International Series 221, ed. M. Angold (Oxford, 1984), 254–66. A few triconch churches have been noted in Asia Minor, but they are different in design and their original contexts have not been determined.

41. R. Bergman, "Byzantine Influence and Private Patronage in a Newly Discovered Medieval Church in Amalfi: S. Michele Arcangelo in Pogenola," *JSAH* 50 (1994): 421–45.

42. Kuniholm, "First Millenium," 5.

43. F. Benoit, *L'architecture: L'orient médiévale et moderne* (Paris, 1912), fig. 97.

44. See, among others, H. Maguire, "Truth and Convention in Byzantine Descriptions of Works of Art," *DOP* 28 (1974): 113–40; A. Hohlweg, "Ekphrasis," *RBK* (1971): 34–75; L. James and R. Webb, "'To Understand Ultimate Things and Enter Secret Places': Ekphrasis and Art in Byzantium," *Art History* 14, no. 1 (1991): 1–17.

45. *Vita Basilii*, ed. I. Bekker, *CSHB*, chaps. 83–85, pp. 325–27; trans. in Mango, *Sources*, 194–95.

46. See Angold, "Inventory," 254–66. Two versions of the text survive: this one in Greek and another preserved only in Latin translations; cf. F. Miklosich and J. Muller, *Acta et diplomata Graeca mediiaevi* (Vienna, 1865), 3:55–57, and x–xv.

47. For an assessment, see R. Ousterhout, "Reconstructing Ninth-Century Constantinople," in *Byzantium in the Ninth Century: Dead or Alive?*, ed. L. Brubaker (Aldershot, 1998), 115–30; also P. Magdalino, "Observations on the Nea Ekklesia of Basil I," *JöB* 37 (1987): 51–64.

48. M. Psellos, *Chronographia*, 3.14–19, 4.31, 6.185–88; translated passages are from E. R. A. Sewter, trans., *Fourteen Byzantine Rulers: The Chronographia*, rev. ed. (Harmondsworth, 1966), 71–75, 105–6, 250–52.

49. J. Mavrogordato, *Digenes Akrites* (Oxford, 1956), reprinted in Mango, *Sources*, 215–16.

50. O. Wulff, "Das Raumerlebnis im Spiegel der Ekphrasis," *BZ* 30 (1929–30): 531–39.

51. As emphasized by James and Webb, "To Understand Ultimate Things," 1–17.

52. L. Petit, "Typikon du monastère de la Kosmosotira près d'Aenos (1152)," *IRAIK* 13 (1908): 17–75; English trans. by N. P. Ševčenko in *BMFD*, forthcoming, cf. chaps. 75, 79, 82.

53. R. Krautheimer, "Introduction to an 'Iconography of Medieval Architecture,'" in *Studies in Early Christian, Medieval, and Renaissance Art* (New York, 1969), 115–50.

54. Vatican Library, MS gr. 1162, fol. 2v; Monastery of Saint Catherine, Sinai, MS gr. 339, fol. 4v; Monastery of John the Theologian, Patmos, cod. 707, roll 1; for illustrations, see H. C. Evans and W. D. Wixom, eds., *The Glory of Byzantium: Art and Culture of the Middle Byzantine Era, A.D. 843–1261*, exh. cat., Metropolitan Museum of Art (New York, 1997), 4, 107–11; A. Cutler and J.-M. Spieser, *Byzance médiévale 700–1204* (Paris, 1996), figs. 290–93.

55. Vatican Library, MS gr. 1613, p. 353; illustrated in Cutler and Spieser, *Byzance médiévale*, fig. 120.

56. A. Cutler, "Originality as a Cultural Phenomenon," in *Originality in Byzantine Literature, Art and Music*, ed. A. Littlewood (Oxford, 1996), 203–16; see also A. Kazhdan, "Innovation in Byzantium," in ibid., 1–14.

57. Mango, *Byzantine Architecture*, 249.

Chapter Two

1. Cassiodorus, *Variae*, vii.5, *The Letters of Cassiodorus*, trans. T. Hodgkin (London, 1886), 323; quoted in M. S. Briggs, *The Architect in History* (Oxford, 1927), 48. The recent, abridged translation by Barnish omits this passage.

2. Vitruvius, *The Ten Books on Architecture*, esp. 1.1–1.2; trans. M. H. Morgan (Cambridge, Mass., 1914), 5–12.

3. I. Ševčenko, "Alexios Makrembolites and His 'Dialogue between the Rich and the Poor,'" *ZRVI* 6 (1960): 200.

4. Vatican Library, MS lat. 4939, fol. 28v. I thank Mark Johnson for this reference.

5. See I. Dujcev, *Die Miniaturen der Manasses-Chronik* (Sofia, 1965); Vatican Library, MS slav. 2, fol. 109r (a similar scene, badly flaked, of Justinian directing the construction of Hagia Sophia); and C. Havice, "The Hamilton Psalter in Berlin, Kupferstichkabinett 78. A.9" (Ph.D. diss., Pennsylvania State University, 1978), 437–38, for fol. 174r (David supervising the building of the Temple).

6. Procopius, *The Buildings*, 1.1.66–78; trans. H. P. Dewing (Cambridge, Mass., 1940), 28–33.

7. G. Dagron, *Constantinople imaginaire* (Paris, 1984), 265–69; see also the useful discussion by C. Mango, "Byzantine Writers on the Fabric of Hagia Sophia," in *Hagia Sophia from the Age of Justinian to the Present*, ed. R. Mark and A. Çakmak (Cambridge 1992), 41–56.

8. *Vita Basilii*, in *Theophanes Continuatus*, ed. I. Bekker (Bonn, 1838), 211–353; significant portions trans. in Mango, *Sources*, 192–99.

9. Ibid.; Mango, *Sources*, 192.

10. Psellos, *Chronographia*, 6.143–51 (Sewter, 250–52).

11. Suetonius, *The Twelve Caesars*, 6.31; trans. R. Graves (Harmondsworth, 1957), 224. Although Suetonius's work may not have been known to the Byzantines, other Roman biographies

were; cf. R. Jenkins, "The Classical Background of the Scriptores Post Theophanem," *DOP* 8 (1954): 13–30, who suggests that the *Vita Basilii* relied on biographies of Mark Anthony and Nero.

12. John Kinnamos, *Deeds of John and Manuel Comnenus*, 1.14; trans. C. Brand (New York, 1976), 17.

13. I. Ševčenko and N. Ševčenko, eds. and trans., *The Life of Saint Nicholas of Sion* (Brookline, Mass., 1984), 68–69.

14. D. Sullivan, *The Life of Saint Nikon* (Brookline, Mass., 1987), 119.

15. J. Noret, ed., *Vitae duae antiquae Sancti Athanasii Athonitae* (Turnhout, 1982), Vita A: 74–76; Vita B: 25.

16. Psellos, *Chronographia*, 6.54–58 (Sewter, 182–83): "He always had a pretext for these visits—that he was supervising some detail of the building—and several times a month he would go there, nominally to watch the progress of the work, but in reality to be with his mistress."

17. For comments on the limitations in determining the role of the patron in art, see R. Cormack, "Patronage and New Programs of Byzantine Iconography," *The 17th International Byzantine Congress, Major Papers* (New York, 1986), 609–38; also A. Cutler, "Uses of Luxury: On the Functions of Consumption and Symbolic Capital in Byzantine Culture," in *Byzance et les images*, ed. A. Guillou and J. Durand (Paris 1994), 289–327.

18. See R. Ousterhout, "Collaboration and Innovation in the Arts of Byzantine Constantinople," *BMGS* 21 (1997): 93–112, esp. 98–100; see also below, Chapter 8.

19. G. Downey, "Byzantine Architects: Their Training and Methods," *Byzantion* 18 (1946): 99–118, esp. 105–9.

20. Ibid., 112–14; also A. Cameron, "Isidore of Miletus and Hypatia: On the Editing of Mathematical Texts," *GRBS* 31 (1990): 103–27, esp. 122.

21. K. P. Mentzou, *Symbole eis ten meleten tou oikonomikou kai koinoikou biou tes proimou byzantines periodou* (Athens 1975), 169–94, lists professions recorded from Early Christian inscriptions; workshops include *oikodomos* and *technites*, which were very common, as well as *maistor, ktistai, ergodotai, ergolaboi, tektones, epistektones, latomoi, leptourgoi-xylikarioi, marmararioi,* and *lithxooi-akonetai.*

22. Architects measure the capacity of granaries: *De ceremoniis*, 2.51 (ed. Reiske, 701).

23. Downey, "Byzantine Architects," 109 n. 2; I. Bekker, ed., *Anecdota graeca* (Berlin, 1814–21), 1:202 (no. 5).

24. M. Johnson et al., "Architect," *ODB*, 1:157.

25. A. Kazhdan, "Technites," *ODB*, 3:2020.

26. A. Kazhdan and A. Cutler, "Carpenter," *ODB*, 1:382–83; A. Kazhdan, "Mason," *ODB*, 3:1311–12.

27. Paris gr. 29, fol. 4r: S. Dufrenne, *L'illustration des Psautiers grecs du Moyen-Age* (Paris, 1966).

28. O. Demus, *The Mosaic Decoration of San Marco, Venice*, ed. H. Kessler (Chicago, 1988), 137.

29. O. Demus, *The Mosaics of Norman Sicily* (London, 1949), pl. 102.

30. *Basilicorum libri LX*, ed. H. J. Scheltema, N. van der Wal, D. Holwerda (Groningen, 1953–58), 15.1.38, and *scholia* 1; also A. Kazhdan and A. Cutler, "Building Industry," *ODB* 1:331–32.

31. Johnson et al., "Architect," *ODB*, 1:157.

32. Contra G. Necipoğlu, *The Topkapı Scroll—Geometry and Ornament in Islamic Architecture* (Los Angeles, 1994), 3, no architectural drawing is mentioned; trans. in Mango, *Sources*, 160.

33. Mango, *Byzantine Architecture*, 351 n. 14.

34. Johnson et al., "Architect," *ODB*, 1:157.

35. Chap. 42; ed. G. Moravcik and R. Jenkins (Washington, D.C. 1967), 184–85.

36. Trans. N. Ševčenko, in *BMFD*, forthcoming.

37. G. Moravcsik, *Szent László Leánya és a Bizánci Pantokrator-Monostor* (Budapest, 1923), 44, 50.

38. Anna Comnena, *The Alexiad*, 6.10 (ed. Migne, 503–4); trans. E. R. A. Sewter (Harmondsworth, 1969), 203–4, with slight modification.

39. G. Pachymeres, *Relations historiques*, ed. A. Failler, French trans. V. Laurent (Paris, 1984), 1:233.8–11; A.-M. Talbot, "The Restoration of Constantinople under Michael VIII," *DOP* 47 (1993): 243–61, esp. 247, 251.

40. Cyril of Scythopolis, *Vita Sabae*, chap. 73 (ed. Schwartz, 177); see also J. P. Thomas, *Private Religious Foundations in the Byzantine Empire* (Washington, 1987), 45.

41. J. Koder, ed. and German trans., *To Eparchikon Biblion* (Vienna, 1991).

42. *AASS* (May 3), 9*.

43. For the *typikon*, see P. Gautier, "Le typikon du Christ Sauveur Pantocrator," *REB* 32 (1974): 1–145, esp. 127–29; noted by Thomas, *Private Religious Foundations*, 45.

44. Koder, *Eparchikon Biblion*, 139–43.

45. A. Kazhdan, "Guilds," *ODB*, 2:887.

46. M. McCormick, *Eternal Victory: Triumphal Rulership in Late Antiquity, Byzantium and the Early Medieval West* (Cambridge, 1986), 204–5.

47. A. Kazhdan and A. Epstein, *Change in Byzantine Culture in the Eleventh and Twelfth Centuries* (Berkeley, 1985), 52.

48. S. Vryonis, "Byzantine *Demokratia* and the Guilds of the Eleventh Century," *DOP* 17 (1963): 289–314.

49. N. Oikonomidès, *Hommes d'affaires grecs et latins à Constantinople (XIIIe–XVe siècles)* (Montreal, 1979), 108–14.

50. Z. Pljakov, "La production artisanale dans la ville byzantine aux XIIIe–XIVe siècles," *Bulgarian Historical Review* 16 (1988): 34–55, esp. 44.

51. Ibid.

52. See comments by A. Kazhdan, "Book of the Eparch," *ODB*, 1:308.

53. Koder, *Eparchikon Biblion*, 139–43.

54. Mango, *Sources*, 96–97.

55. Theophanes, *Chronographia*, am. 6258; trans. C. Mango and R. Scott, *The Chronicle of Theophanes the Confessor* (Oxford, 1997), 607–9.

56. Ibid., 608.

57. C. Mango, "Isaurian Builders," in *Polychronion: Festschrift F. Dölger zum 75. Geburtstag*, ed. P. Wirth (Heidelberg, 1966), 358–65, esp. 361.

58. Ševčenko and Ševčenko, *Saint Nicholas*, 76–77.

59. L. Petit, "Vie et office de St. Euthyme le jeune," *Bibliothèque hagiographique orientale* 5 (1904): 38–39.

60. For the text, see G. P. Kremos, *Phokika. Proskynetarion tes en te Phokidi mones tou Osiou Louka*

toupiklen Steirioto, 3 vols. (Athens, 1874–80), 1:ιδ'. See L. Boura, *O Glyptos Diakosmos tou Naou tes Panagias sto Monasteri tou Osiou Louka* (Athens, 1980), 8–9 (and English summary, p. 124), who doubts the number of masons but finds the legend otherwise satisfactory; she identifies the building in question as the Theotokos church. See also P. A. Mylonas, "Gavits arméniens et Litae byzantines: Observations nouvelles sur le complexe de Saint-Luc en Phocide," *CA* 38 (1990), 107–116, esp. 115–16, who probably correctly interprets this building as having been the predecessor of the katholikon.

61. Kremos, *Phokika*, 1:ιδ'. I thank Paul Mylonas for this reference.

62. For convenient summary and further bibliography, see L. Shelby, "Masons and Builders," *DMA*, 8:172–80; also J. Harvey, *The Mediaeval Architect* (London, 1972); P. du Colombier, *Les chantiers des cathédrales* (Paris, 1973); and D. Kimbel, "Le développement de la taille en série dans l'architecture médiévale et son rôle dans l'histoire économique," *Bulletin monumental* 135, no. 3 (1977): 195–222.

63. Shelby, "Masons," 172–80.

64. Koder, *Eparchikon Biblion*, 139–43.

65. *AASS* (May 24), 415–17; discussed by H. Magoulias, "Trades and Crafts in the Sixth and Seventh Centuries as Viewed in the Lives of the Saints," *Byzantinoslavica* 37 (1976): 11–13.

66. K. Vogel, ed., *Ein byzantinisches Rechenbuch des frühen 14. Jahrhunderts* (Vienna, 1968); H. Hunger and K. Vogel, eds., *Ein byzantinisches Rechenbuch des 15. Jahrhunderts* (Vienna, 1963).

67. See for example, *Actes du Protaton*, ed. D. Papachryssanthou (Paris, 1975), 213 [*typikon* of John Tzmiskes dated 972], no. 7, lines 141–42; 260: [Manuel Palaiologos's chrysobull of 1406], no. 13, lines 74–75.

68. Oikonomidès, *Hommes d'affaires*, 73–74.

69. R. Janin, *La géographie ecclésiastique de l'Empire Byzantin: Les églises et monastères* (Paris, 1969), 361 (hereafter cited as *Eglises et monastères*).

70. See, for example, M. Bartusis, "State Demands for Building and Repairing Fortifications in Late Byzantine and Medieval Serbia," *Byzantinoslavica* 49 (1988): 205–12.

71. Ibid., 205.

72. A. Lampros, *Palaiologeia kai Peloponnesiaka*, 4 vols. (Athens, 1912–30), 3:298; cited in Bartusis, "State Demands," 210.

73. A. Papadopoulos-Kerameus, *Analekta Ierosolymitikes Stachoulogias* (St. Petersburg, 1891–98), 1:433; cited in Bartusis, "State Demands," 210.

74. Sullivan, *Life of Saint Nikon*, 114–19.

75. Ibid., 114–35.

76. Ibid., 128–29.

77. *AASS* (May 3), 9*.

78. For the text, see H. Delehaye, "Constantini Acropolitai Hagiographi Byzantini Epistularum Manipulus," *AB* 51 (1933): 279–84, esp. 280; trans. A.-M. Talbot, in *BFMD* (forthcoming).

79. Ibid.

80. F. Dölger, *Aus den Schatzkammern des heiligen Berges* (Munich, 1948), 102.

81. A. Kazhdan, "Nov'ie Material'i po Vnutrennei Istorii Bizantii X–XV vv.," *VizVrem* 26 (1965): 81; A. Kazhdan and A. Cutler, "Building Industry," *ODB*, 1:331–32. An *aspron* is a coin of small denomination.

12. Downey, "Byzantine Architect," 99–118.

13. Briggs, *Architect in History*, 48.

14. Cassiodorus, *Variae*, vii.5 (Hodgkin, 323); see also Briggs, *Architect in History*, 47–50.

15. Mark the Deacon, *Vita Porphyrii*, ed. H. Grégoire and M. A. Kugener (Paris, 1930), 59–79.; trans. in Mango, *Sources*, 30–32.

16. See G. Stričević, "The Methods of the Early Byzantine Architect," *BSCA* 19 (1993): 79–80, who has noted numerous possible examples of this phenomenon.

17. See D. Koco, "Nouvelles considérations sur l'église de Sainte Sophie à Ohrid," *Archaeologia Iugoslavica* 2 (1956): 139–44.

18. *AASS* (Nov. 3), 160 and 9*.

19. *PG* 116:77.

20. *AASS* (Nov. 2), 402c.

21. Mango, "Isaurian Builders," 360.

22. M. R. James, *The Apocryphal New Testament* (Oxford, 1924), 371–72.

23. Harvey, *Mediaeval Architect*, 97, 101. Note also that in the vision of Ezekiel, his guide showed him the reconstruction and measurements of the Temple with a line of flax and a measuring reed: Ezekiel 40:3; similarly Revelation 11:1. In his insistence on the use of drawings, Harvey used a broad definition of drawings, including the laying out of the building at full scale.

24. J. J. Coulton, "Incomplete Preliminary Planning in Greek Architecture: Some New Evidence," in *Le dessin d'architecture dans les sociétés antiques*, ed. T. Thieme (Strasbourg, 1985), 103–21.

25. L. Haselberger, "The Construction Plans for the Temple of Apollo at Didyma," *Scientific American*, December 1985, 126–32; also Haselberger, "Deciphering a Roman Blueprint," *Scientific American*, June 1995, 84–89.

26. I. Bayer, "Architekturzeichnungen auf dem Boden der Basilica," in *Die Basilika des Heiligen Kreuzes in Resafa-Sergiupolis*, ed. T. Ulbert (Mainz, 1986), 155–56 and figs. 73–75.

27. D. Sullivan, ed., *The Poliorcetica of Heron of Byzantium: Text, Translation, and Commentary* (Washington, D.C., forthcoming); also D. Sullivan, "Originality in the *Poliorcetica* of 'Heron' of Byzantium," *BSCA* 18 (1993): 32–33: For illustrations, see C. Wescher, *Poliorcétique des grecs* (Paris, 1867). I have benefited greatly from numerous discussions with Denis Sullivan.

28. Sullivan, *Poliorcetica*.

29. One wonders if this has implications for understanding art after Iconoclasm; see C. Barber, "From Transformation to Desire: Art and Worship after Byzantine Iconoclasm," *Art Bulletin* 75 (1993): 7–16, who emphasizes the representational aspect of the art.

30. Again, I thank Denis Sullivan for this observation; *Poliorcetica*, chap. 27.

31. See also *Poliorcetica*, chap. 34, for additional confusions on plans and elevations.

32. Dennis, *Three Byzantine Military Treatises*, 248–49 and figs. 5–9 (Vat. gr. 1164).

33. Ibid., 329.

34. *Les regestes des actes du Patriarchat de Constantinople*, ed. V. Grumel, V. Laurent, and J. Darrouzès (Paris, 1932–79), vol. 2, pt. 6, no. 2997; F. Miklosich and J. Müller, *Acta et diplomata graeca medii aevi sacra et profana* (Vienna, 1860–90), 2:246–48; W. Regel, *Fontes rerum byzantinarum* (reprint, Leipzig, 1982), 32–34. I thank Alice-Mary Talbot for this reference.

35. E. McGeer, "The Syntaxis Armatorum Quadrata: A Tenth-Century Tactical Blueprint," *REB* 50 (1992): esp. 227; Sullivan, *Poliorcetica*, "Introduction."

36. For these references, and much that follows, see Necipoğlu, *Topkapı*, 3–4.

37. J. Lassner, *The Topography of Baghdad in the Early Middle Ages* (Detroit, 1970), 292 n. 32.

38. Cited in Harvey, *Mediaeval Architect*, 98.

39. Lassner, *Topography*, 79.

40. For discussion of these, see O. Grabar, *The Mediation of Ornament* (Princeton, 1992), 155–93 and figs. 160–61.

41. H.-C. Graf von Bothmer, "Architekturbilder im Koran," *Pantheon* 45 (1987): 4–20.

42. Grabar, *Mediation*, 155–93, with a useful essay on the interpretation of medieval architectural representations.

43. According to the Persian historian Bayhaqi (995–1071), quoted by Necipoğlu, *Topkapı*, 4.

44. According to the thirteenth-century historian Ibn Bibi, quoted by Necipoğlu, *Topkapı*, 4.

45. Necipoğlu, *Topkapı*, 4–5 and fig. 1.

46. See the provocative study by G. Necipoğlu-Kafadar, "Plans and Models in 15th- and 16th-Century Ottoman Architectural Practice," *JSAH* 45 (1986): 224–43.

47. W. Djobadze, "The Georgian Churches of Tao-Klarjet'i: Construction Methods and Materials," *Oriens Christianus* 62 (1978): 114–34.

48. Ibid., 116.

49. It is noteworthy that the tenth-century Armenian architect Trdat produced an exact copy in Ani of a church in Zvartznotz: here the exactitude suggests the use of a plan; L. Der Manuelian, "Trdat," *DMA* 12:164–65.

50. As has been suggested by Yasser Tabbaa in his studies of Islamic architecture: Y. Tabbaa, "Geometry and Memory in the Design of the Madrasat al-Firdows in Aleppo," in *Theories and Principles of Design in the Architecture of Islamic Societies* (Cambridge, Mass., 1988), 23–34.

51. Ibid., 23.

52. Ibid., for further bibliography; see also R. Holod, "Text, Plan, and Building: On the Transmission of Architectural Knowledge," in *Theories and Principles*, 1–12 (note 50, above).

53. H. Buchwald, "The Geometry of Middle Byzantine Churches and Some Possible Implications," *JöB* 42 (1992): 293–321, esp. 293.

54. Both procedures may have occurred at the monastery of Lips in Constantinople: a template was probably used for the tenth-century cornices, but when they were imitated in the late thirteenth century, they were carved freehand. See the "Additional Notes" by C. Mango and E. J. W. Hawkins in T. Macridy et al., "The Monastery of Lips (Fenari Isa Camii) at Istanbul," *DOP* 18 (1964): 299–315, esp. 307, 310.

55. G. L. Huxley, *Anthemius of Tralles: A Study in Later Greek Geometry* (Cambridge, 1959).

56. K. Krumbacher, *Geschichte der byzantinsichen Literature von Justinian bis zum Ende des oströmischen Reiches* (Munich, 1897), 620–21; quoted by C. L. Striker, "Applied Geometry in Later Byzantine Architecture," in *Festschrift Hallensleben*, 31–37, esp. 31.

57. E. M. Bruins, ed., *Codex Constantinopolitanus Palatii Veteris, No. 1*, 3 vols. (Leiden, 1964).

58. Ibid., esp. fols. 40v–52r; 1:76–99.

59. Ibid., 3:121–23; Bruins confusingly identifies this as a pendentive rather than as a pendentive dome.

60. Sullivan, *Poliorcetica*.

61. Ibid.: *Geodesia*, chap. 8; illustration fol. 50v.

62. Dennis, *Three Byzantine Military Treatises*, 248–49.

63. P. A. Underwood, "Some Principles of Measurement in the Architecture of the Period of Justinian," *CA* 3 (1948): 64–74, notes that fifty Byzantine feet was a common measurement in the architecture of Justinian.

64. E. Schilbach, *Byzantinische Metrologie* (Munich, 1970), esp. 13–36. Larger units were the *schoinion* and the *orgyia*, whose interrelationship varied. Various trades and crafts may have relied on their own systems.

65. H. Buchwald, "Sardis Church E—A Preliminary Report," *JöB* 26 (1977): 265–99, esp. 271–72 and fig. 7.

66. M. Restle, *Studien zur frühbyzantinische Architektur Kappadokiens*, 3 vols. (Vienna, 1979), 1:89–135, with additional comments on measurements and proportions (both real and imagined) in the Cappadocian churches.

67. Buchwald, "Geometry," 296–302.

68. P. I. Kuniholm and C. L. Striker, "Dendrochronology and the Architectural History of the Church of the Holy Apostles in Thessaloniki," *Architectura* 2 (1990): 1–26, esp. fig. 8.

69. Ibid., 14–15.

70. Ph. Koukoules, "Peri ten Byzantinen Oikian," *Epeteris Etaireias Byzantinon Spoudon* 12 (1936): 84.

71. C. L. Striker, "Applied Geometry in Later Byzantine Architecture," in *Festschrift Hallensleben*, 31–37, esp. 34; W. Wiemer, "Digitale Bildverarbeitung in der Kunstwissenschaft: Eine Datenbank zur Proportionsanalyse mittelalterliche Kirchen," *Kunstchronik* 43 (1990): 55–62.

72. Striker, "Applied Geometry," 35.

73. M. Velte, *Die Anwendung der Quatratur und Triangulatur be der Grund- und Aufrissgestaltung der gotischen Kirchen* (Basel, 1951); H. R. Hahnloser, *Villard d'Honnecourt* (Graz-Vienna, 1934), among others.

74. Buchwald, "Sardis Church E," fig. 4; note the discrepancies between the foundation grid and the more regular measurements of the superstructure.

75. H. Hallensleben, "Untersuchungen zur Genesis und Typologie des 'Mistratypus,'" *Marburger Jahrbuch für Kunstwissenschaft* 18 (1969): 105–18, esp. 113–15.

76. Buchwald, "Geometry," 298–99 and figs. 11–12.

77. Kuniholm and Striker, "Dendrochronology," 14–15 and fig. 8.

78. Ousterhout, *Kariye*, 24 and pl. 49.

79. Ibid., 45–46. The dome was rebuilt in the fourteenth century, and the upper portion replaced in the seventeenth century, but it seems to reflect the proportions of the twelfth-century dome; its height is just under eighteen meters.

80. N. K. Mutsopulos, "Harmonische Bauschnitte in der Kirchen vom Typus kreuzförmigen Innenbaus im Griechischen Kernland," *BZ* 55 (1962): 274–91; my illustrations are his figs. 20 (Hagios Ioannes Theologos, Athens) and 21 (Panagia Chalkeon, Thessaloniki).

81. Striker, "Applied Geometry," 35.

82. Buchwald, "Geometry," 299–300 and fig. 13.

83. But see H. Buchwald, "Lascarid Architecture," *JöB* 28 (1979): 261–96.

84. A. Van Millingen, *Byzantine Churches in Constantinople* (London, 1912), 212–16; also R. Ousterhout, "Some Notes on the Construction of Christos ho Pantepoptes (Eski Imaret Camii) in Istanbul," *DChAE* 16 (1991–92): 47–56.

85. K. Weitzmann, *Ancient Book Illumination* (Cambridge, Mass., 1959), 8–10; D. Sullivan, "Technical Illustration and Neo-Platonic Levels of Reality in Vaticanus Graecus 1605," *BSCA* 19 (1993): 96–97.

86. *Poliorcetica*, chap. 30.

87. Ibid., chap. 38.

88. Ibid.

89. Ibid., chap. 29.

Chapter Four

1. *Typikon* of the Kosmosoteira monastery, chap. 75; trans. N. P. Ševčenko in *BMFD* (forthcoming).

2. Ibid., chap. 89. See N. P. Ševčenko, "The Tomb of Isaak Komnenos at Pherrai," *GOTR* 29 (1984): 135–40. The architectural form and the implications of the "extension" are discussed at the end of this chapter.

3. Much of what follows is expanded from my essay, "Beyond Hagia Sophia: Originality in Byzantine Architecture," in *Originality in Byzantine Literature, Art and Music*, ed. A. Littlewood (Oxford, 1995), 167–85.

4. *Vita Basilii* (ed. Bekker), 321ff.; trans. in Mango, *Sources*, 192–99.

5. Ibid. The text names thirty-one churches that were restored in and around Constantinople.

6. Ibid.

7. Ibid.

8. It is interpreted this way by J. J. Norwich, *Byzantium: The Apogee* (New York, 1992), 96, who states, "Many other, humbler shrines were similarly restored and in several cases re-roofed, the older wooden roofs—always a dangerous fire risk—being replaced by new ones of stone, frequently domed."

9. Psellos, *Chronographia*, 3.14–19 (Sewter, 72). For what is known of the Peribleptos, see Janin, *Eglises et monastères*, 218–22.

10. Ibid.

11. *Chronographia*, 4.31 (Sewter, 105); see comments by Janin, *Eglises et monastères*, 286–89.

12. *Chronographia*, 4.31 (Sewter, 105).

13. Ibid., 6.185–88 (Sewter, 250–52). For the limited archaeological remains, see R. Demangel and E. Mamboury, *Le quartier des Manganes et la premier région de Constantinople* (Paris, 1939), 19–37; for an attempt at reconstruction, see Ch. Bouras, "Typologikes paratereseis sto Katholiko tes Mones ton Manganon," *AD* 31 (1976): 136–51.

14. *Chronographia*, 6.185–88 (Sewter, 250–52).

15. J.-P. Adam, "La basilique byzantine de Kydna de Lycie," *Revue archéologique* 1 (1977): 53–78.

16. C. S. Lightfoot and E. Ivison, "The Amorium Project: The 1995 Excavation Season," *DOP* 51 (1997): 291–300, esp. fig. B.

17. S. Eyice, "Amasra 'Büyükadasında bir Bizans kilisesi," *TTKB* 15 (1951): 469–96; I thank Y. Ötüken for observations on the site.

18. N. Fıratlı, "Découverte d'une église byzantine à Sébaste de Phrygie," *CA* 29 (1969): 151–56.

19. U. Peschlow, *Die Irenenkirche in Istanbul: Untersuchungen zur Architektur* (Tübingen, 1977), 212–13.

20. P. A. Mylonas, "Le plan initial du catholicon de la Grande-Lavra au Mont Athos et la genèse du type du catholicon athonite," *CA* 32 (1984): 89–112.

21. Ibid.

22. Ibid. But see S. Mamaloukos, "E architektonike tou Katholikou," in *Iera Megiste Mone Batopediou. Paradose—Istoria—Techne* (Mount Athos, 1996), 172, who notes, without further explanation, that at least the lower portions of the Vatopedi choroi are contemporaneous with the naos construction.

23. B. G. Barskij, *Stranstvovanija . . . Barskago po svjatym mjestam Vostoka* (St. Petersburg, 1887), vol. 3, pl. facing p. 76.

24. Mylonas, "Plan initial," 103, 108–9.

25. D. Oates, "A Summary Report on the Excavations of the Byzantine Institute in the Kariye Camii: 1957 and 1958," *DOP* 14 (1969): 223–31. For a fuller analysis, see Ousterhout, *Kariye*, 15–32, esp. 20–22.

26. Ousterhout, *Kariye*, 15–20. This interpretation of the archaeological evidence has recently been questioned in a review by C. Mango in *BZ* 83 (1990): 126–28.

27. Oates, "Summary Report," 226–28.

28. R. Ousterhout, "The Byzantine Church at Enez: Problems in Twelfth-Century Architecture," *JöB* 35 (1985): 262–80, esp. 267–70; also Ousterhout, *Kariye*, 31–32.

29. C. Mango, "The Monastery of St. Abercius at Kurşunlu (Elegmi) in Bithynia," *DOP* 22 (1968): 169–76; S. Eyice, "Remarques sur deux anciennes églises byzantines d'Istanbul: Koca Mustafa Paşa Camii et l'église du Yuşa Tepesi," in *Actes du XIe Congrès international d'etudes byzantines* (Thessaloniki, 1953), 190–95.

30. Bouras, *Nea Moni on Chios*, 21–32.

31. For the mosaics, see D. Mouriki, *The Mosaics of Nea Moni on Chios* (Athens, 1985).

32. R. Ousterhout, "Originality in Byzantine Architecture: The Case of Nea Moni," *JSAH* 51 (1992): 48–60, esp. figs. 10–11 (view toward sanctuary; detail of revetments).

33. This problem is discussed in greater detail in ibid.

34. H. Maguire, "The Mosaics of Nea Moni: An Imperial Reading," *DOP* 46 (1992): 205–14.

35. See A. K. Orlandos, *Monuments byzantins de Chios*, vol. 2, *Planches* (Athens, 1930), for numerous illustrations; see also Ch. Bouras, "Twelfth and Thirteenth Century Variations of the Single Domed Octagon Plan," *DChAE* 9 (1977–79): 21–34.

36. P. A. Mylonas has come to the same conclusion about Nea Moni; see P. A. Mylonas, "Domike erevna sto ekklesiastiko syngrotema tou Osiou Louka Phokidos," *Archaiologia* 36 (1990): 6–30, esp. 19–20 and n. 51.

37. Mylonas, "Plan initial," 95; see also Ćurčić, "Architectural Significance," 94–110.

38. Mylonas, "Plan initial," 102–3.

39. T. Papazotos, "The Identification of the Church of 'Profitis Elias' in Thessaloniki," *DOP* 45 (1991): 121–28.

40. G. Velenis, "Thirteenth-Century Architecture in the Despotate of Epirus: The Origins of

the School," in *Studenica et l'art byzantin autour de l'année 1200* (Belgrade, 1988), 279–85, esp. 280–81; L. Theis, *Die Architektur der Kirche der Panagia Paregoretissa in Arta/Epirus* (Amsterdam, 1991), esp. 76–77.

41. Velenis, "Thirteenth-Century Architecture," 280–81; Theis, *Paregoretissa*, 56–71.

42. Hallensleben, "Untersuchungen zur Genesis," 105–18.

43. Van Millingen, *Byzantine Churches*, 219–42; J. Ebersolt and A. Thiers, *Les églises byzantines de Constantinople* (Paris, 1913), 185–207; and, for clarification of the chronology of construction, A. H. S. Megaw, "Notes on Recent Work of the Byzantine Institute in Istanbul," *DOP* 17 (1963): 335–64. See also L. Butler, "The Pantocrator Monastery: An Imperial Foundation" (M.A. thesis, Oberlin College, 1980); and R. Cormack, *Writing in Gold: Byzantine Society and Its Icons* (London, 1985), 194–214.

44. For further observations, see R. Ousterhout, "The Byzantine Churches of Constantinople in Context," *DOP*, forthcoming.

45. I. Zonaras, *Epitome historiarum*, 3 vols., in *CSHB*, 3:767; see also P. Magdalino, "The Byzantine Aristocratic *Oikos*," in *The Byzantine Aristocracy IX to XIII Centuries*, BAR International Series 221, ed. M. Angold (Oxford, 1984), 92–111.

46. Ousterhout, *Kariye*, 91–96.

47. I. Ševčenko, "Theodore Metochites, the Chora, and the Intellectual Trends of His Time," in *The Kariye Djami*, vol. 4, ed. P. A. Underwood (Princeton, 1975), 17–55.

48. Ousterhout, *Kariye*, 96–100; frontispiece and pl. 110.

49. A. H. S. Megaw, "The Original Form of the Theotokos Church of Constantine Lips," *DOP* 18 (1964): 279–98.

50. Ćurčić, "Architectural Significance," 94–110.

51. A. I. Komech, *Drevnerusskoe Zodchestvo Kontsa X–Nachala XII v.* (Moscow, 1987), 181–232; H. Logvin, *Kiev's Hagia Sophia* (Kiev, 1971), 8–12.

52. Mango, *Byzantine Architecture*, 324–28, emphasizes the inherently Byzantine character, stating, "I fail to see any feature of St. Sophia that is not Byzantine" (325).

53. Komech, *Drevnerusskoe*; Mango, *Byzantine Architecture*, 324–40.

54. S. Ćurčić, *Gračanica: King Milutin's Church and Its Place in Late Byzantine Architecture*, (University Park, Pa., 1979), esp. 71–74.

55. Kuniholm and Striker, "Dendrochronology."

56. Ćurčić, *Gračanica*, 73 n. 15; *Thessaloniki and Its Monuments* (Thessaloniki, 1985), 95–98.

57. Ousterhout, *Kariye*.

58. Ibid., esp. 142–44.

59. Macridy et al., "Monastery of Lips," 251–98; H. Belting, C. Mango, and D. Mouriki, *The Mosaics and Frescoes of St. Mary Pammakaristos (Fethiye Camii) at Istanbul* (Washington, D.C. 1987), esp. 1–38.

60. Bouras, "Twelfth and Thirteenth Century Variations," 21–34.

61. Ibid., 28–30.

62. For illustrations, see Orlandos, *Monuments byzantins de Chios*, 2:30–34, 42–45, 53–54. The projected text volume was never published.

63. Information about the tombs discussed here is limited. Although it was common to have a tomb marker above the floor, the actual burials in this period would have been *below* the floor.

Of the burials discussed here in Constantinople and Pherrai, no archaeological examination has been conducted.

64. See the comments by S. Ćurčić, "Medieval Royal Tombs in the Balkans: An Aspect of the 'East or West' Question," *GOTR* 29 (1984): 175–94, esp. 183, who suggests that such restrictions ultimately reflect the controversy following the burial of Emperor Constantine in the church of the Holy Apostles.

65. Macridy et al., "Monastery of Lips," figs. 70–71.

66. Van Millingen, *Byzantine Churches*, 201–7.

67. Ćurčić, "Twin-Domed Narthex," 333–44.

68. Ćurčić, "Architectural Significance," 102–3.

69. See most recently, I. Sinkević, "Alexios Angelos Komnenos: A Patron Without History?" *Gesta* 35 (1996): 34–42.

70. Ćurčić, "Architectural Significance," 102–3.

71. For the *typikon*, see Gautier, "Typikon," 1–145.

72. Megaw, "Recent Work," esp. 343–44, who believed that Eirene died in 1124; but see P. Gautier, "L'obituaire du typikon du Pantocrator," *REB* 27 (1969): 247–48, for clarification.

73. Gautier, "Typikon," lines 728–32; for the chronology, see Megaw, "Recent Work," esp. 344.

74. The four arcosolia are framed by projecting masonry below the cornice. It appears they were understood as a set.

75. A *verde antico* sarcophagus that once stood in front of the church is sometimes said to be that of Eirene; it is now in the narthex of Hagia Sophia. See E. Grosvenor, *Constantinople* (Boston, 1895), 2:426. It would have been too large to fit into any of the arcosolia in the church.

76. Gautier, "Typikon," lines 883–98.

77. Ibid., lines 270–88.

78. Niketas Choniates, *Nicetae Choniatae historia*, ed. J. L. van Dieten, 2 vols. (Berlin, 1975), 1:115; John Kinnamos, *Epitome*, ed. A. Meineke, *CSHB*, 202; also P. Magdalino, *The Empire of Manuel I Komnenos 1143–1180* (Cambridge, 1993), 65, 117.

79. C. Mango, "Notes on Byzantine Monuments: Tomb of Manuel I Comnenos," *DOP* 23–24 (1969–70): 372–75; and C. Mango, "Three Imperial Sarcophagi Discovered in 1750," *DOP* 16 (1962): 397–402.

80. Gautier, "Typikon," lines 867–68.

81. Ibid., lines 863–64.

82. Ibid., lines 867–68.

83. In addition to the daily lighting of lamps and saying of the *Trisagion* and commemorative prayers at the tombs of the founders, the *heroon* was used for liturgy three days a week and for the Saturday commemorations of the dead, in which the names of those to be remembered were recited during the services. A more elaborate ceremony and procession occurred on the anniversary of their deaths, in which the icon of the Hodegitria was ceremonially installed in the *heroon*, with a vigil and a liturgy in its presence; Gautier, "Typikon," lines 883–903.

84. R. Ousterhout, "Temporal Structuring in the Chora Parekklesion," *Gesta* 34 (1995): 63–76.

85. S. Sinos, *Die Klosterkirche der Kosmosoteira in Bera (Vira)* (Munich, 1985); and my review in *Speculum* 63 (1988): 229–31.

86. L. Petit, "Typikon du monastère de la Kosmosotira près d'Ainos (1152)," *IRAIK* 13 (1908): 17–75; now superseded by G. Papazoglou, *Typikon Isaakiou Alexiou Komnenou tes Mones Theotokou tes Kosmosoteiras (1151/52)* (Komotini, 1994), 31–154. Citations are from N. P. Ševčenko's translation in *BMFD* (forthcoming).

87. *Typikon*, chaps. 89–90; see also discussion by Ševčenko, "Tomb of Isaak," 135–40.

88. See Ousterhout, *Kariye*, 20–32, 97–100.

89. Various scholars have stated firmly that Isaak's tomb was in the narthex of the Chora; see T. Uspenskij, "L'octateuque de la Bibliothèque du Sérail à Constantinople," *IRAIK* 12 (1907): 21–22; Janin, *Eglises et monastères*, 534; and K. Varzos, *He Genealogia ton Komnenon* (Thessaloniki, 1984), 252. Although this location seems most likely, their claim is ultimately based on Uspenskij's misreading of the Kosmosoteira *typikon*.

90. *Typikon*, chap. 89; see also P. A. Underwood, "The Deisis Mosaic in the Kariye Cami at Istanbul," in *Late Classical and Medieval Studies in Honor of A. M. Friend, Jr.*, ed. K. Weitzmann (Princeton, 1955), 254–60.

91. *Typikon*, chaps. 89–90.

92. See Sinos, *Klosterkirche*, pls. 6, 8, 10, 63, 71. A line of foundations was once visible along the north side of the church, but this may be the remains of an Ottoman portico. The west facade of the church has suffered from much rebuilding and the area to the west of the church is paved with concrete, making examination difficult. The Twelfth Ephoreia of Byzantine Antiquities has recently undertaken a thorough cleaning and restoration of the building, and I am grateful to them for allowing me access to it.

93. *Typikon*, chap. 107.

94. R. Ousterhout, "Where Was the Tomb of Isaak Komnenos?" *BSCA* 11 (1985): 34.

95. *Typikon*, chap. 86.

96. Sinos, *Klosterkirche*, 204, pl. 56.

97. Ibid., 202–3, pl. 140.

98. See Ćurčić, "Medieval Royal Tombs," fig. 1.

99. *Typikon*, chap. 90.

100. See comments by Ćurčić, *Gračanica*, 130–32.

101. Ćurčić, "Medieval Royal Tombs," 183–84, fig. 7.

102. For the identification of the founder, see C. Mango in Belting, Mango, and Mouriki, *Mosaics and Frescoes*, 5–10. The church was studied simultaneously by H. Hallensleben, "Untersuchungen zur Baugeschichte der ehemaligen Pammakaristoskirche, der heutigen Fethiye Camii in Istanbul," *IM* 13–14 (1963–64): 128–93; and C. Mango and E. J. W. Hawkins, "Report on Field Work in Istanbul and Cyprus, 1962–63," *DOP* 18 (1964): 319–33, with slightly different conclusions. We here accept Mango's date but Hallensleben's reconstruction of the original church.

103. Mango, in Belting, Mango, and Mouriki, *Mosaics and Frescoes*, 39–42.

104. Macridy et al., "Monastery of Lips," 251–315 passim.

105. Hallensleben, "Untersuchungen zur Baugeschicte," 170–73, figs. 5–7; for the section, see Ebersolt and Thiers, *Églies byzantines*, pl. 56/2.

106. See the discussion in Magdalino, *Empire of Manuel*, 180–227.

107. Janin, *Églises et monastères*, 517–18.

Chapter Five

1. K. Theocharidou, "Symbole ste Melete tes Paragoges Oikodomikon Keramikon Proionton sta Byzantina kai Metabysantina Chronia," *DChAE* 13 (1988): 97–112, provides a useful overview of brick production.

2. K. Harmenopoulos, *Procheiron Nomon e Exabiblos*, ed. G. Pitsake (Athens, 1971), 2.15, p. 116; cited by Theocharidou, "Symbole," 98–99.

3. Theophanes, *Chronographia*, am. 6258 (Mango and Scott, 607–9).

4. *Actes de Lavra* (Paris, 1970), 1.4:23–24: "ergasterion pros keramon kataskeven epitedeion meta kai chorafiaion topon kai tes kathedras auton te thalasse geitonouses . . ."

5. *Actes d'Iviron* (Paris, 1985), 4:117–29, 12:175–79.

6. Theocharidou, "Symbole," 100–101, outlines the process.

7. Vatican Library, MS gr. 747, fol. 78v; reproduced in *ODB*, 1:322.

8. J.-P. Adam, *Roman Building: Materials and Technique* (Bloomington, Ind., 1995), 58–65.

9. Theocharidou, "Symbole," 100.

10. Ibid., 106 and fig. 16; Rappoport, *Churches*, 10–30.

11. For example, Vatican Library, MS gr. 746, fol. 61r. The illustration in the Smyrna Octateuch, fol. 24r, is almost identical; see D.-C. Hesseling, *Miniatures de l'Octateuque grec de Smyrne* (Leiden, 1909).

12. Demus, *Mosaics of Norman Sicily*, fig. 32b.

13. Theocharidou, "Symbole," 104.

14. Rappoport, *Churches*, 29.

15. Ibid., 30.

16. J. B. Ward Perkins, "Notes on the Structure and Building Methods of Early Byzantine Architecture," in *The Great Palace of the Byzantine Emperors, Second Report* (St. Andrews, 1954), 52–104, esp. 55–57; also Mango, *Architecture*, 11.

17. Theocharidou, "Symbole," fig. 17.

18. For brick dimensions in Constantinople, see most recently Y. Kâhya, "İstanbul Bizans Mimarsinde Tuğla Boyutları Üzerine," in *Prof. Doğan Kuban'a Armağan* (Istanbul, 1996), 171–82.

19. Adam, *Building*, 64–65.

20. C. Mango, "Byzantine Brickstamps," *AJA* 54 (1950): 19–27; A. Kazhdan, "Brick," *ODB*, 1:322–23; more recently J. Bardill, "A Catalogue of Stamped Bricks in the Ayasofya Collection," *Anatolian Archaeology* 1 (1995): 28–29.

21. S. Hill, "The Brickstamps," in *Excavations at Saraçhane in Istanbul*, ed. R. M. Harrison (Princeton, 1986), 1:207–25, esp. 224–25.

22. Rappoport, *Churches*, 31–46.

23. See Adam, *Building*, 65–76, for an excellent introduction.

24. Ibid., 69–70.

25. Rappoport, *Churches*, 59–68.

26. O. Lampsidou, *O ek Pontou Osios Nikon o Metanoeite*. Pegai tes Istorias ton Ellenon tou Pontou, vol. 4 (Athens, 1982), 251–56, esp. 253–54.

27. *AASS* (Nov. 3), 527F: "lakkon poiesai eis kausin asbestou."

28. E. Reusche, "Geschichte der Bau- und Baustofftechnik als Hilfswissenschaft," *Zograf* 13 (1982): 53–58, fig. 6; A. Deroko, *Monumentalna i dekorativna arhitektura u srednje-vekovnoj Srbiji* (Belgrade, 1962), 28.

29. G. J. Vzdornov, *Kievskaia Psaltir 1397 goda* (Moscow, 1978): MS 1252F, fol. 134r, St. Petersburg Public Library; note also MS Taphou 53, fol. 138v, Greek Patriarchal Library, Jerusalem; Kievski Psalter, MS 1252F VI, fol. 134r, St. Petersburg Public Library; Tomic Psalter, MS 2752, fol. 163v, Moscow Historical Museum. Workers with hods and trowels also appear in the Serbian Psalter, Cod. Slav. 4, fol. 124v, Bayerische Staatsbibliothek, Munich.

30. Demus, *Mosaic Decoration of San Marco*, fig. 72; Demus, *Mosaics of Norman Sicily*, figs. 32B, 102.

31. J. Waldbaum, *Metalwork from Sardis* (Cambridge, Mass., 1983), nos. 106–7.

32. Adam, *Building*, 72–73.

33. Rappoport, *Churches*, 65.

34. R. Folk and S. Valastro, Jr., "Successful Technique for Dating of Lime Mortar by Carbon-14," *Journal of Field Archaeology* 3 (1976): 203–8.

35. Adam, *Building*, 73.

36. Vitruvius, *Architecture*, 2.5.1 (Morgan, 45).

37. F. Dölger, *Aus den Schatzkammern des Heiligen Berges* (Munich, 1948), 102, translates *ostrakon* as mussel shells, although potsherds would make much more sense in this context.

38. Rappoport, *Churches*, 66.

39. A. Çakmak and R. Mark, "Mechanical Tests of Material from the Hagia Sophia Dome," *DOP* 48 (1994): 277–79.

40. G. Baronio, L. Binda, and C. Tedeschi, "Thick Mortar Joints in Byzantine Buildings: Study of Their Composition and Mechanical Behaviour," in *Ancient Structures*, 235–44.

41. Ibid., 238.

42. *Anastylose ton byzantinon kai metabyzantinon mnemeion ste Thessalonike* (Thessaloniki, 1985), 39–46, 77–83, 91–101.

43. Vatican Library, MS gr. 746, fol. 61v. The Smyrna Octateuch, fol. 24v, is almost identical; see Hesseling, *Miniatures*, pl. 41.

44. Dölger, *Aus den Schatzkammern*, 102.

45. Waldbaum, *Metalwork*, nos. 109–10.

46. F. Halkin, "Invention des reliques et miracles de Sainte Photeine la Samaritaine," in *Hagiographica inedita decem* (Brepols-Turnhout, 1989), 121; translated in A.-M. Talbot, "The Posthumous Miracles of St. Photeine," *AB* 112 (1994): 98.

47. To be discussed further in the next chapter; Noret, *Vitae duae antiquae*, Vita A, 234, p. 113.

48. Baronio, Binda, and Tedeschi, "Thick Mortar Joints," 243–44; also M. Karaveziroglou, C. Barboutis, and V. Kranas, "Behaviour of Masonry with Full Bricks and Lime Mortars," in *Ancient Structures*, 225–33.

49. Ward Perkins, "Notes on the Structure," 53–57.

50. Information from K. Erguvanlı et al., "The Significance of Research on Old Quarries for the Restoration of Historic Buildings with Special Reference to the Marmara Region, Turkey," in *The Engineering Geology of Ancient Works, Monuments and Historical Sites*, ed. P. Marinos and G. Koukis (Rotterdam, 1988), 2:631–38.

51. A. Van Millingen, *Byzantine Constantinople* (London, 1899), 44.

52. A. Kazhdan, "Mason," *ODB*, 2:1311–12.

53. *Chronographia*, 3.15 (Sewter, 72).

54. Bouras, *Nea Moni*, 148–49.

55. P. Diaconu and E. Zah, "Les carrières de pierre de Păcuiul lui Soare," *Dacia* 15 (1971): 289–306.

56. Ibid.

57. R. Ousterhout, "The 1996 Survey at Akhisar-Çanlı Kilise," in *XV. AST* (Ankara, 1998), 47 and fig. 4.

58. N. Asgari, "Roman and Early Byzantine Marble Quarries of Proconessus," in *Proceedings of the 10th International Congress of Classical Archaeology* (Ankara, 1978), 1:467–80, outlines the process. See also J. B. Ward Perkins, "Quarries and Stoneworking in the Early Middle Ages: The Heritage of the Ancient World," *Settimane di Studi del Centro Italiano di Studi sull'alto Medioevo* 17, vol. 2 (1971): 525–44; and Adam, *Building*, 20–43.

59. Waldbaum, *Metalwork*, 47–54. Similar tools were used for woodworking. An early fourteenth-century poem by Manuel Philes lists the tools of carpenters (*tektones*): the chisel, the drill, the axe, the saw, and the cord painted red with clay (*spartion kokkinon ek ges ostrakon*). It is not entirely clear what the last item is. Modern carpenters utilize a string coated in chalk, which can be stretched taut and then snapped to mark a straight line onto a surface prior to cutting. The red cord may be something similar to this, used to mark surfaces. Manuel Philes, *Carmina*, ed. E. Miller, 2 vols. (Paris, 1855–57), 2:182. For this reference, I thank Prof. K.-P. Metschke, whose "Builders and Building in Late Byzantine Constantinople" will appear in the symposium volume *Byzantine Constantinople: Monuments, Topography, and Everyday Life*, ed. N. Necipoğlu (Istanbul, forthcoming).

60. N. Thierry, "Illustration de la construction d'une église. Les sculptures de Korogo (Georgie)," in *Artistes, Artisans, et Production Artistique au Moyen Age*, ed. X. Barral I Altet (Rennes, 1983), 1136–39; R. Mepisachvili, "Le monument de Korogo," *Sovetskaia Archeologiia* 4 (1969): 219–33 (in Russian with French summary).

61. Mango, *Architecture*, 12–14.

62. Theophanes Continuatus, ed. I. Bekker, *CSHB*, 139ff.; trans. in Mango, *Sources*, 161–65.

63. A. Dworakowska, *Quarries in Roman Provinces* (Wrocław, 1983), 26, for quarries in western Asia Minor; also A. Dworakowska, *Quarries in Ancient Greece* (Wrocław, 1975); L. Moens, P. de Paepe, and M. Waelkens, "Survey in the White Marble Quarries of Anatolia," in *IV. AST* (Ankara, 1987), 113–126; J.-P. Sodini, A. Lambraki, and T. Kozelj, *Les carrières à l'époque paléochrétienne*, in *Aliki* (Paris, 1980), 1:79–143.

64. Asgari, "Roman and Early Byzantine Marble Quarries."

65. A. Kazhdan, "Prokonnesos," *ODB*, 3:1730–31.

66. P. Magdalino, *Constantinople médiévale* (Paris, 1997), 46.

67. Megaw, "Notes on Recent Work," 344–47.

68. W. Müller-Wiener, "Spoliennutzungen in Istanbul," in *Beiträge zur Altertumskunde Kleinasiens. Festschrift für Kurt Bittel*, ed. R. Boehmer and H. Hauptmann (Mainz, 1983), 369–82.

69. K. Rheidt, *Die Byzantinische Wohnstadt*, Altertümer von Pergamon, 15, no. 2 (Berlin, 1991).

70. Leo the Deacon, *Historiae libri X*, ed. C. B. Hase (Bonn, 1828), 128–9; C. Mango, *The Brazen House* (Copenhagen, 1959), 148.

71. *Historia*, ed. I. Bekker, *CSHB*, 580–81; trans. in Mango, *Sources*, 236–37.

72. Angold, "Inventory," 254–66.

73. Ousterhout, *Kariye*, 39–42.

74. For the Pantokrator example, see Van Millingen, *Byzantine Churches*, fig. 75.

75. Ousterhout, *Kariye*, 137–41.

76. O. Hjort, "The Sculpture of the Kariye Camii," *DOP* 33 (1979): pls. 90–91. Note other two-sided pieces, such as ibid., pls. 93–96.

77. Ousterhout, "Byzantine Church at Enez," fig. 26.

78. Pekak, "Zeytinbagı/Trilye," 1:307–38.

79. As does H. Belting, "Eine Gruppe konstantinopler Reliefs aus dem 11. Jahrhundert," *Pantheon* 30 (1972): 263–71; but see Hjort, "Sculpture," 237–42.

80. Ch. Bakirtzis, "To Episkopeion ton Philippon," in *E Kavala kai e Perioche tes* (Kavala, 1987), 149–57.

81. C. Pulak, "1993 Sualtı Araştırması," in *XII. AST* (Ankara, 1994), 1–12, esp. 3–4; see also G. Kapitan, "The Church Wreck off Marzamemi," *Archaeology* 22 (1969): 122–32, for a similar wreck, interpreted as the furnishings for a church under construction.

82. As J. W. Barker suggested in his paper, "Byzantine War Trophies and Venetian Political Iconography," Dumbarton Oaks Symposium, 1993. For another suggestion of an ideological context for *spolia*, see D. Kinney, "Spolia from the Baths of Caracalla in Sta. Maria in Trastevere," *Art Bulletin* 68 (1986): 379–97.

83. S. Redford, "The Seljuqs of Rum and the Antique," *Muqarnas* 10 (1993): 149–56.

84. R. Ousterhout, "Ethnic Identity and Cultural Appropriation in Early Ottoman Architecture," *Muqarnas* 13 (1995): 48–62.

85. As discussed in Chapter 4.

86. Mango and Hawkins, "Additional Notes," 310 and fig. 39.

87. For further discussion of interior decorations, see Chapter 8.

88. Sinos, *Klosterkirche*, 92–93.

89. Ousterhout, "Byzantine Church at Enez," 265–66 and figs. 11–12.

90. *BHG* 236a; *PG* 127, col. 481D–484A.

91. For Lazaros, see *AASS* (Nov. 3), 403B; for Dorotheos, see *BHG* 979, col. 581B.

92. Halkin, *Hagiographica*, 120; Talbot, "Posthumous Miracles," 96–97 and n. 32.

93. R. Ginouvès and R. Martin, *Dictionnaire méthodique de l'architecture grecque et romaine* (Rome and Paris, 1985), 1:113–14 and pls. 27–29.

94. A. K. Orlandos, *He xylostegos palaiochristianike basilike* (Athens, 1954), esp. 262–338 and fig. 313 (Basilica A, Philippi).

95. Macridy et al., "Monastery of Lips," figs. 13, 54, 56.

96. See Adam, *Building*, 213–15, for the Roman system; T. Gregory and S. Claire, "Tiles," *ODB*, 3:2084–85.

97. Rheidt, *Byzantinische Wohnstadt*, pl. 14, esp. fig. 12; also K. Rheidt, "Bautechnik und Bautradition im byzantinischen Pergamon," in *Bautechnik der Antike* (Mainz, 1991), 189–96.

98. Theocharidou, "Symbole," 100 and fig. 2.

99. M. M. Mango et al., "Lead," *ODB*, 2:1199–1200.

100. Sinos, *Klosterkirche*, 152 and fig. 93.

101. Ousterhout, *Kariye*, 88–90.

102. Mango, *Architecture*, fig. 218.

103. S. Vogiatzes, "Neotera Stoicheia gia ten Oikodomike Istoria tou Katholikou tes Neas Mones Chiou," *DChAE* 14 (1989): 159–72.

104. Lefort et al., *Actes d'Iviron*, 1:61–63; following the *vita* of George.

105. V. Djurić, "Architects et maîtres maçons de Dubrovnik dans la Serbie médiévale," *Zbornik za umetnosto zgodovino* 3 (1967): 87–106; in Serbian with French summary, 104–6.

106. Van Millingen, *Byzantine Churches*, 227–28.

107. Ousterhout, "Byzantine Churches" forthcoming; also R. Ousterhout, Z. Ahunbay, and M. Ahundbay, "Study and Restoration of the Zeyrek Camii in Istanbul: First Report, 1997–98," *DOP* (forthcoming).

108. Rappoport, *Churches*, 149–56.

109. Ibid., 149; in such citations, the words for *tin* and *lead* are sometimes confused, but tin would not withstand the cold Russian winter.

110. Ousterhout, *Kariye*, 88–90.

111. W. Loerke et al., "Window," *ODB*, 3:2198–99.

112. For a recent survey of the evidence on glass production, see J. Henderson and M. M. Mango, "Glass at Medieval Constantinople: Preliminary Scientific Evidence," in *Constantinople and Its Hinterland*, ed. C. Mango and G. Dagron (Aldershot, 1995), 333–56.

113. G. Davidson, *The Minor Objects*, Corinth: Results of Excavations Conducted by the American School of Classical Studies at Athens, vol. 12 (Princeton, 1952), 144, nos. 1061–66.

114. A. von Saldern, *Ancient and Byzantine Glass from Sardis* (Cambridge, Mass., 1980), 98–102.

115. Halkin, *Hagiographica*, 122–24; Talbot, "Posthumous Miracles," 100–102.

116. H. Franz, "Transennae als Fensterverschluss, ihre Entwicklung von der frühchristlichen biz zur islamischen Zeit," *IM* 8 (1958): 65–81.

117. Macridy et al., "Monastery of Lips," 266–67 and fig. 58.

118. E. Stikas, *To Oikodomikon Chronikon tes Mones Osiou Louka Phokidos* (Athens, 1970), 188, fig. 98, and pl. 122.

119. Hallensleben, "Untersuchungen zur Baugeschichte," 180–81 and fig. 11.

120. Ibid.

121. Ousterhout, *Kariye*, 89.

122. Ibid., fig. 96.

123. Ibid., fig. 94.

124. Ćurčić, *Gračanica*, 61–62, figs. 64, 77, 78.

125. S. Gabelić, "Lesnovski Prozop y Narodnom Muzeiy," *Zbornik Narodnog Muzeia* (Belgrade) 15, no. 2 (1994): 37–41.

126. S. Visots'kii, "Vikonna rama ta shibki Kiivs'koi Sofii," in *Kiivs'ka starovina* (Kiev, 1972), 54; cited in Rappoport, *Churches*, 142–44.

127. Megaw, "Notes," 349–64.

128. Ibid., 349–67.

129. Ibid., 364–65.

130. Henderson and Mango, "Glass," 349–56; additional information from an unpublished analysis by Robert Brill of the Corning Museum, courtesy of Susan Boyd of Dumbarton Oaks, who organized an exhibit of the Byzantine stained glass from the Chora and Pantokrator in 1998.

131. Megaw, "Notes," 349–64; G. Vikan, "Stained Glass," *ODB*, 2:853–54, with additional bibliography. Note also the evidence for painted stained glass from the early Umayyad palace at Khirbet al Mafjar in Palestine; see N. Brosh, "Glass Window Fragments from Khirbat Al-Mafjar," in *Annales du 11e congrès de l'Association internationale pour l'histoire du verre* (Amsterdam, 1990), 247–56. I thank Susan Boyd for this reference.

Chapter Six

1. R. Mark, ed., *Architectural Technology up to the Scientific Revolution* (Cambridge, Mass., 1993), 16–50, for preliminary remarks on soils and foundation systems.

2. R. Ousterhout, "The 1994 Survey at Akhisar-Çanlı Kilise," in *XII. AST* (Ankara, 1996), 165–80; and Ötüken and Ousterhout, "Byzantine Church," 85–92.

3. Ousterhout, *Kariye*, fig. 121.

4. Macridy et al., "Monastery of Lips," 260–61.

5. Buchwald, "Church E," 273–75.

6. Ibid., 273.

7. Ibid., 274–75.

8. A. Pasadaios, *Epi duo byzantinon mnemeion tes Konstantinoupoleos agnostou onomatos* (Athens, 1965), 56–108.

9. S. Eyice, "Tuzla'nin Değirmenaltı Mevkiinde bir Bizans Kalıntısı," *Sanat Tarihi Yıllğı* 5 (1973), 27–78.

10. Ousterhout, *Kariye*, fig. 73.

11. Buchwald, "Church E," 274.

12. R. Ousterhout, "A Byzantine Church at Didymoteicho and Its Frescoes," *Milion* 5 (1999): forthcoming.

13. Buchwald, "Church E," 274.

14. S. Mikailov, "Arkheologicheski materiali ot Pliska," *Izvestiia na arkheologicheskiia institut* (Sofia) 20 (1955): 114–15; and S. Mikailvov, "Dvortsovata ts'rkva v Pliska," 250–51, in the same volume.

15. Rappoport, *Churches*, 89–98, figs. 45–50.

16. Ibid., 92.

17. Ousterhout, "Byzantine Church at Enez," 272–76.

18. Ousterhout, "Some Notes," 47–56.

19. Magdalino, *Constantinople médiévale.*

20. Ousterhout, *Kariye*, 12–15.

21. C. L. Striker and Y. D. Kuban, *Kalenderhane in Istanbul: The Buildings, Their History, Architecture, and Decoration* (Mainz, 1997), esp. 95.

22. S. Eyice, "Encore une fois l'église d'Alexis Apokauque à Selymbria (=Silivri)," *Byzantion* 48 (1978): 406–16.

23. Y. Ötüken and R. Ousterhout, "Notes on the Monuments of Turkish Thrace," *Anatolian Studies* 39 (1989): 138–39.

24. A. M. Mansel, *Side* (Ankara, 1978), 257–91.

25. M. I. Tunay et al., "Kurşunlu Hagios Aberkios Manastırı," *Rehber Dünyası* (August 1996): 19–25.

26. Striker, *Myrelaion*, 25–31.

27. Ibid., fig. 7.

28. Müller-Wiener, *Bildlexikon*, 188–89.

29. Ibid., 108.

30. Ibid., 81.

31. Mylonas, "Domike," 6–30.

32. Mijatev, *Mittelalterliche Baukunst*, 160–62, 190–92.

33. H. Schäfer, *Die Gül Camii in Istanbul: Ein Beitrag zur mittelbyzantinischen Kirchenarchitektur Konstantinopels* (Tübingen, 1973), 37–61.

34. Striker, *Myrelaion*, 13–16, figs. 26, 67–76.

35. H. Tezcan, *Topkapı Sarai ve Çevresinin Bizans Devri Arkeolojisi* (Istanbul, 1989).

36. Mango and Hawkins, "Report," 319–33.

37. See also Tezcan, *Topkapı*, figs. 15–15a; W. Müller-Wiener, "Zur Lage der Allerheiligenkirche in Konstantinopel," in *Lebendige Altertumswissenschaft. Festgabe zur Vollendung des 70. Lebensjahres von Herman Vetters* (Mainz, 1985), 333–36; A. Berger, "Die mittelbyzantinische Kirche bei der Mehmet Fatih Camii in Istanbul," IM 47 (1997): 455–60.

38. R. Demangel and E. Mamboury, *Le Quartier des Manganes et le premièr région de Constantinople* (Paris, 1939).

39. A. Ricci, "The Road from Baghdad to Byzantium and the Case of the Bryas Palace in Istanbul," in *Byzantium in the Ninth Century: Dead or Alive?*, ed. L. Brubaker (Aldershot, 1998), 131–49.

40. Ousterhout, *Kariye*, 61 and figs. 92–93.

41. Ibid., 36.

42. Ibid., 127; B. Aran, "The Church of Saint Theodosia and the Monastery of Christ Euergetes," *JöB* 28 (1979): 211–28.

43. G. Velenis, *Ermeneia tou Exoterikou Diakosmou ste Byzantine Architektonike* (Thessaloniki, 1984), 1–12, 45–49.

44. Ousterhout, "The 1994 Survey," 167.

45. Ötüken and Ousterhout, "Byzantine Church," 85–91.

46. R. Ousterhout, "The Palaeologan Architecture of Didymoteicho," *Byzantinische Forschungen* 14 (1989): 429–43.

47. Krautheimer, *Early Christian*, 378–89.

48. For illustrations, see *Thessaloniki and Its Monuments* (Thessaloniki, 1985), 99–120.

49. R. Ousterhout, "Observations on the Recessed Brick Technique during the Palaeologan Period," *AD* 39 (1990): 163–70, for much of what follows. See also Y. Ötüken, "Bizans Duvar Tekniğinde Tektonik ve Estetik Çözümler," *Vakıflar Dergisi* (1990): 395–410.

50. Velenis, *Ermeneia*, 65–106; Sinos, *Klosterkirche*, 90; Y. Ötüken, "İsa Kapı Mescidi und Medresesi in Istanbul" (Ph.D. diss., University of Bonn, 1974), 105–17, esp. 113.

51. Velenis, *Ermeneia*, 68; U. Peschlow, "Neue Beobachtungen zur Architektur und Ausstattung der Koimesiskirche in Iznik," *IM* 22 (1972): 164–65; Krautheimer, *Early Christian*, 339.

52. Velenis, *Ermeneia*, 66–81.

53. Ousterhout, "Some Notes," 49–50.

54. F. Sear, *Roman Architecture* (Ithaca, N.Y., 1982), fig. 40.

55. As Sinos has suggested, *Klosterkirche*, 90.

56. Ousterhout, "Observations," 164–66.

57. Ibid., 165–66.

58. Buchwald, "Lascarid Architecture," 261–96.

59. Schäfer, "Architekturhistorische Beziehungen," 197–224.

60. Rappoport, *Churches*, 10–30.

61. Schäfer, "Architekturhistorische Beziehungen"; R. Ousterhout, "Rebuilding the Temple," 66–78.

62. Ousterhout, "Observations," 166 and pl. 70.

63. See P. Miljkovič-Pepek, *Veljusa* (Skopje, 1981), pls. 9–20.

64. Ch. Bakirtzis and N. Zikos, "Anaskafai Polystylou Abderon," *AD Chronika* 41 (1986): 198–290 and pl. 135.

65. Mango, *Byzantine Architecture*, 180 and fig. 265; V. Korač, "Les origines de l'architecture de l'école de la Morava," in *L'école de la Morava et son temps* (Belgrade, 1972), 157–68.

66. Van Millingen, *Byzantine Churches*, 212–17.

67. Ousterhout, "Some Notes," 52–56.

68. Velenis, *Ermeneia*, pls. 38–39; Ousterhout, "Some Notes," 52–56; Ötüken and Ousterhout, "Byzantine Church," fig. 7.

69. Ötüken, "Bizans Duvar," 403.

70. Ibid., fig. 5.

71. Schäfer, "Architekturhistorische Beziehungen," pls. 97–99.

72. Adam, *Building*, figs. 325–26.

73. Ibid., 220–27.

74. Ötüken, "Bizans Duvar," 398–403; Schäfer, "Architekturhistorische Beziehungen," 223–24 and pl. 101.

75. Ousterhout, "Rebuilding the Temple," fig. 13.

76. Ibid. Similar incisions appear in the eleventh-century repairs to Hagia Sophia in Nicaea, but they are more difficult to interpret; see Ötüken, "Bizans Duvar," fig. 2.

77. See Adam, *Building*, 81–87, esp. fig. 182, for Roman scaffoldings.

78. Velenis, *Ermeneia*, 13–44.

79. Petit, "Vie et office," 39–40 (chap. 2, note 59, above).

80. See Talbot, "Posthumous Miracles," 99.

81. Adam, *Building*, 174–77.

82. *AASS* (Nov. 3), 882; trans. in Mango, *Sources*, 201–2.

83. Noret, ed., *Vitae duae antiquae*, Vita A, chap. 234; Vita B, chap. 66.

84. Ibid., Vita B, chap. 66.

85. V. Djuric, *Zidno Slikarstvo Manastira Dečana* (Belgrade, 1995), fig. 15, facing p. 352.

86. Velenis, *Ermeneia*, figs. 3–21

87. Ousterhout, "Observations," pls. 70–71.

88. Ousterhout, "Constantinople, Bithynia, and Regional Developments in Later Palaeologan Architecture," in *Twilight of Byzantium*, ed. S. Ćurčić and D. Mouriki (Princeton, 1991), 78–79, figs. 9–10.

89. For photographs, see T. F. Mathews, *The Byzantine Churches of Istanbul: A Photographic Survey* (University Park, Pa., 1976), 73–101, 130–134; Schäfer, *Gül Camii*, pls. 1–28.

90. Restle, *Studien*, vol. 2, pls. 147–53.

91. Ibid., vol. 2, pl. 157.

92. P. I. Kuniholm and C. L. Striker, "Dendrochronological Investigations in the Aegean and Neighboring Regions," *Journal of Field Archaeology* 10 (1983): 411–20; 14 (1987): 385–98; and Kuniholm, "First Millenium A.D. Oak Chronologies."

93. Velenis, *Ermeneia*, 45–64.

94. Ibid., vol. 2, figs. 22–30.

95. Mathews, *Byzantine Churches*, figs. 35-45, 35-46.

96. Ibid., fig. 17-2.

97. Ibid., fig. 30-3.

98. R. Nigbor, A. Çakmak, and R. Mark, "Measured to the Max," *Civil Engineering* (November 1992): 44–47.

99. Baronio, Binda, and Tedeschi, "Thick Mortar Joints," esp. 244.

100. In rare instances, iron reinforcements were also used, as will be discussed in the next chapter in the section devoted to the reinforcement of arches and vaults.

101. Millet, *L'école grecque*, esp. 1–13.

102. Velenis, *Ermeneia*, passim.

103. See comments by Krautheimer, *Early Christian*, 354–69.

104. A. Pasadaios, *O Keramoplastikos Diakosmos ton Byzantinon Kterion tes Konstantinopouleos* (Athens, 1973); also Y. Ötüken, "İstanbul son devir Bizans mimarisinde cephe süslemeleri," *Vakıflar Dergisi* 12 (1978): 213–33.

105. Demangel and Mamboury, *Quartier des Manganes*, 24 and fig. 23.

106. Ibid., 49–53 and figs. 50–52.

107. Ousterhout, *Kariye*, fig. 7.

108. A. Rachénov, *Églises de Mesemvria* (Sofia, 1932), with many illustrations.

109. Mathews, *Byzantine Churches*, figs. 10-47, 13-4.

110. Ibid., fig. 35–42; Ousterhout, *Kariye*, 135 and fig. 140.

111. Ousterhout, "Some Notes," 53–54.

112. Bakirtzis and Zikos, "Anaskafai," pl. 135.

113. R. Ousterhout, "The Byzantine Heart," *Zograf* 17 (1986): 36–44.

114. Ibid.

115. Velenis, "Thirteenth-Century Architecture," 279–84.

116. See, among others, G. C. Miles, "Classification of Islamic Elements in Byzantine Architectural Ornamentation in Greece," in *Actes du XIIe Congrès international des études byzantines, Ohride 1961* (Belgrade, 1964), 3:281–87; N. Nikonanos, "Keramoplastikes kouphikes diakosmeseis sta mnemeia tes perioches ton Athenon," in *Aphieroma ste mneme Stylianou Pelikanide* (Thessaloniki, 1983), 330–52.

117. P. Vocotopoulos, "The Role of Constantinopolitan Architecture during the Middle and Late Period," *XVI. Internationaler Byzantinistenkongress, Akten I/2*; 31, no. 2 (1981): 551–73.

118. Velenis, *Ermeneia*, 65–108, fig. 31.

119. Ousterhout, "Constantinople, Bithynia," 78–80, 83–84.

120. For illustrations, see Velenis, *Ermeneia*, figs. 83, 110.

121. Ibid., esp. chart, fig. 44.

122. Vocotopoulos, "Role of Constantinopolitan Architecture," for example, does not make a distinction between the two.

Chapter Seven

1. A. Choisy, *L'art de bâtir chez les Byzantins* (Paris, 1893).

2. Mark and Çakmak, *Hagia Sophia*, includes numerous relevant studies; note review by R. Ousterhout in *JSAH* 53 (1994): 245–46. See also M. Ahunbay et al., "Non-Destructive Testing and Monitoring in Hagia Sophia, Istanbul," in *Ancient Structures*, 177–86; M. Erdik, E. Durukal, and A. Çakmak, "Assessment of the Earthquake Performance of Hagia Sophia," in *Ancient Structures*, 407–16.

3. For a recent analysis that suggests avenues of approach for the structural examination of later Byzantine churches, see E. E. Toumbakari, "Structural Analysis of the Church of Aghia Triada, Astros, Peloponnesos, Greece," in *Ancient Structures*, 507–16. Although her subject is a provincial post-Byzantine church, its cross-in-square plan has dimensions comparable to Middle and Late Byzantine churches.

4. See Krautheimer, *Early Christian*, 205–57, 285–300, for discussion.

5. Peschlow, *Die Irenenkirche*, 212–13.

6. Krautheimer, *Early Christian*, 285–300.

7. Ousterhout, "Byzantine Church at Enez," 261–80.

8. Ousterhout, *Kariye*, 20–32.

9. As above, Chapter 4.

10. Krautheimer, *Early Christian*, 385–88.

11. For definition of terms and structural analysis, see R. Mainstone, "Squinches and Pendentives: Comments on Some Problems of Definition," *AARP: Art and Archaeology Research Papers* 4 (1973): 131–37.

12. See R. Ousterhout, "Innovation in Byzantine Architecture: The Case of Nea Moni," *JSAH* 51 (1992): 48–60, esp. 58–60; also Krautheimer, *Early Christian*, 340; C. Mango, "Les monuments de l'architecture du XIe siècle et leur signification historique et sociale," *Travaux et mémoires* 6 (1976): 351–65.

13. See R. Schultz and S. Barnsley, *The Monastery of Saint Luke of Stiris, Near Phocis* (London, 1901), for illustrations.

14. Striker, *Myrelaion*, esp. pls. 19, 20, 28.

15. See my comments on similarities with Western medieval developments and the misconceptions these might cause: R. Ousterhout, "An Apologia for Byzantine Architecture," *Gesta* 35 (1996): 21–33.

16. S. Ćurčić, "Articulation of Church Facades during the First Half of the Fourteenth Century," in *L'art byzantin au début du XIVe siècle* (Belgrade, 1978), 17–27.

17. Ousterhout, *Kariye*, 116–26.

18. Ćurčić, "Articulation," 17–27.

19. Bouras, *Nea Moni*, 102–10.

20. Ousterhout, *Kariye*, 135.

21. Krautheimer, *Early Christian*, 248–41.

22. M. Restle, *Studien zur frühbyzantinischen Architektur Kappadokiens* (Vienna, 1979), for numerous examples.

23. Demangel and Mamboury, *Quartier des Manganes*, figs. 26 and 30.

24. Choisy, *L'art de bâtir*, 115–22.

25. Kuniholm and Striker, "Dendrochronology and the Holy Apostles," 1–26.

26. Rappoport, *Churches*, 135–39.

27. Ousterhout, *Kariye*, 45–46 and pls. 50–54; information from an unpublished structural report of 1954, in the author's possession.

28. L. Butler, "Hagia Sophia's Nave Cornices as Elements of Its Design and Structure," in *Hagia Sophia from the Age of Justinian to the Present*, ed. R. Mark and A. Çakmak (Cambridge, 1992), 57–77.

29. Ibid., 62–65.

30. For example, K. Theocharidou, "The Structure of Hagia Sophia in Thessaloniki from Its Construction to the Present," in *Hagia Sophia from the Age of Justinian to the Present*, ed. R. Mark and A. Çakmak (Cambridge, 1992), 92, suggests that the cornices of Hagia Sophia in Thessaloniki were also pinned together but provides no evidence.

31. Ousterhout, *Kariye*, fig. 57.

32. Striker and Kuban, *Kalenderhane*, pl. 55 and fol. 3.

33. Megaw, "Original Form," 296.

34. P. I. Kuniholm and C. L. Striker, "The Tie-Beam System in the Nave Arcade of St. Eirene: Structure and Dendrochronology," in U. Peschlow, *Die Irenenkirche in Istanbul: Untersuchungen zur Architektur* (Tübingen, 1977), 229–35, fig. 31, foldout 2.

35. Rappoport, *Churches*, 133–44, esp. fig. 55.

36. See R. Mainstone, *Developments in Structural Form* (London, 1975), 122–25, for wooden reinforcements and the Florence dome.

37. Megaw, "Original Form," 296 and fig. 9.

38. Ibid., 296.

39. Sinos, *Klosterkirche*, 85–87, 94–95, and pls. 26–27.

40. Ibid., pls. 34–45.

41. R. Van Nice, *Saint Sophia in Istanbul: An Architectural Survey* (Washington, D.C., 1965), pls. 4–5; E. H. Swift, *Hagia Sophia* (New York, 1940), 87–88. R. J. Mainstone, *Hagia Sophia: Architecture, Structure and Liturgy of Justinian's Great Church* (New York, 1988), 104–5, suggests that the western flying buttresses may be ninth or tenth century in date, marking the independent development of the flying buttress in Byzantium.

42. Ousterhout, *Kariye*, 85, 132–33, and figs. 5, 142.

43. Choisy, *L'art de bâtir*, 32–47; R. Ousterhout, "The Construction of Vaulting in Later Byzantine Architecture," in *Ancient Structures*, 305–14, esp. 309–12.

44. Adam, *Roman Building*, 174–77; also Mainstone, *Developments*, 73–75.

45. Striker, *Myrelaion*, 27.

46. R. Ousterhout and Th. Gourides, "Ena Byzantino Ktirio dipla ston Agio Athanasio Didymoteichou," *To Archaiologiko Ergo ste Makedonia kai Thrake* 5 (1991): 515–25.

47. Note the extensive discussion of this problem in Gothic architecture in J. Fitchen, *The Construction of Gothic Cathedrals* (Chicago, 1961), 123–74.

48. P. Sanpaolesi, "Strutture a cupola autoportanti," *Palladio* 21 (1971): 3–64.

49. I thank former student John Rushing for his expertise on structures; see also Mainstone, *Developments*, 73–75.

50. Megaw, "Notes on Recent Work," 347 and figs. 13–14.

51. Ousterhout, *Kariye*, figs. 102–3.

52. Hallensleben, "Untersuchungen zur Baugeschichte," 146–56, figs. 5–7, and pl. 62.

53. W. George, *The Church of St. Irene in Constantinople* (London, 1913), 44.

54. Schäfer, *Gül Camii*, 37–41, pls. 24, 25, 27; Müller-Wiener, *Bildlexikon*, figs. 130–31.

55. Ousterhout, *Kariye*, pl. 98.

56. Stiker and Kuban, *Kalenderhane*, 96–97 and fol. 2; Mathews, *Byzantine Churches*, fig. 18–16.

57. Sanpaolesi, "Strutture," esp. figs. 5–6.

58. Mango, "Monastery of St. Abercius," 169–76; and Mango, *Architecture,* pl. 197.

59. Mathews, *Byzantine Churches*, fig. 16–15.

60. Macridy et al., "Monastery of Lips," figs. 24–26.

61. Mathews, *Byzantine Churches*, fig. 35–37.

62. Ibid., figs. 17–3, 18–17.

63. Ibid., figs. 10–47, 13–4; Ousterhout, "Byzantine Church at Enez," fig. 8.

64. Ousterhout, "Rebuilding the Temple," fig. 17.

65. Sanpaolesi, "Strutture," figs. 86–87.

66. Velenis, *Ermeneia*, 65–106 passim.

67. Ousterhout, *Kariye*, 70–78.

68. Ibid., pls. 54, 56, 106, 107, 113; Mathews, *Byzantine Churches*, fig. 35–26.

69. For definitions, see Mainstone, "Squinches and Pendentives," 131–37.

70. S. Nenadović, "Les pots résonnants dans les églises médiévales serbes," *Zbornik Architektonskog Fakulteta* 5 (1960): 3–11 (in Serbo-Croatian with French summary).

71. Vitruvius, *Architecture*, 5.5.1–5 (Morgan, 143–45).

72. Macridy et al., "Monastery of Lips," fig. 23; Ousterhout, *Kariye*, pl. 152; Demangel and Mamboury, *Quartier des Manganes*, 44–46.

73. Rappoport, *Churches*, 78–82.

74. I thank Vsevolod Rozhniatovsky for his on-site demonstration.

75. Striker and Kuban, *Kalenderhane*, pl. 50.

76. Demangel and Mamboury, *Quartier des Manganes*, figs. 28, 49.

77. S. Bogiatzes, "Neotera Stoicheia gia ten Oikodomike Istoria tou Katholikou tes Neas Mones Chiou," *DChAE* 14 (1989): 159–72 and fig. 7.

78. Logvin, *Kiev's Hagia Sophia*, 10.

79. A. Pasadaios, "Peri tinos asynethous byzantinou tholou," in *Charisterion eis A. K. Orlandon* (Athens, 1965), 1:187–92.

80. Ousterhout, *Kariye*, pl. 67.

81. Sinos, *Klosterkirche*, pl. 93; Mango, *Architecture*, fig. 261.

Chapter Eight

1. See S. Kostof, *Caves of God*, 2nd ed. (Oxford, 1989); and L. Rodley, *Cave Monasteries of Byzantine Cappadocia* (Cambridge, 1985), for numerous examples.

2. Ousterhout, *Kariye*, 86–87; Megaw, "Original Form," 288; Bouras, *Nea Moni*, 125–30; perhaps there were connections with other monastic buildings at these points.

3. Ousterhout, *Kariye*, pl. 112.

4. Striker and Kuban, *Kalenderhane*, 117–19 and pls. 16–31; there is much evidence for reuse in both the revetments and the sculptural decoration.

5. Ousterhout, *Kariye*, 39–46.

6. A similar patching with a different type of stone is evident in the *painted* imitation revetment in the southeast parekklesion tomb; see Underwood, *Kariye Djami*, vol. 3, pl. 526-b.

7. Ibid., 1:39–42.

8. Bouras, *Nea Moni*, 79–89.

9. As is frequently suggested; see most recently Mylonas, "Domike erevna," 6–30.

10. Schultz and Barnsley, *Monastery of St. Luke*, 27–31, believed the revetments came directly from the quarry or the marble yard.

11. M. Chatzidakis, "A propos de la date et du fondateur de Saint-Lue," *CA* 29 (1969): 127–50, esp. 141. I thank Vassilis Marinis for bringing this inscription to my attention.

12. Ousterhout, *Kariye*, 66–67, 138, and fig. 114.

13. Underwood, *Kariye Djami*, 1:117–20.

14. Demus, *Byzantine Mosaic Decoration*, 12.

15. Henderson and Mango, "Glass," 339. For technical analyses, see papers in *III Colloquio internazionale sul mosaico antico. Ravenna 6–10 settembre 1980*, ed. R. Farioli Campanati (Ravenna, 1983).

16. Underwood, *Kariye Djami*, 1:172–83.

17. Ibid., 1:173.

18. Ibid., 1:172.

19. Ibid., 1:174.

20. Ibid., 1:175.

21. See Logvin, *Kiev's Hagia Sophia*, 16, for what follows.

22. Underwood, *Kariye Djami*, 1:173.

23. Cutler's calculation of 2.5 million tesserae for the apse mosaic of Hagia Sophia in Constantinople seems reasonable: A. Cutler, "Mosaic," *ODB*, 2:1412–13; Mango's estimate of "over one million" at Monreale seems too few: C. Mango, quoted in Henderson and Mango, "Glass," 339.

24. Logvin, *Kiev's Hagia Sophia*, 16.

25. Underwood, *Kariye Djami*, 1:300–309.

26. For the frescoes, see Y. Ötüken, "Akhisar-Çanlı Kilise Freskoları," in *Bedrettin Cömert'e Armağan* (Ankara, 1980), 303–20. I am preparing a new study of the frescoes.

27. A. Wharton, "Fresco Technique," *ODB*, 2:805–6.

28. Quoted in Underwood, *Kariye Djami*, 1:301.

29. Ibid., 1:303.

30. Rappoport, *Churches*, 178; T. Tsarevskaia, "Nekotoriie Osobennosti Ikonografiieskoi Programmii Rospisei Tserkvi Blagovesheniia na Miachine ("v Arkazhakh") bliz Novgoroda," in *Drevnerusskoe Iskusstvo* (Moscow, 1997), 83–95.

31. W. C. Brumfield, *A History of Russian Architecture* (Cambridge, 1993), 35–37; Rappoport, *Churches*, 178. I thank Tatiana Tsarevskaia for her on-site observations.

32. For these paintings, see T. Chatzidakis-Bacharas, *Les peintures murales de Hosios Loukas* (Athens, 1982); and C. Connor, *Art and Miracles in Medieval Byzantium* (Princeton, 1991).

33. Underwood, *Kariye Djami*, passim.

34. For overlap, see R. Gettens and G. Stout, "A Monument of Byzantine Wall Painting: The Method of Construction," *Studies in Conservation* 3, no. 3 (1958): 116–17. For the artists, see S. Young, "Relations between Byzantine Mosaic and Fresco Technique," *JöB* 25 (1976): 269–78; and O. Demus, "The Style of the Kariye Djami and Its Place in the Development of Palaeologan Art," in *The Kariye Djami*, vol. 4, ed. P. A. Underwood (Princeton, 1975), 109–60.

35. A. K. Orlandos, *Archeion Byzantinon Mnemeion tes Ellados*, (Athens, 1935), 1:152–60; more recently, P. Koufopoulos, "Sympleromatika stoichia gia tis orthomarmaroseis tou naou tes Odegitrias ston Mystra," in *Ebdomo Symposio Byzantines kai Metabyzantines Archaiologias kai Technes* (Athens, 1987), 40.

36. A. Xyngopoulos, *He Psephidote Diakosmesis tou Naou ton Hagion Apostolon Thessalonikes* (Thessaloniki, 1953), 3–4, 65.

37. Above all, C. Stephan, *Die Mosaiken und Fresken der Apostelkirche zu Thessaloniki* (Worms, 1986); also *Thessaloniki and Its Monuments* (Thessaloniki, 1985), 99–108.

38. Demus, *Byzantine Mosaic Decoration*, 14–16.

39. Ibid., 16.

40. Mathews, "Sequel to Nicaea II," 11–23.

41. Maguire, "Mosaics of Nea Moni," 205–14, notes that Demus follows Byzantine terminology: in the eleventh century John Mauropous wrote an *ekphrasis* called *Eis pinakas megalous ton heorton* ("on the pictures of the great feasts"); ed. P. De Lagarde, *Iohannis Euchaitorum Metropolitae quae in codice vaticano graeco* 676 *supersunt* (Göttingen, 1882), 2–8, nos. 2–11.

42. Much of what follows derives from my paper "Collaboration and Innovation in Byzantine Art," *BMGS* 21 (1997): 93–112. I thank Leslie Brubaker for her useful comments.

43. A. W. Epstein, "The Fresco Decoration of the Column Churches, Göreme Valley, Cappadocia," *CA* 29 (1980–81): 27–45.

44. M. Restle, *Byzantine Wall Painting in Asia Minor* (Greenwich, Conn., 1967), 2:183–84.

45. Striker, *Myrelaion*, 23–25.

46. Belting, Mango, and Mouriki, *Mosaics and Frescoes*, esp. figs. 5, 6, 10, 11.

47. Ousterhout, "Originality," 48–60.

48. As discussed in Chapter 3.

49. As noted by E. Kitzinger, "Reflections on the Feast Cycle in Byzantine Art," *CA* 36 (1988): 51–73, esp. 57–58.

50. See W. M. Ramsay and G. Bell, *The Thousand and One Churches* (London, 1909), 404–18; H. Rott, *Kleinasiatische Denkmäler aus Pisidien, Pamphilien, Kappadokien und Lykien* (Leipzig, 1908), 257–62; Ötüken, "Akhisar Çanlı Kilise," 303–20.

51. Ousterhout, "The 1994 Season," 165–80.

SELECTED BIBLIOGRAPHY

Adam, J.-P. "La basilique byzantine de Kydna de Lycie." *Revue archéologique* 1 (1977): 53–78.

———. *Roman Building: Materials and Technique*. Bloomington, Ind., 1995.

Ahunbay, M., Z. Ahunbay, D. Almesberger, A. Rizzo, M. Tončić, and Ü. İzmirligil. "Non-Destructive Testing and Monitoring in Hagia Sophia, Istanbul." In *Ancient Structures*, 177–86.

Anastylose ton byzantinon kai metabyzantinon mnemeion ste Thessalonike. Thessaloniki, 1985.

Andaloro, M., and G. Naselli Flores. *I mosaici di Monreale: Restaure e scoperte 1965–1972*. Palermo, 1986.

Angold, M. "Inventory of the So-called Palace of Botaniates." In *The Byzantine Aristocracy IX to XIII Centuries*. BAR International Series 221, ed. M. Angold. Oxford, 1984.

Aran, B. "The Church of Saint Theodosia and the Monastery of Christ Euergetes." *JöB* 28 (1979): 211–28.

Asdracha, C. "Inscriptions byzantines de la Thrace orientale et de l'île d'Imbros (XIIe–XVe siècles)." *AD* 43 (1995): 261–67.

Asdracha, C., and Ch. Bakirtzis. "Inscriptions byzantines de la Thrace (VIIIe–XVe siècles). Edition et commentaire historique." *AD* 35 (1986): 271–76.

Asgari, N. "Roman and Early Byzantine Marble Quarries of Proconessus." In *Proceedings of the 10th International Congress of Classical Archaeology*, Vol. 1. Ankara, 1978.

Babić, G. *Les chapelles annexes des églises byzantines*. Paris, 1969.

Bakirtzis, C. "To Episkopeion ton Philippon." In *E Kavala kai e Perioche tes*, Kavala, 1987.

Bakirtzis, Ch., and N. Zikos. "Anaskafai Polystylou Abderon." *AD Chronika* 41 (1986): 198–290.

Bardill, J. "A Catalogue of Stamped Bricks in the Ayasofya Collection." *Anatolian Archaeology* 1 (1995): 28–29.

Baronio, G., L. Binda, and C. Tedeschi. "Thick Mortar Joints in Byzantine Buildings: Study of Their Composition and Mechanical Behaviour." In *Ancient Structures*, 235–44.

Bartusis, M. "State Demands for Building and Repairing Fortifications in Late Byzantine and Medieval Serbia," *Byzantinoslavica* 49 (1988): 205–12.

Bayer, I. "Architekturzeichnungen auf dem Boden der Basilica." In *Die Basilika des Heiligen Kreuzes in Resafa-Sergiupolis*, ed. T. Ulbert. Mainz, 1986.

Belting, H. "Eine Gruppe konstantinopler Reliefs aus dem 11. Jahrhundert." *Pantheon* 30 (1972): 263–71.

Belting, H., C. Mango, and D. Mouriki. *The Mosaics and Frescoes of St. Mary Pammakaristos (Fethiye Camii) at Istanbul*. Washington, D.C., 1987.

Berger, A. "Die mittelbyzantinische Kirche bei der Mehmet Fatih Camii in Istanbul." *IM* 47 (1997): 455–60.

Bergman, R. "Byzantine Influence and Private Patronage in a Newly Discovered Medieval Church in Amalfi: S. Michele Arcangelo in Pogenola." *JSAH* 50 (1994): 421–45.

Bogdanović, D., V. Djurić, and D. Medaković, eds. *Chilandar*. Belgrade, 1978.

Bošković, D. "Sur quelques maîtres-maçons et maître-peintres des premieres décades du XIVe s. en Serbie et en Macédoine." *Starinar*, n.s., 9–10 (1958–59): 125–31.

Boura, L. *O Glyptos Diakosmos tou Naou tes Panagias sto Monasteri tou Osiou Louka*. Athens, 1980.

Bouras, Ch. *Nea Moni on Chios: History and Architecture*. Athens, 1982.

———. "Twelfth and Thirteenth Century Variations of the Single Domed Octagon Plan." *DChAE* 9 (1977–79): 21–34.

Briggs, M. S. *The Architect in History*. Oxford, 1927.

F. E. Brightman, ed. *Historia mystagogica*. *Journal of Theological Studies* 9 (1908): 248–67, 387–97.

Brosh, N. "Glass Window Fragments from Khirbet Al-Mafjar." In *Annales du 11e congrès de l'Association internationale pour l'histoire du verre*. Amsterdam, 1990.

Bruins, E. M., ed. *Codex Constantinopolitanus Palatii Veteris, No. 1*. 3 vols. Leiden, 1964.

Brumfield, W. C. *A History of Russian Architecture*. Cambridge, 1993.

Buchwald, H. "The Geometry of Middle Byzantine Churches and Some Possible Implications." *JöB* 42 (1992): 293–321.

———. "Lascarid Architecture." *JöB* 28 (1979): 261–96.

———. "Sardis Church E—A Preliminary Report." *JöB* 26 (1977): 265–99.

———. "Western Asia Minor as a Generator of Architectural Forms in the Byzantine Period: Provincial Back-Wash or Dynamic Center of Production." *JöB* 34 (1984): 200–234.

Butler, L. "Hagia Sophia's Nave Cornices as Elements of Its Design and Structure." In *Hagia Sophia from the Age of Justinian to the Present*, ed. R. Mark and A. Çakmak. Cambridge, 1992.

Çakmak, A., and R. Mark. "Mechanical Tests of Material from the Hagia Sophia Dome." *DOP* 48 (1994): 277–79.

Cameron, Av. "Isidore of Miletus and Hypatia: On the Editing of Mathematical Texts." *GRBS* 31 (1990): 103–27.

Carty, C. "The Role of Gunzo's Dream in the Building of Cluny III." *Gesta* 27 (1988): 113–23.

Chatzidakis-Bacharas, T. *Les peintures murales de Hosios Loukas*. Athens, 1982.

Choisy, A. *L'art de bâtir chez les Byzantins*. Paris, 1883.

Colombier, P. de. *Les chantiers des cathédrales*. Paris, 1973.

Conant, K. J. *Cluny. Les églises et la maison du chef d'ordre*. Mâcon, 1968.

———. "Mediaeval Academy Excavations at Cluny. IX: Systematic Dimensions of the Buildings." *Speculum* 38 (1963): 8–11.

Connor, C. *Art and Miracles in Medieval Byzantium*. Princeton, 1991.

Cormack, R. "Patronage and New Programs of Byzantine Iconography." In *The 17th International Byzantine Congress, Major Papers*. New York, 1986.

———. *Writing in Gold: Byzantine Society and Its Icons*. London, 1985.

Coulton, J. J. *Ancient Greek Architects at Work: Problems of Structure and Design*. Ithaca, N.Y., 1977.

———. "Incomplete Preliminary Planning in Greek Architecture: Some New Evidence." In *Le dessin d'architecture dans les sociétés antiques*, ed. T. Thieme. Strasbourg, 1985.

Ćurčić, S. "Architectural Significance of Subsidiary Chapels in Middle Byzantine Churches." *JSAH* 36 (1977): 94–110.

———. "Articulation of Church Facades during the First Half of the Fourteenth Century." In *L'art byzantin au début du XIVe siècle*. Belgrade, 1978.

———. *Gračanica: King Milutin's Church and Its Place in Late Byzantine Architecture*. University Park, Pa., 1979.

———. "Medieval Royal Tombs in the Balkans: An Aspect of the 'East or West' Question." *GOTR* 29 (1984): 175–94.

———. "The Twin-Domed Narthex in Paleologan Architecture." *ZRVI* 13 (1971): 333–44.

———. "What Was the Real Function of Late Byzantine *Katechoumena*?" *BSCA* 19 (1993): 8–9.

Ćurčić, S., and E. Hadjitriphonas, eds. *Secular Medieval Architecture in the Balkans 1300–1500 and Its Preservation*. Thessaloniki, 1997.

Cutler, A. "Originality as a Cultural Phenomenon." In *Originality in Byzantine Literature, Art and Music*, ed. A. Littlewood. Oxford, 1996.

———. "Uses of Luxury: On the Functions of Consumption and Symbolic Capital in Byzantine Culture." In *Byzance et les images*, ed. A. Guillou and J. Durand. Paris, 1994.

Cutler, A., and J.-M. Spieser. *Byzance médiévale 700–1204*. Paris, 1996.

Dagron, G. *Constantinople imaginaire*. Paris, 1984.

Davidson, G. *The Minor Objects*. Corinth: Results of Excavations Conducted by the American School of Classical Studies at Athens, vol. 12. Princeton, 1952.

Demus, O. *Byzantine Mosaic Decoration*. London, 1948.

———. *The Mosaic Decoration of San Marco, Venice*. Ed. H. Kessler. Chicago, 1988.

———. *The Mosaics of Norman Sicily*. London, 1949.

Dennis, G. *Three Byzantine Military Treatises*. Washington, D.C., 1985.

Devoko, A. *Monumentalna I dekorativna architektura u srednje-vekovnoj Srbiji*. Belgrade, 1962.

Diaconu, P., and E. Zah. "Les carrières de pierre de Păcuiul lui Soare." *Dacia* 15 (1971): 289–306.

Djobadze, W. "The Georgian Churches of Tao-Klarjet'I: Construction Methods and Materials." *Oriens Christianus* 62 (1978): 114–34.

Dölger, F. *Aus den Schatzkammern Heiligen Berges*. Munich, 1948.

Downey, G. "Byzantine Architects: Their Training and Methods." *Byzantion* 18 (1946): 99–118.

Duncan-Flowers, M. J. "The Mosaics of Monreale: A Study of Their Monastic and Funerary Contexts." Ph.D. diss., University of Illinois at Urbana-Champaign, 1994.

Dworakowska, A. *Quarries in Ancient Greece*. Wrocław, 1975.

———. *Quarries in Roman Provinces*. Wrocław, 1983.

Ebersolt, J., and A. Thiers. *Les églises byzantines de Constantinople*. Paris, 1913.

Epstein, A. W. "The Fresco Decoration of the Column Churches, Göreme Valley, Cappadocia." *CA* 29 (1980–81): 27–45.

Erguvanlı, E., I. Eris, M. Ahunbay, and Z. Ahunbay. "The Significance of Research on Old Quarries for the Restoration of Historic Buildings with Special Reference to the Marmara Region, Turkey." In *The Engineering Geology of Ancient Works, Monuments and Historical Sites,* ed. P. Marinos and G. Koukis. Rotterdam, 1988.

Ettinghausen, R., and O. Grabar. *The Art and Architecture of Islam 650–1250*. Harmondsworth, 1987.

Evans, H. C., and W. D. Wixom, eds. *The Glory of Byzantium: Art and Culture of the Middle Byzantine Era,* A.D. 843–1261. Exh. cat., Metropolitan Museum of Art. New York, 1997.

Eyice, S. "Amasra 'Büyükadasında bir Bizans kilisesi." *TTKB* 15 (1951): 469–96.

———. "L'église cruciforme de Side en Pamphylie." *Anatolia* 3 (1958): 35–42.

———. "Encore une fois l'église d'Alexis Apokauque à Selymbria (=Silivri)." *Byzantion* 48 (1978): 406–16.

———. "Remarques sur deux anciennes églises byzantines d'Istanbul: Koca Mustafa Paşa Camii et l'église du Yuşa Tepesi." In *Actes du XIe Congrès international d'études byzantines*. Thessaloniki, 1953.

———. "Tuzla'nin Değirmenaltı Mevkiinde bir Bizans Kalıntısı." *Sanat Tarihi Yıllığı* 5 (1973): 27–78.

Farioli Campanati, R., ed. *III Colloquio internazionale sul mosaico antico. Ravenna 6–10 settembre 1980*. Ravenna, 1983.

Fıratlı, N. "Découverte d'une église byzantine à Sébaste de Phrygie." *CA* 29 (1969): 151–56.

Fitchen, J. *The Construction of Gothic Cathedrals*. Chicago, 1961.

Folk, R., and S. Valastro, Jr. "Successful Technique for Dating of Lime Mortar by Carbon-14." *Journal of Field Archaeology* 3 (1976): 203–8.

Franz, H. "Transennae als Fensterverschluss, ihre Entwicklung von der frühchristlichen biz zur islamischen Zeit." *IM* 8 (1958): 65–81.

Frothingham, A. L. "Byzantine Architects in Italy from the Sixth to the Fifteenth Century." *AJA* 9 (1894): 32–52.

Gabelić, S. "Lesnovski Prozop y Narodnom Muzeiy." *Zbornik Narodnog Muzeia* (Belgrade) 15, no. 2 (1994): 37–41.

Gautier, P. "Le typikon du Christ Sauveur Pantocrator." *REB* 32 (1974): 1–145.

———. "L'obituaire du typikon du Pantocrator." *REB* 27 (1969): 235–62.

George, W. *The Church of St. Irene in Constantinople*. London, 1913.

Gettens, R., and G. Stout. "A Monument of Byzantine Wall Painting: The Method of Construction." *Studies in Conservation* 3, no. 3 (1958): 116–17.

Ginouvès, R., and R. Martin. *Dictionnaire méthodique de l'architecture grecque et romaine*. Rome and Paris, 1985.

Grabar, O. *The Mediation of Ornament*. Princeton, 1992.

Graf von Bothmer, H.-C. "Architekturbilder im Koran." *Pantheon* 45 (1987): 4–20.

Grape, W. "Zum Stil der Mosaiken in der Kilise Camii in Istanbul." *Pantheon* 32 (1974): 3–13.

Hallensleben, H. "Untersuchungen zur Baugeschichte der ehemaligen Pammakaristoskirche, der heutigen Fethiye Camii in Istanbul." *IM* 13–14 (1963–64): 128–93.

———. "Untersuchungen zur Genesis und Typologie des 'Mistratypus.'" *Marburger Jahrbuch für Kunstwissenschaft* 18 (1969): 105–18.

Harvey, J. *The Mediaeval Architect*. London, 1972.

Haselberger, L. "The Construction Plans for the Temple of Apollo at Didyma." *Scientific American*, December 1985, 126–32.

———. "Deciphering a Roman Blueprint." *Scientific American*, June 1995, 84–89.

Havice, C. "The Hamilton Psalter in Berlin, Kupferstichkabinett 78. A.9." Ph.D. diss., Pennsylvania State University, 1978.

Henderson, J., and M. M. Mango. "Glass at Medieval Constantinople: Preliminary Scientific Evidence." In *Constantinople and Its Hinterland*, ed. C. Mango and G. Dagron. Aldershot, 1995.

Hesseling, D.-C. *Miniatures de l'Octateuque grec de Smyrne*. Leiden, 1909.

Hill, S. "The Brickstamps." In *Excavations at Saraçhane in Istanbul*, vol. 1, ed. R. M. Harrison. Princeton, 1986.

Hjort, O. "The Sculpture of the Kariye Camii." *DOP* 33 (1979): 199–290.

Hohlweg, A. "Ekphrasis." *RBK* 2 (1971): 34–75.

Holod, R. "Text, Plan, and Building: On the Transmission of Architectural Knowledge." In *Theories and Principles of Design in the Architecture of Islamic Societies* (Cambridge, Mass., 1988), 1–12.

Huber, P. *Bild und Botschaft*. Zurich, 1973.

Hunger, H., and K. Vogel, eds. *Ein byzantinisches Rechenbuch des 15. Jahrhunderts*. Vienna, 1963.

Huxley, G. L. *Anthemius of Tralles: A Study in Later Greek Geometry*. Cambridge, 1959.

James, L., and R. Webb. "'To Understand Ultimate Things and Enter Secret Places': Ekphrasis and Art in Byzantium." *Art History* 14, no. 1 (1991): 1–17.

Janin, R. *La géographie ecclésiastique de l'Empire Byzantin: Les églises et monastères*. Paris, 1969.

Jenkins, R. "The Classical Background of the Scriptores Post Theophanem." *DOP* 8 (1954): 13–30.

Kâhya, Y. "İstanbul Bizans Mimarsinde Tuğla Boyutları Üzerine." In *Prof. Doğan Kuban'a Armağan*. Istanbul, 1996.

Kalopissi-Verti, S. *Dedicatory Inscriptions and Donor Portraits in Thirteenth-Century Churches of Greece*. Vienna, 1992.

Kapitan, G. "The Church Wreck off Marzamemi." *Archaeology* 22 (1969): 122–32.

Karaveziroglou, M., C. Barboutis, and V. Kranas. "Behaviour of Masonry with Full Bricks and Lime Mortars." In *Ancient Structures*, 225–33.

Kazhdan, A. "Nov'ie Material'i po Vnutrennei Istorii Bizantii X–XV vv." *VizVrem* 26 (1965): 77–99.

Kazhdan, A., and A. Epstein. *Change in Byzantine Culture in the Eleventh and Twelfth Centuries*. Berkeley, 1985.

Kimbel, D. "Le développement de la taille en série dans l'architecture médiévale et son rôle dans l'histoire économique." *Bulletin monumental* 135, no. 3 (1977): 195–222.

Kinney, D. "Spolia from the Baths of Caracalla in Sta. Maria in Trastevere." *Art Bulletin* 68 (1986): 379–97.

Kitzinger, E. *The Mosaics of Monreale*. Palermo, 1960.

———. "Reflections on the Feast Cycle in Byzantine Art." *CA* 36 (1988): 51–73.

Kleinbauer, W. E. "Pre-Carolingian Concepts of Architectural Planning." In *The Medieval Mediterranean: Cross-Cultural Contacts*, ed. M. J. Chiat and K. L. Reyerson. St. Cloud, Minn., 1988.

Koco, D. "Nouvelles considérations sur l'église de Sainte Sophie à Ohrid." *Archaeologia Iugoslavica* 2 (1956): 139–44.

Koder, J., ed. and trans. *To Eparchikon Biblion*. Vienna, 1991.

Komech, A. I. *Drevnerusskoe Zodchestvo Kontsa X–Nachala XII v.* Moscow, 1987.

Korać, V. "Les origines de l'architecture de l'école de la Morava." In *L'école de la Morava et son temps*. Belgrade, 1972.

Kostof, S. *Caves of God.* 2nd ed. Oxford, 1989.

Koufopoulos, P. "Sympleromatika stoichia gia tis orthomarmaroseis tou naou tes Odegitrias ston Mystra." In *Ebdomo Symposio Byzantines kai Metabyzantines Archaiologias kai Technes*. Athens, 1987.

Koukoules, Ph. "Peri ten Byzantinen Oikian." *Epeteris Etaireias Byzantinon Spoudon* 12 (1936): 76–138.

Krautheimer, R. *Early Christian and Byzantine Architecture*. 4th rev. ed., with S. Ćurčić. Harmondsworth, 1986.

———. "Introduction to an 'Iconography of Medieval Architecture.'" In *Studies in Early Christian, Medieval, and Renaissance Art*. New York, 1969.

Krönig, W. *The Cathedral of Monreale and Norman Architecture in Sicily.* Palermo, 1965.

Krumbacher, K. *Geschichte der byzantinsichen Literature von Justinian bis zum Ende des oströmischen Reiches*. Munich, 1897.

Kuniholm, P. I. "First Millenium A.D. Oak Chronologies." Typescript report, Wiener Lab, Cornell University, Ithaca, N.Y., 14 March 1995.

Kuniholm, P. I., and C. L. Striker. "Dendrochronology and the Architectural History of the Church of the Holy Apostles in Thessaloniki." *Architectura* 2 (1990): 1–26.

———. "Dendrochronological Investigations in the Aegean and Neighboring Regions." *Journal of Field Archaeology* 10 (1983): 411–20; 14 (1987): 385–98.

———. "The Tie-Beam System in the Nave Arcade of St. Eirene: Structure and Dendrochronology." In U. Peschlow, *Die Irenenkirche in Istanbul: Untersuchungen zur Architktur.* Tübingen, 1977.

Lange, I. D. "Theorien und Entstehung der byzantinischen Kreuzkuppelkirche." *Architectura* 16 (1986): 93–113.

Laourdas, B. "Metrophranes, Bios tou hosiou Dionysiou tou Athonitou." *Archeion Pontou* 21 (1956): 43–79.

Lassner, J. *The Topography of Baghdad in the Early Middle Ages*. Detroit, 1970.

Lefort, J., et al. *Géometries du fisc byzantin*. Paris, 1991.

Lightfoot, C. S., and E. Ivison. "The Amorium Project: The 1995 Excavation Season." *DOP* 51 (1997) 291–300.

Logvin, H. *Kiev's Hagia Sophia*. Kiev, 1971.

Macridy, T., et al. "The Monastery of Lips (Fenari Isa Camii) at Istanbul." *DOP* 18 (1964): 251–98.

Magdalino, P. "The Byzantine Aristocratic *Oikos*." In *The Byzantine Aristocracy IX to XIII Centuries*. BAR International Series 221, ed. M. Angold. Oxford, 1984.

———. *Constantinople médiévale*. Paris, 1997.

———. *The Empire of Manuel I Komnenos 1143–1180*. Cambridge, 1993.

———. "Observations on the Nea Ekklesia of Basil I." *JöB* 37 (1987): 51–64.

Magoulias, H. "Trades and Crafts in the Sixth and Seventh Centuries as Viewed in the Lives of the Saints." *Byzantinoslavica* 37 (1976): 11–13.

Maguire, H. "The Mosaics of Nea Moni: An Imperial Reading." *DOP* 46 (1992): 205–14.

———. "Truth and Convention in Byzantine Descriptions of Works of Art." *DOP* 28 (1974): 113–40.

Mainstone, R. *Developments in Structural Form*. London, 1975.

———. "Squinches and Pendentives: Comments on Some Problems of Definition." *AARP: Art and Archaeology Research Papers* 4 (1973): 131–37.

Mango, C. "Approaches to Byzantine Architecture." *Muqarnas* 8 (1991): 41.

———. *Art of the Byzantine Empire 312–1453: Sources and Documents*. Englewood Cliffs, N.J., 1972.

———. *The Brazen House*. Copenhagen, 1959.

———. *Byzantine Architecture*. New York, 1976.

———. "Byzantine Brickstamps." *AJA* 54 (1950): 19–27.

———. "Byzantine Writers on the Fabric of Hagia Sophia." In *Hagia Sophia from the Age of Justinian to the Present*, ed. R. Mark and A. Çakmak. Cambridge, 1992.

———. "Isaurian Builders." In *Polychronion: Festschrift F. Dölger zum 75. Geburtstag*, ed. P. Wirth. Heidelberg, 1966.

———. *Materials for the Study of the Mosaics of St. Sophia in Istanbul*. Washington, D.C., 1963.

———. "The Monastery of St. Abercius at Kurşunlu (Elegmi) in Bithynia." *DOP* 22 (1968): 169–76.

———. "Les monuments de l'architecture du XIe siècle et leur signification historique et sociale." *Travaux et mémoires* 6 (1976): 351–65.

———. "Notes on Byzantine Monuments: Tomb of Manuel I Comnenos." *DOP* 23–24 (1969–70): 372–75.

———. Review of *The Architecture of the Kariye Camii in Istanbul*, by Robert Ousterhout. *BZ* 83 (1990): 126–28.

———. "Three Imperial Sarcophagi Discovered in 1750." *DOP* 16 (1962): 397–402.

———. "The Work of M. I. Nomidis in the Vefa Kilise Camii." *Mesaionica kai neaellenika* 3 (1990): 421–29.

Mango, C., and E. J. W. Hawkins. "Report on Field Work in Istanbul and Cyprus, 1962–63. *DOP* 18 (1964): 319–33.

Mango, C., and R. Scott. *The Chronicle of Theophanes the Confessor*. Oxford, 1997.

Mango, C., and I. Ševčenko. "Some Churches and Monasteries on the South Shore of the Sea of Marmara." *DOP* 18 (1964): 279–98.

Mansel, A. M. *Die Ruinen von Side*. Berlin, 1963.

———. *Side*. Ankara, 1978.

Mark, R., ed. *Architectural Technology Up to the Scientific Revolution*. Cambridge, Mass., 1993.

Mark, R., and A. Çakmak, eds. *Hagia Sophia from the Age of Justinian to the Present*. Cambridge, 1992.

Mathews, T. F. *The Byzantine Churches of Istanbul: A Photographic Survey*. University Park, Pa., 1976.

———. *The Early Churches of Constantinople: Architecture and Liturgy*. University Park, Pa., 1971.

Mathews, T. F. "The Sequel to Nicaea II in Byzantine Church Decoration." *Perkins Journal* 41, no. 3 (1988): 11–23.

Matthews, J. T. "The Byzantine Use of the Title Pantocrator." *Orientalia Christiana Periodica* 44 (1978): 442–62.

McCormick, M. *Eternal Victory: Triumphal Rulership in Late Antiquity, Byzantium and the Early Medieval West*. Cambridge, 1986.

McGeer, E. "The Syntaxis Armatorum Quadrata: A Tenth-Century Tactical Blueprint." *REB* 50 (1992): 219–30.

Megaw, A. H. S. "Notes on Recent Work of the Byzantine Institute in Istanbul." *DOP* 17 (1963): 335–64.

———. "The Original Form of the Theotokos Church of Constantine Lips." *DOP* 18 (1964): 279–98.

Mentzou, K. P. *Symbole eis ten meleten tou oikonomikou kai koinoikou biou tes proimou byzantines periodou*. Athens, 1975.

Mepisachvili, R. "Le monument de Korogo." *Sovetskaia Archeologiia* 4 (1969): 219–33.

Mijatev, K. *Die mittelalterliche Baukunst in Bulgarien*. Sofia, 1974.

Mikailov, S. "Arkheologicheski materiali ot Pliska." *Izvestiia na arkheologicheskiia institut* (Sofia) 20 (1955): 114–15.

———. "Dvortsovata ts'rkva v Pliska," *Izvestiia na arkheologicheskiia institut* (Sofia) 20 (1955): 250–51.

Miles, G. C. "Classification of Islamic Elements in Byzantine Architectural Ornamentation in Greece." In *Actes du XIIe Congrès international des études byzantines, Ohride 1961*, vol. 3. Belgrade, 1964.

Millet, G. *L'ancien art serbe: Les églises*. Paris, 1919.

———. *L'école grecque dans l'architecture byzantine*. Paris, 1916.

Moens, L., P. de Paepe, and M. Waelkens. "Survey in the White Marble Quarries of Anatolia." In *IV. AST*. Ankara, 1987.

Moravcsik, G. *Szent László Leánya és a Bizánci Pantokrator-Monostor*. Budapest, 1923.

Morganstern, J. *The Byzantine Church at Dereağzı and Its Decoration*. Tübingen, 1983.

Mouriki, D. *The Mosaics of Nea Moni on Chios*. Athens, 1985.

Müller-Wiener, W. *Bildlexikon zur Topographie Istanbuls*. Tübingen, 1977.

———. "Spoliennutzungen in Istanbul." In *Beiträge zur Altertumskunde Kleinasiens. Festschrift für Kurt Bittel*, ed. R. Boehmer and H. Hauptmann. Mainz, 1983.

———. "Zur Lage der Allerheiligenkirche in Konstantinopel." In *Lebendige Altertumswissenschaft. Festgabe zur Vollendung des 70. Lebensjahres von Herman Vetters*. Mainz, 1985.

Mutsopulos, N. K. "Harmonische Bauschnitte in der Kirchen vom Typus kreuzförmigen Innenbaus im Griechischen Kernland." *BZ* 55 (1962): 274–91.

Mylonas, P. A. "Armenika Gkavit kai Byzantines Lites." *Archaiologia* 32 (Sept. 1989): 52–68.

———. "Domike erevna sto ekklesiastiko synkrotema tou Osiou Louka Phokidos." *Archaiologia* 36 (1990): 6–30.

———. "Gavits arméniens et Litae byzantines: Observations nouvelles sur le complexe de Saint-Luc en Phocide." *CA* 38 (1990): 107–16.

———. "Le plan initial du catholicon de la Grande-Lavra au Mont Athos et la genèse du type du catholicon athonite." *CA* 32 (1984): 89–112.

Necipoğlu, G. *The Topkapı Scroll—Geometry and Ornament in Islamic Architecture.* Los Angeles, 1994.

Necipoğlu-Kafadar, G. "Plans and Models in 15th- and 16th-Century Ottoman Architectural Practice." *JSAH* 45 (1986): 224–43.

Nenadović, S. "Les pots résonnants dans les églises médiévales serbes." *Zbornik Architektonskog Fakulteta* 5 (1960): 3–11.

Nigbor, R. A., A. Çakmak, and R. Mark. "Measured to the Max." *Civil Engineering* (November 1992): 44–47.

Nikonanos, N. "Keramoplastikes kouphikes diakosmeseis sta mnemeia tes perioches ton Athenon." In *Aphieroma ste mneme Stylianou Pelikanide.* Thessaloniki, 1983.

Noret, J., ed. *Vitae duae antiquae Sancti Athanasii Athonitae.* Turnhout, 1982.

Oates, D. "A Summary Report on the Excavations of the Byzantine Institute in the Kariye Camii: 1957 and 1958." *DOP* 14 (1969): 223–31.

Oikonomidès, N. *Hommes d'affaires grecs et latins à Constantinople (XIIIe–XVe siècles).* Montreal, 1979.

Orlandos, A. K. *He xylostegos palaiochristianike basilike.* Athens, 1954.

———. *Monuments byzantins de Chios.* Vol. 2, *Planches.* Athens, 1930.

Ötüken, Y. "Akhisar-Çanlı Kilise Freskoları." In *Bedrettin Cömert'e Armağan.* Ankara, 1980.

———. "Bizans Duvar Tekniğinde Tektonik ve Estetik Çözümler." *Vakıflar Dergisi* (Istanbul) 21 (1990): 395–410.

———. "İsa Kapı Mescidi und Medresesi in Istanbul." Ph.D. diss., University of Bonn, 1974.

———. "İstanbul son devir Bizans mimarisinde cephe süslemeleri." *Vakıflar Dergisi* (Istanbul) 12 (1978): 213–33.

Ötüken, Y., and R. Ousterhout. "The Byzantine Church at Çeltikdere." In *Festschrift Hallensleben.*

———. "Notes on the Monuments of Turkish Thrace." *Anatolian Studies* 39 (1989): 138–39.

Ousterhout, R. "An Apologia for Byzantine Architecture." *Gesta* 35 (1996): 21–33.

———. *The Architecture of the Kariye Camii in Istanbul.* Washington, D.C., 1987.

———. "Beyond Hagia Sophia: Originality in Byzantine Architecture." In *Originality in Byzantine Literature, Art and Music*, ed. A. Littlewood. Oxford, 1995.

———. "A Byzantine Church at Didymoteicho and Its Frescoes." *Milion* 5 (1999): forthcoming.

———. "The Byzantine Church at Enez: Problems in Twelfth-Century Architecture." *JöB* 35 (1985): 262–80.

———. "The Byzantine Churches of Constantinople (843–1453) in Context." *DOP* 54 (2000), forthcoming.

———. "The Byzantine Heart." *Zograf* 17 (1986): 36–44.

———. "Collaboration and Innovation in the Arts of Byzantine Constantinople." *BMGS* 21 (1997): 93–112.

———. "Constantinople, Bithynia, and Regional Developments in Later Palaeologan Architecture." In *Twilight of Byzantium*, ed. S. Ćurčić and D. Mouriki. Princeton, 1991.

———. "The Construction of Vaulting in Later Byzantine Architecture." In *Ancient Structures*, 305–14.

———. "Ethnic Identity and Cultural Appropriation in Early Ottoman Architecture." *Muqarnas* 13 (1995): 48–62.

———. "Innovation in Byzantine Architecture: The Case of Nea Moni." *JSAH* 51 (1992): 48–60.

———. "Observations on the Recessed Brick Technique during the Palaeologan Period." *AD* 39 (1990): 163–70.

———. "Originality in Byzantine Architecture: The Case of Nea Moni." *JSAH* 51 (1992): 48–60.

———. "The Palaeologan Architecture of Didymoteicho." *Byzantinische Forschungen* 14 (1989): 429–43.

———. "Rebuilding the Temple: Constantine Monomachus and the Holy Sepulchre." *JSAH* 48 (1989): 66–78.

———. "Reconstructing Ninth-Century Constantinople." In *Byzantium in the Ninth Century: Dead or Alive?*, ed. L. Brubaker. Aldershot, 1998.

———. "Some Notes on the Construction of Christos ho Pantepoptes (Eski Imaret Camii) in Istanbul." *DChAE* 16 (1991–92): 47–56.

———. "Temporal Structuring in the Chora Parekklesion." *Gesta* 34 (1995): 63–76.

———. "The Virgin of the Chora: An Image and Its Contexts." In *The Sacred Image East and West.* Illinois Byzantine Studies 4, ed. R. Ousterhout and L. Brubaker. Urbana and Chicago, 1995.

———. "Where Was the Tomb of Isaak Komnenos?" *BSCA* 11 (1985): 34.

———. "The 1994 Survey at Akhisar-Çanlı Kilise." In *XIII. AST.* Ankara, 1996.

———. "The 1995 Survey at Akhisar-Çanlı Kilise." In *XIV. AST.* Ankara, 1997.

———. "The 1996 Survey at Akhisar-Çanlı Kilise." In *XV. AST.* Ankara, 1998.

Ousterhout, R., Z. Ahunbay, and M. Ahunbay. "Study and Restoration of the Zeyrek Camii in Istanbul: First Report, 1997–98." *DOP* 54 (2000), forthcoming.

Ousterhout, R., and Th. Gourides. "Ena Byzantino Ktirio dipla ston Agio Athanasio Didymoteichou." *To Archaiologiko Ergo ste Makedonia kai Thrake* 5 (1991): 515–25.

Panić, D. "L'inscription avec les noms de protomaîstres dans l'exonarthex de la Vierge-Ljeviška à Prizren." *Zograf* 1 (1966): 21–23. (In Serbian, with French summary p. 47)

Papazoglou, G. *Typikon Isaakiou Alexiou Komnenou tes Mones Theotokou tes Kosmosoteiras (1151/52).* Komotini, 1994.

Papazotos, Th. "The Identification of the Church of 'Profitis Elias' in Thessaloniki." *DOP* 45 (1991): 121–28.

Pasadaios, A. *Epi duo byzantinon mnemeion tes Konstantinoupoleos agnostou onomatos.* Athens, 1965.

———. *O Keramoplastikos Diakosmos ton Byzantinon Kterion tes Konstantinopouleos.* Athens, 1973.

———. "Peri tinos asynethous byzantinou tholou." In *Charisterion eis A. K. Orlandon.* Athens, 1965.

Pekak, M. S. "Zeytinbağı/Trilye Bizans Döneme Kiliseleri." In *XIII. AST.* Ankara, 1996.

Peschlow, U. *Die Irenenkirche in Istanbul: Untersuchungen zur Architektur.* Tübingen, 1977.

———. "Die mittelbyzantinischen Ambo aus archäologischer Sicht." In *Thymiama ste mneme tes Laskarinas Boura.* Athens, 1994.

———. "Neue Beobachtungen zur Architektur und Ausstattung der Koimesiskirche in Iznik." *IM* 22 (1972): 164–65.

Petit, L. "Typikon du monastère de la Kosmosotira près d'Ainos (1152)." *IRAIK* 13 (1908): 17–75.

———. "Vie et office de St. Euthyme le jeune." *Bibliothèque hagiographique orientale* 5 (1904): 14–51.

Pljakov, Z. "La production artisanale dans la ville byzantine aux XIIIe–XIVe siècles." *Bulgarian Historical Review* 16 (1988): 34–55.

Pulak, C. "1993 Sualtı Arastırması." In *XII. AST.* Ankara, 1995.

Rachénov, A. *Églises de Mesemvria.* Sofia, 1932.

Ramsay, W. M., and G. Bell. *The Thousand and One Churches.* London, 1909.

Rappoport, P. A. *Building the Churches of Kievan Russia.* Aldershot, 1995.

Redford, S. "The Seljuqs of Rum and the Antique." *Muqarnas* 10 (1993): 149–56.

Restle, M. *Byzantine Wall Painting in Asia Minor.* 3 vols. Greenwich, Conn., 1967.

———. *Studien zur frühbyzantinischen Architektur Kappadokiens.* 2 vols. Vienna, 1979.

Reusche, E. "Geschichte der Bau- und Baustofftechnik als Hilfswissenschaft." *Zograf* 13 (1982): 53–58.

Rheidt, K. "Bautechnik und Bautradition im byzantinischen Pergamon." In *Bautechnik der Antike.* Mainz, 1991.

———. *Die byzantinische Wohnstadt.* Altertümer von Pergamon 15, no. 2. Berlin, 1991.

Ricci, A. "The Road from Baghdad to Byzantium and the Case of the Bryas Palace in Istanbul." In *Byzantium in the Ninth Century, Dead or Alive?*, ed. L. Brubaker. Aldershot, 1998.

Rodley, L. *Cave Monasteries of Byzantine Cappadocia.* Cambridge, 1985.

Rott, H. *Kleinasiatische Denkmäler aus Pisidien, Pamphilien, Kappadokien und Lykien.* Leipzig, 1908.

Ruggieri, V. *Byzantine Religious Architecture (582–867): Its History and Structural Elements.* Rome, 1991.

Saldern, A. von. *Ancient and Byzantine Glass from Sardis.* Cambridge, Mass., 1980.

Sanpaolesi, P. "Strutture a cupola autoportanti." *Palladio* 21 (1971): 3–64.

Schäfer, H. "Architekturhistorische Beziehungen zwischen Byzanz und der Kiever Rus im 10. und 11. Jahrhundert." *IM* 23–24 (1973–74): 197–224.

———. *Die Gül Camii in Istanbul: Ein Beitrag zur mittelbyzantinischen Kirchenarchitektur Konstantinopels.* Tübingen, 1973.

Schilbach, E. *Byzantinische Metrologie.* Munich, 1970.

Schmuck, N. "Kreuzkuppelkirche." *RBK* 5 (1991): 356–74.

Schultz, R., and S. Barnsley. *The Monastery of Saint Luke of Stiris, Near Phocis.* London, 1901.

Sear, F. *Roman Architecture.* Ithaca, N. Y., 1982.

Ševčenko, I. "Alexios Makrembolites and his 'Dialogue between the Rich and the Poor.'" *ZRVI* 6 (1960): 187–228.

———. "Theodore Metochites, the Chora, and the Intellectual Trends of His Time." In *The Kariye Djami*, vol. 4, ed. P. A. Underwood. Princeton, 1975.

Ševčenko, I., and N. P. Ševčenko, eds. and trans. *The Life of Saint Nicholas of Sion.* Brookline, Mass., 1984.

Ševčenko, N. "The Tomb of Isaak Komnenos at Pherrai." *GOTR* 29 (1984): 135–40.
Shelby, L. "Masons and Builders." *DMA*, 8:172–80.
Sinkević, I. "Alexios Angelos Komnenos: A Patron without History?" *Gesta* 35 (1996): 34–42.
Sinos, S. *Die Klosterkirche der Kosmosoteira in Bera (Vira)*. Munich, 1985.
Sodini, J.-P. "Les ambons médiévaux à Byzance: Vestiges et problèmes." In *Thymiama ste mneme tes Laskarinas Boura*, 303–7. Athens, 1994.
Sodini, J.-P., A. Lambraki, and T. Kozelj. *Les carrières à l'époque paléochrétienne, Aliki I*. Paris, 1980.
Stephan, A. *Die Mosaiken und Fresken der Apostelkirche zu Thessaloniki*. Worms, 1986.
Stikas, E. *To Oikodomikon Chronikon tes Mones Osiou Louka Phokidos*. Athens, 1970.
Stričević, G. "The Methods of the Early Byzantine Architect." *BSCA* 19 (1993): 79–80.
Striker, C. L. "Applied Geometry in Later Byzantine Architecture." In *Festschrift Hallensleben*, 31–37.
———. "The Byzantine Question in Ottonian Architecture Reconsidered." In *Architectural Studies in Memory of Richard Krautheimer*, ed. C. L. Striker. Mainz, 1996.
———. *The Myrelaion (Bodrum Camii) in Istanbul*. Princeton, 1981.
Striker, C. L., and Y. D. Kuban. *Kalenderhane in Istanbul: The Buildings, Their History, Architecture, and Decoration*. Mainz, 1997.
Sullivan, D. *The Life of Saint Nikon*. Brookline, Mass., 1987.
———. "Originality in the *Poliorcetica* of 'Heron' of Byzantium." *BSCA* 18 (1992): 32–33.
———. "Technical Illustration and Neo-Platonic Levels of Reality in Vaticanus Graecus 1605." *BSCA* 19 (1993): 96–97.
———, ed. *The Poliorcetica of Heron of Byzantium: Text, Translation, and Commentary.* Washington, D.C., forthcoming.
Swift, E. H. *Hagia Sophia*. New York, 1940.
Tabbaa, Y. "Geometry and Memory in the Design of the Madrasat al-Firdows in Aleppo." In *Theories and Principles of Design in the Architecture of Islamic Societies*. Cambridge, Mass., 1988.
Taft, R. "The Frequency of the Eucharist throughout History." *Concilium* 172 (1982): 13–24.
Talbot, A.-M. "The Posthumous Miracles of St. Photeine." *AB* 112 (1994): 85–104.
———. "The Restoration of Constantinople under Michael VIII." *DOP* 47 (1993): 243–61.
Tezcan, H. *Topkapı Sarayı ve Çevresinin Bizans Devri Arkeolojisi*. Istanbul, 1989.
Theis, L. *Die Architektur der Kirche der Panagia Paregoretissa in Arta/Epirus*. Amsterdam, 1991.
———. "Die Flankenräume im mittelbyzantinischen Kirchenbau." Habilitation thesis, University of Bonn, 1996.
Theocharidou, K. "The Structure of Hagia Sophia in Thessaloniki from Its Construction to the Present." In *Hagia Sophia from the Age of Justinian to the Present*, ed. R. Mark and A. Çakmak. Cambridge, 1992.
———. "Symbole ste Melete tes Paragoges Oikodomikon Keramikon Proionton sta Byzantina kai Metabysantina Chronia." *DChAE* 13 (1988): 97–112.
Thessaloniki and Its Monuments. Thessaloniki, 1985.
Thierry, N. "Illustration de la construction d'une église. Les sculptures de Korogo (Georgie)." In *Artistes, Artisans, et Production Artistique au Moyen Age*, ed. X. Barral I Altet. Rennes, 1983.

Thomas, J. P. *Private Religious Foundations in the Byzantine Empire*. Washington, D.C., 1987.

Thomas, J. P., and A. Hero, eds. *Byzantine Monastic Foundation Documents*. Washington, D.C., forthcoming.

Thomson, R. "Architectural Symbolism in Classical Armenian Literature." *Journal of Theological Studies*, n.s., 30 (1979): 101–14.

Toumbakari, E. E. "Structural Analysis of the Church of Aghia Triada, Astros, Peloponnesos, Greece." In *Ancient Structures*, 507–16.

Tsarevskaia, T. "Nekotoriie Osobennosti Ikonografiieskoi Programmii Rospisei Tserkvi Blagovesheniia na Miachine ("v Arkazhakh") bliz Novgoroda." In *Drevnerusskoe Iskusstvo*. Moscow, 1997.

Underwood, P. A. "The Deisis Mosaic in the Kariye Cami at Istanbul." In *Late Classical and Medieval Studies in Honor of A. M. Friend, Jr.*, ed. K. Weitzmann. Princeton, 1955.

———. "Some Principles of Measurement in the Architecture of the Period of Justinian." *CA* 3 (1948): 64–74.

———, ed. *The Kariye Djami*. 3 vols. New York, 1966.

———, ed. *The Kariye Djami*. Vol. 4. Princeton, 1975.

Uspenskij, T. "L'octateuque de la Bibliothèque du Sérail à Constantinople." *IRAIK* 12 (1907): 21–22.

Van Millingen, A. *Byzantine Churches in Constantinople*. London, 1912.

———. *Byzantine Constantinople*. London, 1899.

Van Nice, R. *Saint Sophia in Istanbul: An Architectural Survey*. Washington, D.C., 1965.

Varzos, K. *He Genealogia ton Komnenon*. Thessaloniki, 1984.

Velenis, G. *Ermeneia tou Exoterikou Diakosmou ste Byzantine Architektonike*. 2 vols. Thessaloniki, 1984.

———. "Thirteenth-Century Architecture in the Despotate of Epirus: The Origins of the School." In *Studenica et l'art byzantin autour de l'année 1200*. Belgrade, 1988.

Velte, M. *Die Anwendung der Quatratur und Triangulatur be der Grund- und Aufrissgestaltung der gotischen Kirchen*. Basel, 1951.

Visots'kii, S. "Vikonna rama ta shibki Kiivs'koi Sofii." In *Kiivs'ka starovina*. Kiev, 1972.

Vitruvius. *The Ten Books on Architecture*. Trans. M. H. Morgan. Cambridge, Mass., 1914.

Vocotopoulos, P. "The Role of Constantinopolitan Architecture during the Middle and Late Period." *XVI. Internationaler Byzantinistenkongress, Akten I/2;* published as *JöB* 31, no. 2 (1981): 551–73.

Vogel, K., ed. *Ein byzantinisches Rechenbuch des frühen 14. Jahrhunderts*. Vienna, 1968.

Vogiatzes, S. "Neotera Stoicheia gia ten Oikodomike Istoria tou Katholikou tes Neas Mones Chiou." *DChAE* 14 (1989): 159–72.

Vryonis, S. "Byzantine *Demokratia* and the Guilds of the Eleventh Century." *DOP* 17 (1963): 289–314.

Vzdornov, G. J. *Kievskaia Psaltir 1397 goda*. Moscow, 1978.

Waldbaum, J. *Metalwork from Sardis*. Cambridge, Mass., 1983.

Ward Perkins, J. B. "Notes on the Structure and Building Methods of Early Byzantine Architecture." In *The Great Palace of the Byzantine Emperors, Second Report*. St. Andrews, 1954.

———. "Quarries and Stoneworking in the Early Middle Ages: The Heritage of the Ancient World." *Settimane di Studi del Centro Italiano di Studi sull'alto Medioevo* 17, vol. 2 (1971): 525ff.

Weitzmann, K. *Ancient Book Illumination*. Cambridge, Mass., 1959.

Wescher, C. *Poliorcétique des grecs*. Paris, 1867.

Wiemer, W. "Digitale Bildverarbeitung in der Kunstwissenschaft: Eine Datenbank zur Proportionsanalyse mittelalterliche Kirchen." *Kunstchronik* 43 (1990): 55–62.

Wulff, O. "Das Raumerlebnis im Spiegel der Ekphrasis." *BZ* 30 (1929–30): 531–39.

Wybrew, H. *The Orthodox Liturgy: The Development of the Eucharistic Liturgy in the Byzantine Rite*. London, 1989.

Xyngopoulos, A. *He Psephidote Diakosmesis tou Naou ton Hagion Apostolon Thessalonikes*. Thessaloniki, 1953.

Young, S. "Relations between Byzantine Mosaic and Fresco Technique." *JöB* 25 (1976): 269–78.

INDEX

Architectural structures and ruins are indexed by location.